URBAN SHOCKER

URBAN SHOCKER

Silent Hero of Baseball's Golden Age

STEVE STEINBERG

UNIVERSITY OF NEBRASKA PRESS
Lincoln and London

∞

Library of Congress Cataloging-in-Publication Data
Names: Steinberg, Steve, author.
Title: Urban Shocker: silent hero of
baseball's golden age / Steve Steinberg.
Description: Lincoln: University of Nebraska Press,
2017. | Includes bibliographical references and index.
Identifiers: LCCN 2016038223 (print)
LCCN 2016057128 (ebook)
ISBN 9780803295995 (hardback: alk. paper)
ISBN 9781496200952 (epub)
ISBN 9781496200969 (mobi)
ISBN 9781496200976 (pdf)
Subjects: LCSH: Shocker, Urban, 1890–1928. |
Baseball players—United States—Biography. |
Pitchers (Baseball)—United States—Biography. |
Heart—Diseases—Patients—United States—
Biography. | BISAC: Biography & Autobiography /
Sports. | Sports & Recreation / Baseball / History.
Classification: LCC GV865.S48 S74
2017 (print) | LCC GV865.S48 (ebook)
| DDC 796.357092 [B]—dc23
LC record available at https://
lccn.loc.gov/2016038223

Set in Lyon by Rachel Gould.
Designed by N. Putens.

To Brian, Mat, and Allie, who have patiently endured my travels to and preoccupation with the past in my baseball explorations over the years

Contents

Illustrations

Preface

You've shown the fickleness of Fame,
But with it the eternal worth
Of one who dares to Play the Game
Beyond the scorers of the earth;
Who sees above the maudlin roar
Something beyond the final score.

—from "New Year's Dedication" by Grantland Rice

I first connected with Urban Shocker in 1998. I found him on an old baseball card, when my ten-year-old son and I were frequenting card shows and shops. Shocker's pitching accomplishments, key role with the great 1927 New York Yankees, and untimely death all intrigued me. I soon came across a quote in *The Yankee Encyclopedia*: "Quite possibly Urban was the most courageous man in sports history. Ill with a swollen heart, Urban fought bravely in his last few years to play baseball and indeed for life itself." I was now completely hooked and chose to follow my curiosity, to embark on a search for this forgotten star.

In early 1999 my correspondence with baseball historian Robert Creamer (1922–2012) provided me with encouragement from the start. On March 19, 1999, he wrote,

> If you're fascinated by Shocker and are "crazy" enough to want to do a book on him, sure. . . . It's tedious work, going through microfilm day after day, looking for nuggets of information, but it can be marvelously rewarding. . . . Don't depend only on the *New York Times*, microfilm of which seems to be in every library in the country. Other papers often had more sports detail. Look at as many papers in the same city as you can. . . . I wish I could give you specific leads on Shocker, but I can't. . . . Even though he was one of the best pitchers of his era, he seems remarkably unknown.

I was going through a period of immense change and turmoil at the time. I had recently sold my retail company, which had been a central part of my life for more than twenty years. I was lost without it. I was also approaching the age of fifty and suddenly realized I was no longer young.

I began researching Shocker's life and writing his story. Originally a creative work, it had dialogue between the personalities, as well as my search for Urban and his story, a memoir of sorts. After more than three years, in the fall of 2002, I had written almost 200,000 words. It was long and unwieldy. The story wasn't ready. Neither was I.

I revisited the Shocker manuscript in 2009. At that same time, I was diagnosed with heart failure. It was a complete and inexplicable surprise. My family history is one of great genes and longevity. I had been feeling fine, and none of the symptoms of the disease were present, even at my annual checkups. My cardiologist, who could find no medical explanation for my heart failure, said it may have been caused by a virus.

Had my regular doctor not run an EKG during my 2009 annual physical and noticed an irregularity, I might not have lived to finish this book. I might have simply died in my sleep later that year. For the third time in my life, I had come close to death. The other two were a near-drowning and a very bad car accident decades earlier. For the third time, I have moved forward, in this case because we have been able to treat the disease so successfully.

My illness provides me with a stronger understanding of and connection to Shocker's story. From my first meeting him back in 1998 in a baseball card shop with my son, Shocker and I have reconnected ever more strongly on the same playing field. The discovery of my own heart failure has added another dimension to my understanding of him.

Now more than ever, after collaborating on two books on the Yankees of the 1920s with Lyle Spatz, it is time for Urban Shocker's story to be told. He has been waiting for almost ninety years.

In my correspondence with Shocker's nephew, Roger Shockcor (1920–2003), I was able to pique his interest, and he wrote me on April 19, 1999, "Thank you so much for the articles, cards, etc. about Urban Shocker, which you enclosed with your letter of 3.29.99. I did not realize what a great pitcher Uncle Urb was until after I read and digested the material you sent me. In addition, he was also quite a guy and someone we can be proud of. You have sparked my interest in the story you are trying to put together, and it could have more potential than I originally thought."

Baseball has a unique beauty and rhythm. By understanding this and Urban's story, I have gained perspective on life. I have learned to experience time and make the most of it. By taking the time to go back in time, within the timeless framework of baseball, I have discovered that it is possible to slow time down and savor it. For more than fifteen years, this perspective has guided my life and enriched it immensely.

I have reshaped this book as a traditional nonfiction biography. It is a story of courage, love of the game, and passion for life. Back on April 4, 1999, baseball historian Donald Honig wrote me, "You have picked out one of the more silent stars of baseball's past." During my journey with this book, I have often been asked, "Who? Who's Shocker?" People more familiar with the game and its history have been equally puzzled and asked, "Why? Why Shocker?"

I hope this book answers both of these questions. It certainly has for me.

Acknowledgments

I want to thank my readers for their review and input: Tom Bourke, Judy Cash, and Lyle Spatz. A special thank you to my fact checker, Gabriel Schechter, who has the unique ability to provide big-picture input at the same time that he is making factual and grammatical corrections.

Researchers who provided me with newspapers articles from Shocker's Minor League seasons in Canada were David McDonald, Jim Scheer, and Tony Techko.

Jennifer McCord was an invaluable mentor in my early writing career, when I spent countless hours with drafts of Shocker's story. The following people were generous with their advice and expertise: Art Black, Stephen Boren, Bill Deane, Marshall Eaton, Irv Goldfarb, Bill James, Bill Loughman, Norman Macht, Cyril Morong, Peter Morris, Rob Neyer, Bill Nowlin, Stephan Saks, Jay Sanford, Fred Schuld, Ron Siegel, Barry Sparks, Joe Wancho, Robert Wiggins, and Russell Wolinsky. And the SABR research community continues to be an incredible source of knowledge and support. My apology for any omissions here.

I always want to provide unique images to accompany my work, and many of the images came from my collection. The assortment has been enhanced by photographs from many other sources. Urban Shocker's relatives who provided family photos and information were Linda Jordan, Rene Josephson, Roger Shockcor, and Joan Willenbrock. Private photo collectors who have continued to support my work are Dennis Goldstein and Michael Mumby.

I have also drawn on the images of a number of libraries and museums: Library and Archives of Canada, Cleveland Public Library, Toronto Public Library, Mary Wallace and the Walter P. Reuther Library at Wayne State University, Charlie Brown and the St. Louis Mercantile Library, Missouri History Museum, SABR-Ottoson Photo Archive, and of course John Horne and the National Baseball Hall of Fame Library. I have rounded out the assortment with images from the Associated Press, Diamond Images' Bob Olen Collection, the Rucker Archive, Bill Loughman, and Roland Hemond and Margo Quinn Hemond.

Hillary Levin at the *St. Louis Post-Dispatch* provided photos, as did Alicia Samuel at Bettmann/CORBIS.

All of the above people and institutions helped the story of Urban Shocker come alive. My sincere thanks to all of them.

URBAN SHOCKER

1. Urban Shocker made his home in St. Louis for the last decade of his life, but he longed to be a member of the New York Yankees. His return to the club after the 1924 season "brought balm to his injured spirit." *Cleveland Public Library Photograph Collection.*

1

Passing By and Drawn In

I am the start and the beginning,
I am the first and the final inning,
Soul of the ancient game;
I take them raw and I show the way
That leads in promotion and to pay,
The road that leads to fame.
I catch them young and I send them far
Where great crowds welcome the coming star,
And I am forgotten then;
And when they are old, on the outer rim,
When their arms are gone and their eyes are dim,
I take them back again.

—from "The Bush League Speaks Again" by Grantland Rice

Rennie Heydt had never been to a funeral. He had not seen so many people in one place, except at baseball games at Sportsman's Park here in St. Louis. He watched as a hearse slowly drove past the gates and the archbishop's summer home at St. Louis's Calvary Catholic Cemetery.[1] The hearse wound its way past the small lake and headed north, traversing the road closest to the cemetery's stone walls. It was followed by dozens of automobiles and hundreds of people alighting from streetcars and streaming through the gates of the vast burial grounds.

Rennie, his curiosity prodding him, shoved his bike under a bush and fell in with the somber crowd. They slowly made their way through the rolling green hills, shaded by the majestic oak, gum, and poplar trees.

Rennie was just shy of his tenth birthday, and death was the farthest thing from his mind. Growing up in a row house in St. Louis's Baden neighborhood nearby, he had mixed feelings about his "neighbors" in Calvary Cemetery. Over the years he had not gotten used to them, and they still gave him the creeps. Between this Catholic cemetery and the adjacent nondenominational one, Bellefontaine, there were almost eight hundred acres of land for the dead. Land that could have been a park with ball fields, bike paths, and trails, Rennie thought.

A hush came over the crowd as the casket was lifted out of the hearse. Six well-built young men in dark suits carried the shiny wood box to its final resting place. Archbishop John Joseph Glennon began chanting in Latin:

Requiem aeternam dona ei, Domine
(Eternal rest grant unto him, O Lord)
et lux perpetua luceat ei
(And let perpetual light shine upon him)

Rennie worked his way through the mass of people, squeezing toward the front of the gathering. There must be at least a thousand people here, he thought. A couple of these men looked vaguely familiar, but where had he seen them?

Then, with a start, he realized he was looking at New York Yankees stars Lou Gehrig and Waite Hoyt. He had seen them only in their baseball uniforms, either at the ballpark or in newspaper pictures. They looked different so dressed up. They were somberly leading the other pallbearers to the pit of freshly dug earth.[2]

De profundis clamavi ad te, Domine
(From the depths I have cried unto thee, Lord, Lord hear my prayer)
Domine, exaudi vocem meam
(O Lord, let my prayer come unto thee)

He could hear the sobbing of the women nearest to the casket and the murmurs and hushed remarks of the men nearby. This was the final farewell to St. Louis's great pitcher Urban Shocker, a man the city called one of its own and a man who called St. Louis home, even after he was traded to the Yankees.[3]

In paradisum deducant te angeli
(May the angels lead you into Paradise)
In tuo adventu, suscipiant te martyres
(May the martyrs greet you at your arrival)
et perducant te in civitatem sanctam Jerusalem
(And lead you into the holy city of Jerusalem)

A chill went down Rennie's spine. He had discovered Major League Baseball in the last couple of years. He knew about Shocker, winner of almost twenty games for the Yankees in each of the past two seasons and a star for the St. Louis Browns a few years earlier, before Rennie had become interested in baseball.

Many questions were spinning through Rennie's mind, as he listened to the comments of mourners as the funeral was ending. Was Shocker really as good as these people surrounding the grave were saying? Was he sick while he played for the great Yankees teams of 1926 and 1927? Why did he die so young?

Requiescat in pace
(May he rest in peace)
In nomine Patris, et Filii, et Spiritus Sancti. Amen
(In the name of the Father, and of the Son, and of the Holy Spirit. Amen.)[4]

Rennie went on to learn much more about Shocker. One of St. Louis's leading sportswriters, James Gould, had written, "Shocker's death removes from the world of sport one of the greatest pitchers in the game and one of the game's most colorful figures."[5]

Rennie Heydt never forgot that day in the cemetery. More than seventy years later, the memory was still clear in his mind's eye.

I met Rennie Heydt, the "Candy Man," an eighty-year-old fixture in St. Louis baseball circles, at a spring 1999 St. Louis Browns reunion dinner.

Rennie shared his memories of Shocker's funeral. A longtime employee of the Peter Paul Candy Company, he was so welcome at Busch Stadium that when he invited me to a game that year, we were admitted on sight. In March 2000 Rennie was killed in a car-pedestrian accident on I-270 outside of St. Louis.[6]

2

Midwest Connections

Urban Shocker was born into a large Cleveland family on September 22, 1890.[1] The surname's spelling of "Shockcor" was retained by his siblings.[2] He was the only one to adopt the simplified spelling of "Shocker," probably because newspaper reporters did not get the more complicated spelling right.

He was the fifth of nine children of William Henry and Anna Katherine Shockcor. William was born in Pennsylvania (as were his parents) in 1852 and moved to Cleveland as a young adult. It was here that he met Anna Spies, who was born in 1859 in Ohio. They married on October 8, 1879, and had their first child, also named William, a year later.

William Sr. was a cooper by trade, working at a factory that produced wood barrels. Another William Shockcor, a cousin and also the head of a large family, appears in Cuyahoga County census records and Cleveland city directories in the late nineteenth and early twentieth century.

Two of the many mysteries surrounding Urban Shocker revolve around his name and date of birth. Some baseball records list him as Urbain Jacques Shocker, suggesting a French lineage. There has been some mention among his descendants that the family's "French connection" is to the Alsace-Lorraine region on the French-German border.[3] It is not clear where these French names originated, but they appear to be made out of whole cloth. Urban's birth record and 1900 census record both list him

2. Urban Shocker's parents, William and Anna (seen here with a granddaughter), were born in the Cleveland area. William's family had roots in Philadelphia, while Anna's came from central Germany. *Private collection of the family of Roger Shockcor.*

simply as "Urban J." He may have created the mystery himself (he had a wry sense of humor) while he played for Ottawa in the Canadian League.

Urban's paternal grandparents, William and Mary, appear in the 1860 census record in Philadelphia and were both born in the United States. While Urban's maternal grandparents, Jacob and Elizabeth, were born in Germany, the 1860 census (when they were already in the Cleveland area) records their birthplace as Hesse, a German state far from the French border, in south-central Germany.[4]

A related question is why he was referred to as "Herb" early in his Minor League career. The most logical explanation is that reporters heard him being called "Urb," an unusual moniker, and assumed it was "Herb." Once he came to the Major Leagues, the name "Herb" vanishes from newspaper accounts.

The mystery of Shocker's date of birth is more readily explained. In his baseball career, as he got older, he grew younger. In baseball's *Who's Who* directories, his birth date was listed as September 22, 1891, until the 1923 edition. From 1923 on, it jumped to September 22, 1892. His 1918 World War I draft card lists the 1891 date, and when he later listed his wife as a beneficiary on a military benefits form, he again used the 1891 date (after crossing out 1890).

Shocker got a late start in his baseball career. It was common for ballplayers to lie about their age, in a time when it was hard and inconvenient for management to confirm the actual dates. A younger player appeared more attractive to a club, with the reserve clause giving that club control over the player for his entire career. And if a player was good at age twenty, his manager could expect him to be even better a few years later.

Sporting News columnist John Sheridan addressed the topic in a 1915 column. The baseball guides, which published "Facts for Bugs [Fans]," should really be called "Fakes for Bugs." He wrote, "Every ball player is from two to ten years younger than he really is. . . . The younger the player the greater future he is supposed to have. Hence the younger he is, the more he is worth. . . . As the player approaches 28, he begins to drop two years for every one he gains. At 30 he is 26. At 33 he is 27. He never goes beyond 33."[5]

There is no question that September 22, 1890, is the correct date.[6] That shows up on his birth record. And the federal census enumeration taken in June 1900 states that he was born in September 1890 and was nine at the time.[7] On his marriage license, where Shocker was asked to fill out his age and not his date of birth, he answered accurately, based on the 1890 date. Ironically, his death certificate and most obituaries cited 1891. Is it possible his wife thought that was his birth year?

Shocker attended Dennison Grade School and started playing baseball on the sandlots of Cleveland at an early age, including the largest "sandlot" of them all, Brookside Park.[8] He played for a milk and ice cream club and then for the Leisy Brewing Company team.[9]

Before his twentieth birthday, he started spending time in Detroit, living with his older sister, Cora.[10] He is still listed as part of his parents' household in Cleveland in the 1910 census, but he begins to show up in the Detroit city directory in 1909.[11]

Shocker was a handsome young man, well-built and broad-shouldered, with reddish-brown hair. There were regular references to him during much of his career as "stocky" and even "chunky." The *St. Louis Post-Dispatch* once described Shocker as "roly-poly waist-line and all."[12] While he is listed in baseball databases as 5'10" and 170 pounds, his weight was often mentioned as 180 and even 190.

The baseball opportunities for a youngster were comparable in major midwestern cities at that time. When Urban left Cleveland for Detroit, it was likely to move away from his parents and become independent. His self-assurance, bordering on cockiness, which would become a signature trait, was already evident.

He began working as an electrotyper in a newspaper printing plant in Detroit. Reporters later wrote that this craft demanded precision, not unlike that required of a professional pitcher. Both demanded artistry and accuracy with his hands.[13] Yet while the former paid the bills, the latter was his passion. The fact that baseball paid little or nothing was not important. He loved to play the game.

3

Sandlots and Love of the Game

Before the movies and the automobile became widespread, sandlot baseball games were a big form of entertainment in the Midwest. What better way to spend a summer day than at the ball fields on the edge of the city? The air was clean and refreshing. Streetcars were cheap and convenient, though often crowded. They shuttled thousands of players and fans from the inner cities of Chicago, Cleveland, and Detroit out to these ball fields. As one example of the popularity of these games, the first weekend of September 1909, more than a thousand semipro and amateur games were played in the Chicago area, and the combined attendance was estimated at five hundred thousand.[1]

Fields were open and games were free, and there were literally hundreds of them each summer weekend. Spectators drifted from one ball field to another in these enormous clusters of fields called parks. Fans passed the hat to raise money for the players. Sometimes it went only to players of the winning team. Other times, when the money was in short supply, it went only to the winning pitcher, the man who controlled the flow of the game, and to his catcher, who called the game.

At the end of the first decade of the twentieth century, Detroit seemed like the center of the baseball universe. Ty Cobb and his Tigers, led by manager Hughie Jennings, had won three straight American League pennants between 1907 and 1909.[2] There was no place Urban Shocker would rather have been than Detroit, and there was no team he would rather play for than the Tigers. It was here in the greater Detroit area that he began to make his mark and crossed paths with future Major Leaguers, including future teammates.[3]

Details of Shocker's early career are hazy, in part because accurate records were not kept for semipro games. Many of these sandlot teams were not part of Organized Baseball. And players drifted quite freely from one team to another, even during the same season. They often played three or four games each weekend.

Shocker, who started out as a catcher, first shows up in baseball databases in 1913, when he played for the Windsor Canucks (just across the Detroit River in Ontario) of the Border League. But he was already playing for Windsor in 1911, and he played briefly for Bay City and Saginaw of the Southern Michigan League that year.[4] He probably played against future Yankees teammates Frank Gilhooley and Wally Pipp, who were on Adrian and Kalamazoo, respectively, that season. Because Shocker was a pitcher exclusively after 1913, his statistics as a position player were not preserved.

Glimpses of Shocker's early play can be seen in the local papers. In 1911 he was called "one of Windsor's heavy sluggers," with a batting average of .400.[5] When he left for Bay City a month later (a promotion, since Windsor was in the semipro Public Utilities League that year), the reporter for the Windsor paper lamented, "'Shock' was one of the squarest and brainiest players that ever donned a Windsor uniform."[6]

The following year, when Windsor was in the professional Canadian League, Shocker was suspended and fined for not showing up for three weeks. One report said he was upset the club had added another catcher, who would compete with him for playing time.[7] This is the first documented case of the headstrong Shocker being disciplined by his club. It would not be the last.

In 1913 Shocker split his Windsor season between pitching and catching. He started the season behind the plate, but when the club was short of pitchers in May, he volunteered and quickly developed a reputation not only for effectiveness but also for durability. After he pitched eighteen innings in a doubleheader, the Windsor paper noted, "Shocker has been trying to do all the work for the past month, and the strain has been too much for him."[8] Yet three days later, he tossed a three-hitter against Pontiac.

After the close of the Border League season, Shocker pitched all three games for the S&S Clothing team in the Detroit city championship series, spread out over three weekends. He dominated the Packards, striking out more than thirty men in the series.[9] These performances solidified the position he would play for the rest of his career. He would move permanently from behind the plate to the mound.

His stint as a catcher would contribute to his success as a pitcher: a broken middle finger he suffered in 1913 while catching did not heal properly and left a permanent crook. As Shocker explained years later, "It enabled me to grasp the baseball a little more firmly than ever before. I would fit the baseball in my right hand against the bent finger and then throw. The crooked finger gave the ball an odd twist which fooled the batters."[10] He explained why the pitch was hard to recognize and why reporters would misidentify it throughout his career. "I can get a slow ball to drop just like a spitter."[11]

4

An Emerging Star in the Minors

I saw him first as a kid—
A hard, free-swinging devil in the Bush;
Fast as the winds that sweep the open plains,
As fast as the lightning flashes down the sky.
With rippling muscles wrought of tempered steel,
Steel springs within his arm
And in his legs and in his face
The burning glow of youth.
—from "There—Up—and Back" by Grantland Rice

The relationship of Major League teams with those in the Minors was murky in the early twentieth century. Byzantine, changing rules and no rules at all—governed by informal deals finalized with a handshake—carried the day. Frank Navin, the owner of the Detroit Tigers, had such relationships with clubs in Fort Wayne, Indiana, and Ottawa, Ontario.

After the 1913 season, the Border League disbanded, and Shocker was declared a free agent. Perhaps because of the pitcher's success in the 1913 City finals, Navin made an agreement with him and sent him to Fort Wayne of the Class B Central League the following spring.[1] Shocker, who had played indoor baseball that winter, appeared on the Railroaders' roster in late April.[2] But the club released him shortly thereafter, before the start of the 1914 campaign.[3] They had a veteran pitching staff (three

3. Shag Shaughnessy had a brief Major League career and went on to a long and successful career as a Minor League manager and executive. He was the president of the International League for a quarter century, during which time he invented the Shaughnessy Playoff system with split-season winners. He is a member of the International League Hall of Fame. *Library and Archives, Canada/Alexandra Studio/PA-208415.*

twenty-game winners had led them to the 1913 Central League pennant) and instead wanted Shocker to play in the outfield, which he refused to do.

Shocker was then acquired by Frank "Shag" Shaughnessy, the manager of the Ottawa Senators of the Canadian League, which had just been reclassified up to a Class B league.[4] Shaughnessy, who would go on to a long career as a Minor League executive, had managed Fort Wayne to the 1912 Central League pennant. He still had a close relationship with the owner of that club and had access to players they did not keep.[5] And both clubs had close relationships with the Tigers.

Ottawa had been training in Fort Wayne, and the city's reporters had been writing favorably on how Shocker was performing. He "looks to have everything" and "He has plenty of speed, a good change of pace, and a slow drop" were just two reports praising his pitching.[6]

Shocker's personality and style emerged quickly in Ottawa. After his first win, he was called "cocky" and described as "one of the pluckiest youngsters in the game; he is fortified with a heap of confidence."[7] Another reporter elaborated, "Confidence is Shocker's principal asset."[8] An opposing team's reporter noted that he had "a lot of electricity up his sleeve."[9]

It is unclear just when Shocker developed a spitball. He once said that he learned to throw it as a kid, when a friend showed him how.[10] But years later, Shaughnessy recalled suggesting Shocker try throwing the pitch in the summer of 1914, since his curve ball was not that effective. Shocker chewed some slippery elm and had immediate success with the pitch.[11] Shocker, he said in a 1960 interview, was "as smart as they come. . . . He said he never had [thrown the spitter], but was sure he could throw anything."[12] Shocker tossed a three-hit shutout and "from then on very few teams beat him." The *Ottawa Citizen* reported that he first threw the pitch in that July 19 shutout of the St. Thomas Saints.

Shocker proceeded to dominate the Canadian League and helped lead the Senators to their third straight pennant. For the second year in a row, they clinched the flag on the season's last day, this time thanks to Shocker's twentieth win. He finished the year with a league-best 20-8 record and a 2.17 earned run average. He had been "a real iron man," an Ottawa reporter wrote.[13] In one week in August, Shocker appeared in five games and won four of them.[14] He was reported to be heading to the Detroit Tigers, who would take a close look at him.

Shocker was looking forward to a baseball tour of England that fall. Doc Reisling, a former Major League pitcher and the manager of the London (Ontario) Tecumsehs, was organizing the trip and had invited the Ottawa star along. But when war broke out in Europe in August, the tour was canceled. Unlike the United States, Canada felt the immediate impact of the conflict. As a British Dominion, the country entered the war when Britain declared war on Germany on August 4, 1914. The Senators suffered a 40 percent drop in gate receipts that last month of the season.[15]

Shocker generated positive headlines from exhibition games that fall. In early September, with Major League veteran Frank Bowerman catching, he threw a one-hitter and struck out twenty-three Ann Arbor men.[16] The game came to Ty Cobb's attention, and in his column he wrote of Shocker's performance against a good team. "As an exhibition of pitching efficiency, this ranks with anything that has ever come to my attention.... one of the most remarkable [games] on record."[17] Cobb likely was involved with any column penned under his name and was familiar with Shocker when the two would soon meet face-to-face.[18]

In early October, the Tigers played a benefit game at Navin Field for Eddie Siever, their pitcher who had been crippled in a fall. They beat Shocker and the Otsegos, a well-known semipro team.[19] The Otsegos were owned by millionaire lumberman Tom Stephens, who bet several thousand dollars on Shocker and his club that game.[20] Shocker was thrilled to have held Ty Cobb hitless—and he never forgot that day.

The following spring, there was some question whether Fort Wayne still had control over Shocker. But Claude Varnell had sold the club, and understandings between teams were often based on informalities and personalities. With Varnell gone, Fort Wayne made no claim.[21]

Adjusting to the realities of war, the league shortened its 1915 season and cut the team roster limit to just thirteen players. A highlight for Shocker was a game in early July. He threw 11 innings of no-hit ball but lost in 14 innings, 1–0. His entire month was impressive. In eight starts he gave up just under one walk a game and just over one run a game. The *Detroit Free Press* quoted a reporter from north of the border, who noted that Shocker was drawing attention from Major League scouts. "Shocker is the 'Alexander' of the Canadian circuit, and his pitching the past three weeks has been wonderful.... For a spitballer, his control has been magnificent."[22] Grover Cleveland Alexander of the Phillies was in the midst of a spectacular year with the Phillies: a National League–leading 31 wins, 12 shutouts, 241 strikeouts, and a 1.22 earned run average. This was the first of three straight seasons he won the pitching Triple Crown.

Shocker and the Senators picked up where they had left off in 1914. Ottawa again won the Canadian League pennant, this time decisively. It was the league's final year; in 1916 Ottawa's ballpark was occupied by a military battalion.[23] Shocker again led the league in wins (19) and earned run average (1.99). Perhaps more impressive was his strikeout-to-walk ratio, 3.9:1 (186:48).

In early September the Senators sold Shocker to Kid Elberfeld's Chattanooga Lookouts of the Class A Southern Association for $600.[24] But Shocker said he would not report there (the Southern Association was still playing after the Canadian League season had ended), reportedly because he did not like the weather.

Instead, he played exhibition games with Ottawa and had perhaps his most impressive stretch of pitching. He lost, 1–0, in Toronto against the Maple Leafs of the top-level International League. Shocker then beat strong black teams, the Havana Red Sox and the Cuban Giants, with three wins in six days. He gave up a combined one run and eight hits in those contests. He capped off his baseball year with a 19-strikeout game against a team of Minor League All-Stars in Milford, Pennsylvania.[25]

One reason why Shocker did not report to Chattanooga was that he had gotten word that he had been drafted by a Major League team, though at the time he did not know which club. With the Federal League battling Organized Baseball, the Major Leagues held their draft in secret, to avoid the upstart league's signing the draftees. Such a transaction, which paid Ottawa $750 (a fixed fee based on the class of the Minor League team) would have overridden Shocker's being drafted by a Minor League team.

In early September New York Yankees scout Bobby Gilks told an Ottawa paper, "Shock has everything that goes to make up a good pitcher. His spitter, one of the best, his control of it could not be better, while his change of pace is great. But the best of all . . . he is there with the nerve in a pinch."[26] Why Gilks would make any such public statement before he signed Shocker is unclear. It seems he would not have wanted to draw attention to Shocker, with the Federal League competing for its players. What soon became clear was that the Yankees had indeed drafted Shocker, who signed a contract with the New Yorkers later in September, at an annual salary of $1,350.[27]

Here is one of the mysteries of Shocker's early career: Why was he not picked up by his hometown club, the Tigers, who initially controlled him? Did their manager, Hughie Jennings, give him a tryout, either in 1914 or before the 1915 campaign? Was Jennings not impressed? At the start of Shocker's first year with Ottawa, a reporter wrote that the brash youngster "claims Hughie Jennings let his best pitcher go when he turned him over to the Ottawas and that he could clinch the American League pennant for Detroit."[28]

The Tigers had not won an AL pennant since 1909; they had not even threatened. Ironically, Detroit finally did come close in 1915, when Shocker's arm might have put them over the top.[29] And early that season a Detroit reporter wrote an article entitled, "If Jennings Could Develop One More Pitcher, He'd Be Happy."[30]

Detroit could have purchased Shocker before the draft but chose not to do so. And since Major League teams drafted in reverse order of their position in the standings that season, the Yankees chose before the Tigers. Baseball historian Peter Morris wrote to me, "The Tigers either soured on Shocker or gambled no Major League club would draft him and lost."[31] The former is more likely, since Shocker was drawing a lot of headlines. So what did Jennings think of the pitcher and why?

I have never found a specific reference to a Shocker tryout with the Tigers. But there were some hints. An Ottawa reporter noted in April 1914 that Shocker "managed to put over the strikes on Cobb when with Detroit."[32] The following summer, a *Free Press* reporter wrote, "The Detroit American League club has had an eye on Shocker, and President Navin will probably give the Detroit lad another trial. . . . There is no doubt of his being ripe for much faster company."[33] And an unnamed Tiger had said, "There isn't enough speed on his fast one, and for that reason he will not be a star."[34]

Jennings had his belief system and voiced some platitudes. In early 1914 he was quoted as declaring, "No ball player ever became a star in his home town."[35] More significantly, he told the *Detroit Journal*, "Give me a young fellow with curves, speed, and control, and I'll let the other manager have all the 'spitball kings' he wants."[36] Navin had sent Shaughnessy a telegram: "Mr. Jennings does not like spitball pitchers."[37]

4. Frank Navin (*left*), owner of the Detroit Tigers, took an interest in and signed Shocker early in his career. But despite excelling in Ottawa, Shocker was passed over by Tigers manager Hughie Jennings (*right*). *Private collection of Steve Steinberg.*

Jennings did once note that, while exceedingly rare, a good spitball pitcher would be a great addition to a club, like another Cobb.[38] In his defense, the mid-1910s was an unusual period for spitballers. Two of the best, Ed Walsh and Jack Chesbro, had departed the scene. And a new generation of great or very good ones—Shocker, Coveleski, Douglas, Faber, Grimes, and Quinn—had either not come up or not yet emerged as stars.

Perhaps ruefully but certainly perceptively, Jennings did acknowledge Shocker's greatness in ensuing seasons. In 1926 he picked his all-time team and named Shocker to his third team of all-time great pitchers.[39] Jennings also wrote in his syndicated biography, *Rounding Third*:

> Every batter, no matter how good, has a weakness. It may be a trifle, but it is still there. He will prefer certain balls to others. Now, a pitcher may know a weakness of a batter, but knowing that weakness and being able to pitch to the exact spot that is weak are two different matters. A few inches either way mean disaster for the pitcher. Cobb had a reputation of being weak on low balls pitched inside. Every intelligent pitcher tried to pitch the ball low and inside for Cobb. Sometimes they did, but more often they did not. Urban Shocker, an unusually intelligent pitcher, used to pitch the ball below Cobb's knees for a third strike, hoping he would go after it. If Cobb bit on this low one, he was gone. There was not a chance to hit it. Cobb did not bend his knees enough to enable him to hit low pitching successfully. Smart pitchers knew this. Also, they knew Cobb was eager to hit. But few of them ever put their knowledge into beneficial use as Shocker did. The peculiar part about it was that these balls that could go for third strikes with Shocker pitching to Cobb would all have been called balls if Cobb had ignored them. But he was sure he could hit them and kept on trying.[40]

In all fairness to Cobb, he did not hit Shocker too poorly, with a career .292 batting average against him, in partial career statistics.[41]

5

False Start

"Who is that punk?" the Rookie asked,
"The one who's making that play?
His arm is gone and his legs look bad
And he's turning a little gray."
"You oughter know him," the Veteran said,
With a wrinkle deep in his brow.
"You oughter know him—and know him well—
He's you ten years from now."
—"The Rookie and the Vet Again" by Grantland Rice

Urban Shocker started playing for a Cleveland brewery team as a youth, and now he was joining a club owned by one of the nation's leading brewers, Jacob Ruppert. Just one year into their ownership of the Yankees, Ruppert and his partner, Til Huston, were still perennial losers. Ruppert and Huston made it clear the Yankees were not content being the weak sister of New York City baseball, behind John McGraw's Giants. They would aggressively spend money on talent to build a pennant winner.

And spend they did—over $100,000 combined, an unheard of sum, on established star Frank "Home Run" Baker, Federal League star Lee Magee, emerging pitcher Bob Shawkey, and a large group of promising youngsters.[1] The baseball world was skeptical, openly wondering just

5. Urban Shocker joined the Yankees for 1916 spring training in Macon, Georgia, where he stood out for his daring and pitching excellence. *Private collection of the family of Roger Shockcor*.

how improved the Yankees would be. There were sarcastic comments in the *Sporting News* about the Yankees going after quantity, not quality.[2]

Shocker joined a group of about fifty players who reported to the Yankees' training camp in Macon, Georgia, under the watchful eye of second-year manager Bill Donovan. There were three spitball pitchers Donovan called his "three Rays of sunshine": Ray Caldwell, Ray Fisher, and Ray Keating.[3] There was also a pitcher in camp who would not win his first game for six more years, due to control problems, but would then go on to win 196 more: Charles Arthur "Dazzy" Vance.

Shocker quickly stood out from the crowd for his daring and confidence in intra-squad games. He stunned players and spectators when he threw a spitter to Fritz Maisel with a 3-and-0 count and a slow ball to Wally Pipp on a 3-and-1 count. Sportswriter Harry Schumacher could not figure out whether the rookie had committed "two master bones" [big mistakes] or had shown "real nerve [that] hasn't had an equal on this trip." The reporter explained, "Theoretically both deliveries were ill-advised, to put it mildly. Actually, they were just what the situation called for."[4]

A veteran Yankees infielder took Shocker aside and told him, "Look here, kid, be careful of those slow balls and that spitter against these fellows. They'll murder you." The upstart pitcher snapped back, "You get in there and do the hitting. I'll attend to the pitching."[5]

The good-natured Donovan, a great pitcher for the Tigers a decade earlier, had deep roots in Detroit and had been following Shocker's progress with Ottawa. He spoke highly of his pitcher as "a live wire" who had enormous potential.[6] Early in spring training, he was impressed. "Right now," said Donovan, "Urban Shocker, the young spitball pitcher, looks to have more stuff than any of the other youngsters."[7]

A few days later, Shocker was injured while covering first base, when teammate Tim Hendryx spiked him in the foot. It was a nasty wound, about an inch deep and a couple inches wide. He was expected to be out for a few weeks but returned in just four days. This was a precursor of what he would experience throughout his career: a number of fairly serious injuries from which he would bounce back far sooner than expected.[8]

Donovan decided that the Yankees would send Shocker down to the high Minors for the season to give him regular work. (The Class A league

Richmond Climbers were considered.)[9] The club had to have him pass through waivers first, to permit other Major League teams to claim him before he was sent down. Lee Fohl, the manager of the Cleveland Indians and a savvy evaluator of pitching, claimed Shocker and mailed in the $1,000 claiming fee to the league office.[10] The Yankees hastily withdrew Shocker from waivers.

Did the Indians' claim reach Chicago before Shocker was pulled back? There is reason to believe the Yankees did not act quickly enough. One New York reporter noted that only "rapid work over the telegraph wires at the last minute" saved Shocker for New York.[11] The Indians refused to waive their claim, and league president Ban Johnson may have decided to help the struggling New York club and its new owners.[12]

When Ruppert and Huston had bought the Yankees a year earlier, they were disappointed that Johnson and the league did not provide them with much talent to build around. Johnson also wanted his league to have a strong team in the nation's biggest city. He ruled for New York on this Shocker dispute and returned the $1,000 to Cleveland.

Shocker stayed with the Yankees for the start of the 1916 season. His first Major League appearance came on April 24, when he pitched the final three innings of a lopsided loss to Walter Johnson and the Senators. Nine days later, Shocker appeared in a more meaningful role: he entered in the eighth inning of a 1–1 game against the Athletics.

With a man on base and aging star Napoleon Lajoie at the plate, Shocker's hubris may have gotten the better of him. With two strikes on Lajoie, the oldest regular in the Majors at age forty-one, Shocker grooved a fastball, a pitch he thought the veteran could not get around on. But Lajoie knocked it out of the ballpark for a 3–1 Philadelphia lead.[13] The Athletics held on to win, 3–2, and Shocker got his first loss.

The players who hit home runs off Shocker early in his career were quite a select group of future Hall of Famers. Tris Speaker hit the second one Shocker gave up, and Ty Cobb hit the fourth. Both Babe Ruth and Home Run Baker were in the first ten Shocker allowed. And in 1927 Jimmie Foxx hit his first of 534 home runs off Shocker.

In May 1916, no less a judge than Athletics manager Connie Mack predicted the Yankees would win the American League pennant that

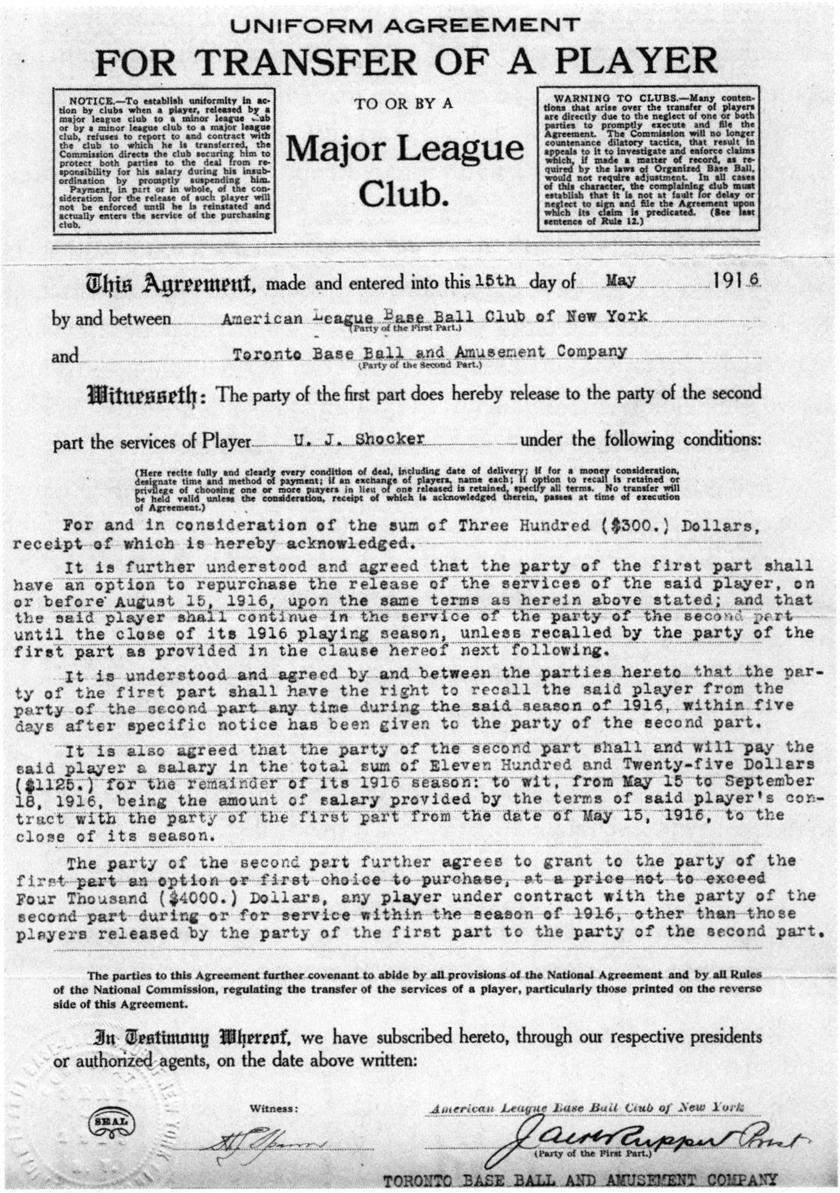

UNIFORM AGREEMENT

FOR TRANSFER OF A PLAYER

TO OR BY A

Major League Club.

NOTICE.—To establish uniformity in action by clubs when a player, released by a major league club to a minor league club or by a minor league club to a major league club, refuses to report to and contract with the club to which he is transferred, the Commission directs the club securing him to protect both parties to the deal from responsibility for his salary during his insubordination by promptly suspending him.
Payment, in part or in whole, of the consideration for the release of such player will not be enforced until he is reinstated and actually enters the service of the purchasing club.

WARNING TO CLUBS.—Many contentions that arise over the transfer of players are directly due to the neglect of one or both parties to promptly execute and file the Agreement. The Commission will no longer countenance dilatory tactics, that result in appeals to it to investigate and enforce claims which, if made a matter of record, as required by the laws of Organized Base Ball, would not require adjustment. In all cases of this character, the complaining club must establish that it is not at fault for delay or neglect to sign and file the Agreement upon which its claim is predicated. (See last sentence of Rule 12.)

This Agreement, made and entered into this 15th day of May 1916

by and between American League Base Ball Club of New York
(Party of the First Part.)

and Toronto Base Ball and Amusement Company
(Party of the Second Part.)

Witnesseth: The party of the first part does hereby release to the party of the second part the services of Player U. J. Shocker under the following conditions:

(Here recite fully and clearly every condition of deal, including date of delivery; if for a money consideration, designate time and method of payment; if an exchange of players, name each; if option to recall is retained or privilege of choosing one or more players in lieu of one released is retained, specify all terms. No transfer will be held valid unless the consideration, receipt of which is acknowledged therein, passes at time of execution of Agreement.)

For and in consideration of the sum of Three Hundred ($300.) Dollars, receipt of which is hereby acknowledged.

It is further understood and agreed that the party of the first part shall have an option to repurchase the release of the services of the said player, on or before August 15, 1916, upon the same terms as herein above stated; and that the said player shall continue in the service of the party of the second part until the close of its 1916 playing season, unless recalled by the party of the first part as provided in the clause hereof next following.

It is understood and agreed by and between the parties hereto that the party of the first part shall have the right to recall the said player from the party of the second part any time during the said season of 1916, within five days after specific notice has been given to the party of the second part.

It is also agreed that the party of the second part shall and will pay the said player a salary in the total sum of Eleven Hundred and Twenty-five Dollars ($1125.) for the remainder of its 1916 season: to wit, from May 15 to September 18, 1916, being the amount of salary provided by the terms of said player's contract with the party of the first part from the date of May 15, 1916, to the close of its season.

The party of the second part further agrees to grant to the party of the first part an option or first choice to purchase, at a price not to exceed Four Thousand ($4000.) Dollars, any player under contract with the party of the second part during or for service within the season of 1916, other than those players released by the party of the first part to the party of the second part.

The parties to this Agreement further covenant to abide by all provisions of the National Agreement and by all Rules of the National Commission, regulating the transfer of the services of a player, particularly those printed on the reverse side of this Agreement.

In Testimony Whereof, we have subscribed hereto, through our respective presidents or authorized agents, on the date above written:

SEAL

Witness:

American League Base Ball Club of New York

Jacob Ruppert Prest

(Party of the First Part.)

TORONTO BASE BALL AND AMUSEMENT COMPANY

6. The Yankees optioned Urban Shocker to Toronto of the International League in May 1916, where he had a spectacular three-month stint. New York recalled him in August, setting off a storm of protest. *Private collection of Steve Steinberg.*

year because of all the talent they had.[14] With the May 15 twenty-five-player limit deadline approaching, the Yankees sent Shocker to Toronto on Option with a Right of Recall.[15] They avoided the waiver route through an arcane procedure that allowed teams to assign a limited number of players to a Minor League club while keeping "strings" on them.

Under the May 15 transfer agreement of "U. J. Shocker" to the Maple Leafs, the Yankees paid Toronto $300 for "an option to repurchase the release of the services of the said player, on or before August 15, 1916, with the right of recall within five days of the Yankees giving such notice."[16]

Why the Yankees' business manager, Harry Sparrow, did not employ such a seemingly foolproof method of protecting Shocker back in March, when he was put on waivers and left exposed, is a legitimate question. Perhaps Sparrow, in his second year on the job, was not familiar with the option route. It is also possible that since a team could send only a limited number of players down on optional assignments, Sparrow wanted to preserve as many of those options as possible.[17]

While the Toronto Maple Leafs were in the highest class International League, Shocker was not happy, to say the least. One New York writer said the young pitcher "raised the howl that a Numidian lion would have been proud to call his own."[18] Ultimately, he had no choice but to report to the Leafs. He would show Donovan that it was a mistake to send him down. Shocker would be back. Soon.

6

A Magical Summer on the Island

The Toronto Maple Leafs played their baseball games in an idyllic setting at Hanlan's Point on Toronto Island.[1] Their waterfront stadium was adjacent to a spectacular amusement park, and all three were owned by entrepreneur Lol Solman. His Toronto Ferry Company shuttled thousands of people across the bay from Toronto, especially on summer weekends. The lights of the park were dazzling when the sun was setting and made the entire scene seem like a fairy tale. It was hard to realize that a horrible war was being fought in Europe.

Shrieks could often be heard from the Big Scream roller coaster and the carousel, while the scenic railroad offered a more leisurely pursuit. The bike path and nearby roller rink seemed to be constantly moving with a series of wheels in motion. The boardwalk was usually crowded, with people getting off and on the side-wheelers, some of which carried more than a thousand people.

There were open-air performances of plays and vaudeville, and the sound of a big band could be heard from the dance pavilion. Informal baseball games were often going on nearby. There were picnics on the beach, while other visitors dined at the more formal tea garden. And nearby were the hotels and the cottages that served as summer residences of the wealthy.

Hanlan's Point Stadium, which seated eighteen thousand, was built in

7. The enchanting island setting of the Toronto Maple Leafs' ballpark made for a surreal backdrop, with an amusement park adjacent. Fans came to the ballgames by boat from the mainland. *Toronto Public Library.*

1910 and replaced the original one, destroyed in a 1909 fire. It was here that Boston Red Sox pitching sensation Babe Ruth hit his first professional home run on September 5, 1914, playing for Bill Donovan's Providence Grays. That home run ball is probably still sitting at the bottom of the nearby bay.[2]

The Leafs had started the season poorly, losing twelve of their first fourteen games. Shocker arrived in Toronto by train at noon on May 17 and rushed to the ballpark. He pitched a complete-game victory in the home opener that afternoon, 5–3. A steady drizzle and a cold wind kept the crowd down, but International League president Ed Barrow was in attendance. After serving three seasons as the manager of the Boston Red Sox, he would join the Yankees as business manager after the 1920 season.

The league's teams were an assortment of players on the way up, on the way down, and those who never had and never would make it in the Majors. A teammate of Shocker's on the way down was former New York

Giants star Red Murray.[3] He had played in nineteen World Series games and surely gave Shocker a sense of postseason play. A teammate who was older than Murray and who was going nowhere in particular was catcher Paul Krichell. He would find decades of success as a Yankees scout, starting in the 1920s.[4]

In his first month with the Leafs, Shocker ran his record to 7-0, including a three-hitter and two four-hitters. The Leafs' season was slowly turning around. Shocker even hit a home run to win one game. It wasn't the Majors, but Toronto was a lot "closer" than Ottawa. He was in the highest level of the Minors.

Shocker was getting noticed, and he enjoyed the attention from the Toronto press. "The progress of the Toronto baseball team seems to be spelled . . . 'Shocker,'" wrote one reporter. "The lesson to a greeny like myself would seem to be—a little more of the Canadian League in class and a good deal less of the worn-out warhorses who are slipping from the big leagues, just grasping this league with a fingernail hold on their downward slide."[5]

The national press was taking notice, too. A *Sporting News* reporter wrote that Shocker was a "life-saver. This boy is ideal in every way, a willing worker, as he has shown in pinches, and a real genuine pitcher."[6]

In late June, Shocker's temper was on display; he was ejected from a game for arguing balls and strikes—while at bat.[7] A couple weeks later, when he won his 10th game, the *Toronto Globe* described his spitter: "The old saliva sling, with the able assistance of copious quantities of slippery elm to lubricate the ball, is what beat the southerners [Richmond]."[8]

There was something special about that win over Richmond, a 3–0 shutout. It was the first of Shocker's five straight shutouts. On July 23, he capped the streak with an 11-inning no-hitter for a 1–0 win over the Rochester Hustlers, in Rochester. In the sixth inning, two Toronto errors almost led to the Leafs' downfall. Shocker walked only one man and hit a triple in the game, though it did not result in a run. His key hit was a successful bunt for a single in the 11th inning that pushed a teammate into scoring position and led to the winning run.

When he was finally scored on in the eighth inning of his next game against the Montreal Royals (with the temperature close to 100°, he cooled himself off with sponges of ice water), Shocker had set a new International League record of 54 consecutive scoreless innings. It was also just an inning short of Walter Johnson's Major League record.[9]

While Shocker was dominating the International League, the Yankees were captivating New York City and surprising the country by moving into first place in late June and staying there for a month. Their high-water mark was a 43-27 record and a 3½-game lead on July 7.

But clouds were forming on the Yankees' horizon. On the very day Shocker was optioned to Toronto, May 15, Fritz Maisel, the club's speedy outfielder, broke his collarbone. In early July the club lost another outfielder when Frank Gilhooley broke his leg, just above the ankle. Less than two weeks later, their star third baseman, Frank Baker, broke some ribs. A few days after that injury, their sensational pitcher, Nick Cullop, collapsed on the mound with a torn stomach muscle.[10] The club also suffered numerous lesser injuries.

The Yankees became, in the words of one sportswriter, "almost helpless at bat."[11] Yet they somehow held onto first place as late as July 28. John McGraw, whose New York Giants were struggling in fourth place in the National League, was moved to say that he had never seen a club show more gameness than the Yankees.[12] But then the bottom fell out. In the next four days the Yankees played six close games with the St. Louis Browns and lost all of them, the last one in 14 innings. They scored a total of only eight runs in the six games. By August 3, they had fallen to fourth place.

They were so shorthanded that they even signed a couple of veterans out of retirement, Rube Oldring (from his New Jersey farm) and Solly Hofman (from his Chicago baseball clinic). The two men contributed little.

Just about everyone who followed baseball in Toronto dreaded the possibility that the Yankees would recall Shocker. A mid-July *Toronto Globe* headline expressed the anxiety: "Pray Donovan to Let Him Stay: We Need Shocker a Million Times Worse Than New York Does."[13] New York hated to hurt the Leafs, who were threatening to move into first place, but they were desperate.

On August 3 the Yankees recalled Shocker and triggered a firestorm of debate across the baseball world. It would not be the last time Urban Shocker would be in the eye of the storm. In this instance it was not an act of his choosing, though the outcome was to his liking. As far as he was concerned, he never should have been sent down by the Yankees. Ultimately the New York owners may have been too sensitive to Toronto's needs and waited too long to salvage a pennant-contending season. Such an outcome may have been lost regardless because of their weakness at bat.

Toronto's president, J. J. McCaffrey, announced he would not return Shocker until the end of the International League season, making the groundless claim that the recall option was illegal.[14] The Leafs were in third place with a 46-41 record at the time and had sentiment on their side. But they had willfully entered into the agreement, which clearly gave the Yankees the right of recall. The National Commission, baseball's governing body, ruled the Leafs had to comply.[15]

Other Minor Leagues and their teams proposed a change to the option regulations. Once a player was optioned out, they argued, he could not be recalled until after the end of that club's season. Such a proposal was not adopted.

The *Sporting News* addressed the subject in an editorial: "It doesn't seem to occur to the minor league critic that if it were not for the optional release system attacked, the minor club probably never would have had the player at all. . . . The advantage of the use of the player until his recall certainly seems to balance the embarrassment that may occur through his recall."[16]

The following week, on August 10, Yankees co-owner Jacob Ruppert wrote an open letter—an apology of sorts—in the baseball weekly, pointing out that the unprecedented wave of injuries had left him no alternative but to recall Shocker.[17] "It is a poor rule that won't work both ways," he said, noting the benefit that the Minor Leagues get from the players sent to them, as well as from the players they sell to the Majors. Of course, he added, the Yankees had every right to recall Shocker anyway.

A week later, a *Sporting News* columnist noted that while Bill Donovan had caused gloom to descend over Toronto, the International League owners "put their own neck in the noose" by accepting players on optional agreements. The arrangement worked both ways, he continued, and the Minor Leagues "had sacrificed their baseball dignity to 'stand in' with the big fellows in the hopes of getting players that will keep them in their pennant races."[18]

The Leafs finished the season in fifth place, 8½ games behind the Buffalo Bisons, the pennant winners. Ironically, Buffalo benefited from the arm of Herb Pennock, a young pitcher that the pennant-winning Boston Red Sox had sent them for the stretch run.[19]

Shocker finished his Toronto season with a 15-3 record and a 1.31 earned run average.[20] For one hundred years, that has remained the lowest earned average for a pitcher in the highest class of the Minor Leagues (Class A at the time; now Class AAA). What is more remarkable is that his last two starts—after he knew he was going back to New York—were poor outings in which he gave up 10 earned runs in 12⅔ innings. Whether he lost focus or interest in his Toronto season at that point is open to debate. Before those two games, his earned run average for the season stood at 0.89.

7

Motor City Mischief

I send you my sons and my favorite ones,
The sons that I love the best;
I send them to you when I know they are due
And ready to tackle the test.
I send you my sons, but it isn't a gift;
It's merely a loan, for when
They have served out their days of "promotion and pay,"
They come back to my arms again.
—from "The Bush to the Big League" by Grantland Rice

Shocker joined the Yankees in his hometown on August 5 and saw the New Yorkers lose their ninth straight game, in 14 innings to the Tigers. Sportswriter Fred Lieb asked him whether he expected more challenges from Major League batters than those in the Minors. Shocker's reply was quick. "I don't know why. One league is just the same as another. They fall for my stuff in one just as they do in the other. . . . I got a ball none of them will do much with."[1]

If things were not difficult enough for the Yankees, their erstwhile star pitcher, Ray Caldwell, who had won 37 games for them in 1914 and 1915, had simply walked out on his team.[2] "When half the team was in the infirmary and the other half on its way," wrote Harry Schumacher, "Caldwell cast aside all restraint to the rip-roaringest rout of them all."[3]

8. New York was the entertainment capital of the country, and celebrities were often in attendance at baseball games. Actress Olive Thomas, whose 1920 death in Paris would generate rumors and conspiracy theories, appeared at a September 1916 benefit game between the Yankees and the Giants. L-R: Angel Aragon, Wally Pipp, Bill Donovan, Charlie Mullen, Nick Cullop, and Fritz Maisel. *Private collection of Steve Steinberg.*

The usually easygoing Bill Donovan fined and suspended Caldwell for fifteen days. Caldwell disappeared and was done for the season.

It was no secret in baseball circles that Caldwell had a drinking problem. Little was understood about alcoholism at the time; it was not looked on as a disease but rather as a character flaw. Typical was the comment by veteran sportswriter Joe Vila: "The trouble with Caldwell is that he has a child's brain. . . . He lacks good common sense. He is easily led, and once he falls, there is no help for him."[4]

Newspapers rarely stated that a player had a drinking problem; the euphemism usually used was that he had "violated training rules." In an act of unusual candor, a *Sporting Life* reporter wrote in 1914 that Caldwell had an "occasional flirtation with that which is amber and foamy."[5]

Shocker had enjoyed Caldwell's company early in the 1916 season, when they relaxed over beers after ballgames, but his absence now meant more opportunities for the rookie. The chance came a week later when Shocker got his first career start at the Polo Grounds.[6] He was sensational, giving up just two hits and one unearned run to the Athletics in eight innings.[7] The sportswriter who used the pseudonym Right Cross described Shocker this way after the game: "Shocker is spindly of leg, powerful of chest, throws with an overarm movement and packs a . . . punch in the shape of a 'spitter' and a Walter Johnson fastball. Shocker is surely ripe for fast company."[8]

Shocker was in the starting rotation now. On August 18 he earned his first Major League victory, and it did not come easily. He went the distance in a 13-inning game against Lee Fohl's Indians. New York first baseman Wally Pipp had tied the score with his eighth home run of the season; it brought him even for the league lead with teammate Frank Baker.

One reporter noted that Pipp had "battered" the ball "far into the populace inhabiting the deepest corner of the [right-field] stand."[9] He would lead the league in home runs that year (the first Yankee to do so; he edged Baker, 12 to 11) and the next. Pipp had been one of the first acquisitions of the new Yankees owners the previous year, and he came with a long-ball reputation. He had led the International League with 27 home runs in 1914, when he played for the Rochester Hustlers. He would become a fixture at first base for the Yankees for a decade, where he excelled defensively, until Lou Gehrig replaced him for an even longer period of time.

Shocker was not sharp in earning his first victory, walking six and giving up 11 hits. But, in the words of one New York reporter, Shocker was "at his best with runners on the bases . . . to show his mettle in a pinch."[10] It was something he would do throughout his career, conserving his energy and bearing down the most when men were on the bases.

In early September Shocker threw his first shutout, a five-hitter over the A's and Joe Bush, a pitcher he would cross paths with over the years. But his biggest game of the season was still to come.

The Tigers were in the 1916 pennant race all season long. On the morning of September 14, they were at home against the Yankees and tied with Boston for first place. Hughie Jennings, aware of Shocker's Detroit roots, had organized Urban Shocker Day for the game. Shocker's many Detroit friends and former semipro teammates were invited, and he would be honored with gifts before the game.

Had Jennings suddenly become magnanimous in the heat of the pennant race? Not at all. The *New York Times* reporter explained Jennings's real intent: "Not to honor Shocker, but to jinx him. What does a ball player do when a celebration is arranged for him and presentations are heaped upon him? Every street Arab [homeless urchin] knows the answer. He blows. Here was Jennings' scheme in all its infamy. Very clever. A diabolical plot." But Shocker did not follow tradition or superstition. After accepting a travel bag from his niece during the pregame ceremony, he handcuffed the Tigers on five hits for a 4–2 Yankees victory. Ty Cobb went hitless. The *Times* reporter noted that Jennings had been thwarted "in regular Frank Merriwell style by Urban Shocker, who made a triumphant return to his hometown."[11]

The key play was the Yankees' double suicide squeeze, one of baseball's most exciting and now rarest plays. With Elmer Miller on third base and Joe Gedeon on second, Detroit pitcher Willie Mitchell went into a "half windup" to Yankees catcher Al Walters. The *New York Tribune* described what happened next: "Walters rolled a slow teaser to [second baseman] Pep Young, and Miller slid over the plate. His dust had only risen, it seemed, when a fresh cloud geysered into the air, hurled up as Gedeon hit the dirt and slid over the plate safely. The play was brought to a perfect ending, for Walters beat the hit out."[12]

A Detroit sportswriter tried to make sense of what Shocker had accomplished. "Urban Shocker is the enigma flinger of the American League," wrote Harold Wilcox. "He seems to be vaccinated against special day jinxes, and he actually is immune from presentation hoodoos. . . . Not even his teammates know if he is a blooming boob embalmed in luck or whether he is the nerviest, gamest slabster in the league."[13]

In case anyone wondered where Donovan's loyalties lay, the former Tigers star said after the game, "I play no favorites. The more we knock down these big fellows, the better I like it."[14] Since the Red Sox lost that day, the Tigers had missed a chance to take sole possession of first place.

After the game, a joyous Shocker told reporters, "I would have pitched my arm off to defeat the Tigers."[15] He could have helped them in the pennant races of 1915 and this year, 1916. As much as he once had wanted to pitch for them, Shocker had put that idea behind him some time back. He had begun to sour on the Tigers' manager in 1914, when he had told an Ottawa reporter that Jennings should have put him on the Detroit roster that season.[16]

Jennings seemed to lack something in the way he ran his club, in Shocker's view. And the Yankees seemed to be a team on the rise. It was not until 1918 that respected Detroit sportswriter H. G. Salsinger went public with the flaws he saw in Jennings's management style, one that, he wrote, had probably cost the Tigers "three or four more pennants."

"Jennings is one of those managers who gives little encouragement . . . but is a strong believer in criticism for misplays," wrote Salsinger. "On the whole, molasses catches more flies than vinegar, and Jennings prefers vinegar. . . . Jennings' criticism of pitching has been keenly unjust many times, and it is unjust criticism that takes the heart out of a man."[17]

The 1916 Tigers finished in third place, four games out of first. The Boston Red Sox repeated as pennant winners and again won the World Series. The Yankees finished in fourth place, 11 games back; it was their first winning season since 1910.

Salsinger wrote in October, "Baseball history fails to reveal one great team that achieved greatness without a good pitching staff. . . . Well, then, why don't they go out and get pitchers? . . . Pitchers are just about as easy to pick as grand opera stars. Their numbers tally very nicely. They just happen, and they do not happen enough to permit a general circulation."[18] Hughie Jennings had let a young "opera star" named Shocker slip right through his grasp.

From Shocker's perspective, he just wanted to be a starting pitcher in the Major Leagues and felt he should have been in that position long before the late summer of 1916. A man in a hurry, he realized the career of a ballplayer was not long, at best. He had started his professional career in his mid-twenties, a relatively late start. Perhaps he had a sense that time was running out even as his career was starting.

8

The Returned Prodigal and the Coming Phenom

The rookie envied the veteran's way,
His ease and timing, his classy style.
He envied the smoothness through each play,
The form that came from a far-off while.
But the veteran watching the rookie play
Thought to himself in the sunny glow—
"I'd trade my head for his legs today,
The legs that I knew ten years ago."
—"The Rookie and the Vet" by Grantland Rice

An air of optimism hung over the Yankees' 1917 spring training camp in Macon. This team had been good enough to compete for the pennant the previous season until they were hit by the rash of injuries, and they were capable of doing so again. But with that optimism came rising expectations. After the 1916 season, one New York reporter said, "The prospect for next season is the finest that the Yankees have ever had to look forward to."[1] Yankees owners Ruppert and Huston were not patient men, nor were they good losers. They were ready for a winner, and they expected one.

A *Sporting News* writer said Ray Caldwell had taken "French leave" [departure without permission] in 1916. He had gone to Central America, where he pitched under an assumed name in Colon and became known as "the pearl of Panama."[2] Surely Frank Chance was thinking of Caldwell when he said, after he had resigned as manager of the Yankees in 1914, "Pitchers—in that one word is half the woes of a baseball manager. Heavens, what temperaments! They are as exacting as grand opera singers; as hard to manage as chorus girls, and a man has just as much chance of guessing their whims as he has in calling the right number at a lottery."[3]

The Yankees reluctantly took Caldwell back. Bill Donovan was more forgiving than the team's owners. "I don't care where he has been," he said. "He declares he has learned his lesson and will take care of himself."[4] But co-owner Til Huston wondered aloud, "Is it worth paying a man like Caldwell a salary of $8,000? Any help we may get from a player of this type is counteracted by the bad influence he will have on the other players."[5]

One of those other players was Urban Shocker. Caldwell admired the skill Shocker was showing and told a reporter, "That fellow has plenty of nerve. He's going to be a great pitcher some day."[6] Shocker, in turn, was drawn to Caldwell, perhaps for his easygoing nature and enormous appetite for life. Shocker looked forward to nights on the town with Caldwell—and what better town than New York City? The question was whether he would learn from the veteran's pitching skills or from his nightlife habits, what the *Sporting News* would call in Caldwell's obituary his "legendary escapades."[7]

During spring training, Donovan called Shocker "a second and better Jack Chesbro," referring to the Yankees' great spitball pitcher of the prior decade.[8] The Yankees had rewarded him with a substantial salary increase, to $2,100 for the 1917 season.[9] Harry Schumacher captured Shocker's progress and promise. "He has well-nigh perfect control to make his varied assortment of dips, slants, and floaters effective. To which he adds a powerful physique, the nerve of a burglar, and a comprehensive knowledge of the pitching trade. There is purpose in every move he makes, and it is impossible to worry or fluster him."[10]

Damon Runyon was more succinct. He simply called Shocker "a coming phenom," before the season began.[11]

The *New York Times* dubbed Caldwell "the returned prodigal."[12] On Opening Day, he was anything but effective. He gave up 10 runs to the world champion Red Sox; Babe Ruth got the easy win for Boston. In 1917 Caldwell would be unpredictable and undependable—terrible at times

9. Urban Shocker had a 12-8 record with a 2.61 earned run average for the 1916–17 Yankees. Yet his off-field activities forced the club's genial manager, Bill Donovan, to fine him. *Private collection of Dennis Goldstein.*

and brilliant at others. An example of the latter came when he won both ends of a doubleheader in late June against the Athletics. Their manager, Connie Mack, had been an admirer of Caldwell; perhaps he felt he could moderate the pitcher's behavior. A week later Mack offered Amos Strunk in a trade for Caldwell. The Yankees turned down the deal.[13]

Shocker had told Fred Lieb about a pitch he threw that hitters could do little with. While at Toronto, he had worked on his slow ball, one that Schumacher called a "tantalizingly, weary slow one."[14] Long before speed guns, one can only wonder how slow it was. When Shocker beat the Senators in his first start, sportswriter Walter Trumbull used vivid language to describe it: "Shocker's drop ball melts away like a pyramid of butter beneath an August sun."[15]

That month the Yankees returned to Toronto for an exhibition game against the Maple Leafs, who were now managed by Napoleon Lajoie. Shocker pitched for New York, and this time it was his home run that beat Lajoie. He may have been a pitcher, but Shocker took pride in his hitting, too.

The promise of the spring did not translate into the regular season for New York. The Yankees hung around first place until mid-May and then began to fall back. Perhaps symbolic of Shocker's season was a game in Cleveland on May 25. He took a 5–0 three-hitter into the ninth inning, when the Indians rose up for six runs. A New York sportswriter was moved to call it "one of the most sensational games ever played here."[16]

On May 30 Shocker saved a 2–0 win for the Yankees by tossing a perfect 15th inning, in relief of Slim Love, who had pitched 14 scoreless innings. One wonders whether Shocker had any feelings for Rube Schauer, the opposing pitcher, who threw all 15 innings and lost a heartbreaker. Schauer, born in Russia with the name Dimitri Ivanovich Dimitrihoff, came to the Majors highly touted, like Shocker. But he had not met expectations.[17]

On June 30 Caldwell and Shocker were out on the town and were not back to their Boston hotel by midnight. The Yankees fined Caldwell $100 and suspended him. They tagged Shocker with a $50 fine but did not suspend him. The next day one reporter wrote—somewhat prematurely as well as wishfully—that Shocker's fine "has no doubt cured that young man."[18]

10. Urban Shocker "buddied" with the Yankees' flamboyant and alcoholic pitcher, 6'2" Ray Caldwell. The club's speedy outfielder, 5'8" Frank "Flash" Gilhooley, stole 22 bases in 1916–17, seasons shortened by injuries. Both men went on to successful Minor League careers in the 1920s. *Private collection of Steve Steinberg.*

But the reaction toward the repeat offender, who now seemed to be corrupting other players, was far harsher. "Caldwell's fall from grace is the last straw," wrote Joe Vila. "He should be traded at once or be permanently barred. . . . The famous boxman must have lost his senses completely."[19] But the Yankees took him back after ten days, and he proceeded to throw 9⅔ innings of shutout ball in relief, in a 17-inning win in St. Louis. Yet early the next morning, Caldwell was arrested, charged with grand larceny for stealing a diamond ring from one Lucy Dick.[20]

The Yankees' serious injury problems did not go away in 1917. After the difficult rehabilitation of his broken leg, Frank "Flash" Gilhooley broke his collarbone in early May and was lost for two months. Armando Marsans broke his leg while sliding into home plate in early August and was done for the year. The Yankees had only recently traded for him.[21] Stereotyping was very common. Harry Schumacher introduced Marsans to Yankees fans as "a temperamental athlete, as fussy and fidgety as only a high-strung Cuban can be."[22]

But perhaps the most bizarre injury befell Shocker. While pitching in Boston in early July, he injured his arm while throwing a curve ball. It was described both as a twisted or torn elbow ligament and as a fracture of the ulna bone below the elbow, which resulted in nerve damage.[23] His arm was put in a sling and he was expected to miss at least two months, but he was out "only" twenty-four days.

Shocker made a study of batters and pitchers and had plenty of time to do so that month. A pitching controversy was raging that summer around Chicago's Eddie Cicotte and his mysterious shine ball.[24] The overwhelming majority opinion, encouraged by Cicotte, was that he really did nothing to affect the ball and only pretended to do so. The shine ball, in this view, was "bunk." Typical was the comment of a *New York Times* reporter, who wrote that the shine ball was the "imagination of superstitious batsmen" and had become "a sort of mental hazard for the batsmen."[25]

One person who did understand the pitch, though it got little coverage in the press, was Urban Shocker. After Cicotte shut out New York, 1–0, that year, Shocker explained that Cicotte's ball had an "emery ball effect," by adding dust and moisture to just one side of the ball.[26]

A week after Shocker came back from his arm injury, Ty Cobb homered against him. Unfortunately there is no record of any repartee they may have had as Cobb rounded the bases. The New York crowd may have appreciated Cobb's skill (he would win his 10th batting title in 1917), but Walter Trumbull noted that Cobb enjoyed the same popularity here "as a porcupine does with a bird dog."[27]

In late September Shocker had another late-game meltdown against the Indians. Working on a one-hitter and up 2–0 after seven innings, he then gave up six runs (five earned). He finished the season with good but not great numbers: an 8-5 record with an earned run average of 2.61, virtually the same he had in 1916. There were hints in the press that his fine may not have "cured" him of improper behavior. A writer from the *New York Evening Journal* sounded as if he were writing of Caldwell when he said, "Shocker should be one of the greatest pitchers in the game. But the young man has not paid strict attention to his work at times this year."[28]

Shocker continued to show his skill and moxie, not only on the mound but also at the plate. He had five sacrifice hits in only 52 plate appearances. More dramatically, papers reported he executed four squeeze plays, two of them with two strikes.[29]

On October 1 Shocker beat the Chicago White Sox, 4–2, who were on their way to the World Series, where they would beat the National League's New York Giants. The key blow was a triple by Yankees outfielder Flash Gilhooley, who then scored to break the 2–2 tie. Gilhooley had 16 stolen bases when he broke his ankle in 1916, and he never fully recovered. "From then on," he later said, "I was just a step slower, and a step in baseball means the difference between a hit and a putout."[30]

As the season moved into September, and the Yankees slipped out of the first division and below .500, it became increasingly clear that manager Bill Donovan would not return in 1918.[31] The official word did not come until after the World Series. The Yankees hired Miller Huggins, the manager of the St. Louis Cardinals and, before that, a scrappy second baseman for the Reds and the Cardinals.

Donovan had many sympathizers, if not supporters, who regretted seeing him replaced. George Daley of the *World* wrote, "It was his misfortune to take over a brittle team. It kept chipping off. Two or three broken bones were all that stood between Donovan and greatness. . . . Fate stood in the way."[32]

One thing Donovan never wavered in was his belief in Shocker. He had gone so far as to say, "I am sure in Shocker the Yanks have a man who will some day be one of the greatest pitchers in the game."[33]

9

The Dream Team

Urban Shocker had to chuckle at his good fortune. He was about to play on an All-Star team managed by Connie Mack, with pitcher Walter Johnson and outfielders Ty Cobb, Tris Speaker, and Joe Jackson.[1] It was quite a collection of baseball talent here in Fenway Park, as the cameras clicked away. And Shocker was in the pictures, next to Speaker and not far from Cobb. He had made it back to the Yankees, and this was where he belonged. These players were the best, and he would be, too.

The September 27, 1917, game was a benefit for the family of noted Boston sportswriter Tim Murnane, who had died suddenly earlier in the year. Murnane was a popular personality in Boston, where he had played before his respected newspaper career. The *Providence Evening Tribune* wrote in his obituary that he was "generally regarded as the greatest authority on the national game in the United States."[2]

This team of mostly American League All-Stars faced the Boston Red Sox and their young star pitcher, Babe Ruth, in an exhibition game. With the big crowd of more than seventeen thousand (the Red Sox averaged less than five thousand per game that season), word was spreading among the players that the game would generate more than $14,000 for Murnane's wife and four children.

Back in 1911, there had been a similar game. Cleveland pitching star Addie Joss had died of tubercular meningitis, and an exhibition game

11. Urban Shocker was a late replacement for the wayward Ray Caldwell on a 1917 All-Star team loaded with baseball's greats. The team played the Boston Red Sox to raise money for the family of the late sportswriter Tim Murnane. Some of those same stars (Walter Johnson, Ty Cobb, and Tris Speaker) had appeared in a benefit game six years earlier for the family of pitcher Addie Joss, who had died of tubercular meningitis. *Private collection of the family of Roger Shockcor.*

had raised about $13,000 for his family. Walter Johnson pitched in that game, and he would pitch today, six years later. Cobb and Speaker had played in that game, too.

It took a little luck for Shocker to land here.[3] The All-Stars had run short of pitchers as the game was approaching. First, Grover Alexander withdrew.[4] Then Ray Caldwell performed one of his disappearing acts. With his history of going off on periodic benders, it was impossible to know how long he would be gone and if he would show up.[5] So Bill Donovan sent Shocker instead.

Fans and players alike enjoyed the pregame activities. The Ziegfeld Follies girls, including Fanny Brice, sold scorecards. Will Rogers performed with his horse and ropes. Former heavyweight boxing champion John L. Sullivan, "the Boston strong boy," would coach third base for the Red Sox.

The ballplayers participated in a series of contests involving baseball skills. The long-distance throwing contest was won by Joe Jackson, with a toss of just under four hundred feet. Ray Chapman won the speed contest, running the bases in 14 seconds. Mike McNally tied a world's record by running to first base in 3.25 seconds. And Babe Ruth, who had hit a couple of home runs during the season, won the hitting contest, with a blow of just over four hundred feet.[6]

Connie Mack gave Shocker the honor of starting the game. He was followed by Howard Ehmke, the only other member of the team (at age twenty-three) who was not considered a star. Mack told his pitchers they would each throw three innings, with Walter Johnson the last of the trio. Shocker held the world champions scoreless, though he gave up a single, double, and triple (one hit per inning) and bore down with men on base. In the first inning, he retired Red Sox star outfielder Duffy Lewis after Dick Hoblitzell had hit a two-out triple.

Ironically, it was star pitcher Walter Johnson who gave up the only runs of the day, on a Lewis triple with two men on base.

Babe Ruth went five innings for the Red Sox and gave up only three hits. Rube Foster held the All-Stars hitless the final four innings, for a 2–0 Boston win.[7] The "dream" outfield of Cobb, Jackson, and Speaker hit only a combined 1-for-11. They switched outfield positions during the contest.

Even though he was not easily rattled on the mound, Shocker probably felt giddy in the dugout. He expected that in a few years, fans everywhere would think of him as belonging in such a group, not as a last-minute replacement.

10

The First Trade

Rail not at Fate for what your hand might be,
For, having drawn, the rest is up to you;
Stand by your cards and let the wide world see
That you can stick until the Game is through.
Play out the Game, whatever else befall,
And at the end, from Heaven unto Hell,
You'll find this test the greatest of them all,
"There goes a man who played a poor hand well."
—from "The Game" by Grantland Rice

On January 22, 1918, in his first official act as the manager of the Yankees, Miller Huggins traded Urban Shocker to the St. Louis Browns as part of a seven-player deal. Fritz Maisel and Nick Cullop, once promising players for the Yankees, went with Shocker, as did second baseman Joe Gedeon and catcher Les Nunamaker.[1] The key acquisition for the Yankees was second baseman Del Pratt, arguably the second best at his position, exceeded only by Chicago's Eddie Collins. The Yankees also got veteran pitcher and 300-game winner Eddie Plank.

Huggins was a former Cardinals second baseman and knew Pratt well, since they both were on St. Louis teams. With a fine all-round shortstop in Roger Peckinpaugh, Huggins wanted to strengthen the other side of his middle infield, and Pratt was the man, a unique combination of power and speed.[2]

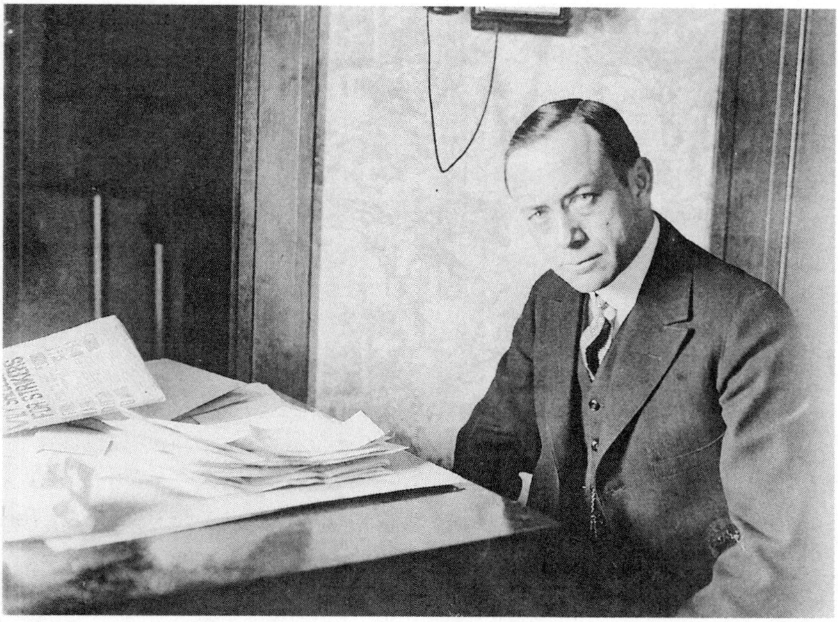

12. Miller Huggins replaced Bill Donovan as manager of the Yankees in late October 1917. Three months later, he sent Urban Shocker to the St. Louis Browns, despite not having seen Shocker pitch. Huggins had been advised to trade the pitcher because he was a troublemaker. Huggins never revealed the source of that input. *Private collection of Steve Steinberg.*

Why did Huggins trade Shocker, a man he apparently never saw pitch? Years later he explained. "I was foolish. I asked advice of too many people. . . . I was told that I would do well to get rid of Shocker as quickly as possible because he was a troublemaker. . . . I later discovered that my informant had done Shocker a very grave injustice. Urban never made trouble for anybody."[3] Huggins never revealed who his "informant" was. It could have been Yankees coach Duke Farrell. It certainly was not Bill Donovan, whose parting words with the Yankees were "Never trade Shocker."[4]

It also could have been the New York sportswriters. They wielded a lot of influence and were quite critical of Shocker, likely influenced by his friendship with Caldwell. A sampling of their remarks shows they supported the trade. Shocker was "a 'bad actor' whose mode of living was equally detrimental to his own interest and the discipline of the New

York club," wrote Harry Schumacher. "A youth of splendid prospects if he reforms, but absolutely worthless to any club unless he does."[5] Joe Vila was equally harsh, calling Shocker "a bitter disappointment" who "misbehaved himself."[6]

The hints that Shocker may have had a drinking problem came through between the lines. Sid Mercer called him "a rather convivial soul."[7] Dan Daniel noted that Shocker had a habit of "getting out of hand every now and then."[8] He added that Huggins wanted to trade Caldwell for the same reason. L. L. Arms noted sarcastically that "Shocker is said to favor the Great White Way. He will get a nice rest in St. Louis."[9]

Huggins's boss, Jacob Ruppert, might have influenced his new manager, if not to get rid of Shocker, at least to do what it took to land Pratt. Ruppert's remarks to *Baseball Magazine* suggested he played an active role in the deal.[10] They also revealed a surprising desperation on the part of the successful brewery owner. "For several years I have had my eye on Pratt," he said. Acknowledging that the Yankees gave up a lot for him, he continued, "But what can you do? I needed the player, everyone knew I needed him. One thing was certain, I couldn't come back empty-handed. . . . I got what I went after, though I had to pay out of all reason for him."[11]

Ruppert added some justification for the deal right after it was made. "One player who will be of assistance to the club is worth more than five who are of no assistance," he said.[12] Clearly he thought little of Shocker. The Browns also felt they were giving up little. Pratt had burned his bridges with his club; he had sued their owner for defamation of character. The Browns' irascible owner, Phil Ball, responded by saying he wanted "all Bolsheviks eliminated."[13] And Plank had turned forty-two and said he was retiring to his Gettysburg home.

Originally Yankees pitcher Ray Fisher was going to be in the trade, but he had enlisted in the Army Signal Corps. There may have been some hesitation on Huggins's part to offer Shocker, because the deal was put on hold for a while.[14] But he finally did pull the string. Years later, Huggins tried to justify the trade by saying he figured Shocker would be drafted, and the prospects for the war's duration were unknown.[15]

There were plenty of dissenting voices on the Yankees' move. Fred Lieb felt they were "held up" on the deal.[16] It did not make things any

13. Second baseman Del Pratt was the key to the Shocker trade for the Yankees. Miller Huggins wanted to strengthen his middle infield, and the durable Pratt seemed like the answer. He brought a hot bat to New York but also earned a reputation as a "clubhouse lawyer" who led an anti-Huggins clique. He would be traded away after the 1920 season. *Private collections of Dennis Goldstein.*

easier when Plank stuck to his retirement plans. "This is not an attempt at a holdout," he said. "An old fellow like me has gotten over that stage."[17] Washington president Clark Griffith said the Yankees would miss Shocker, and the Browns were getting a very valuable player.[18]

St. Louis was pleased with the deal. Sid Keener, the sports editor of the

St. Louis Times, was critical of Pratt's failure to deliver "in the pinches" and was excited about Shocker's "wicked spitball."[19] Bob Quinn, the savvy business manager of the Browns at the time, explained his thinking behind the trade in 1945. "All along, Shocker was the man I really wanted. . . . I knew he drank a little more than was good for him, but that he was a pitching natural. . . . Shocker alone was worth several Pratts."[20]

Shocker was enraged over the deal and vowed revenge on the Yankees. He always held Huggins responsible and did not blame Ruppert. George Daley said Shocker swore he would show that Huggins "had about as much judgment as a fish."[21]

The club's co-owner, Til Huston, who was in France at the time, said he never would have traded him. When Huston ran into Shocker at the 1921 World Series, the first for the Yankees and one the former Yankee missed out on, Huston told him, "My boy, if I hadn't gone to war, you never would have left my Yankee team. Joe Kelley told me that you were a real pitcher, but while I was across the water you were traded. You still look good to me."[22]

Shocker wanted to play in New York, on baseball's biggest stage, for his outsize ego and plans to dominate the game's hitters. Perhaps he sensed the Yankees were a team on the rise. He saw the money their owners were spending to build a winner, and he wanted to be a part of that. One can only wonder if he felt that Huggins would be a better leader than the undemanding Donovan.

This was much more than a player unhappy about a trade. This was an unforgiving player, with real animus, who swore vengeance on the club that "sold him down the river."[23] This was the phrase he used when he spoke to Fred Lieb about the deal. Virtually every New York newspaper knew of Shocker's bitterness and would reference it regularly in the coming years.

Damon Runyon added a bit of New York humor to the subject when he wrote in 1920, "The Yankees condemned Urban Shocker to St. Louis. Urban has never forgiven them for it, and there are people who say they don't blame him. They are people who have been to St. Louis in the summer."[24] One thing was clear: Shocker had wanted to remain a Yankee.

11

Love and War and a Little Baseball

On March 1, 1918, Urban Shocker married Minerva Davenport, a former vaudeville performer from Detroit.[1] It was her second marriage, and it is not known how long he had been acquainted with her.[2] She then accompanied him to spring training in Shreveport, Louisiana. By this time the United States had been in World War I for a year, but only now was the country gearing up for the war effort and ready to send meaningful numbers of soldiers and weapons to Europe.[3]

There is some confusion about Shocker's draft status and options. He registered for the draft, as all men between the ages of twenty-one and thirty-one were required to do, in May 1917. But he supported his parents, and there were reports before his trade to St. Louis that he was entitled to a deferment.[4] He also had four brothers already serving in the armed forces, two of them in France.[5] Yet on his Draft Registration card, Shocker answered the question, "Do you claim an exemption?" with a "no." Early 1918 reports said he had been classified 1-A in the draft, the first group to be taken.[6]

In the meantime, the baseball season got under way. Shocker was joining a team with an even longer tradition of losing than the Yankees. The Browns had not finished in the first division since 1908 and had 100-loss seasons three times since then.[7] Yet, like the Yankees, things seemed to be looking up for them after the 1916 season. Just a year earlier, they had a change of ownership as well as a change of managers.

When the upstart Federal League folded after the 1915 season, Phil Ball, the owner of its St. Louis franchise, the Terriers, bought the American League's Browns. He was a wealthy ice magnate, an irascible and impatient man who loved baseball and aviation.[8] He even piloted his own planes. "Frequently he said things he regretted afterward. He could cuss with anybody," wrote Dick Farrington in Ball's obituary.[9] When he first met Branch Rickey, the manager of the club he had just purchased, Ball is said to have muttered, "So you're the goddamn prohibitionist."[10] In 1916, when Ball accused two of his players, Del Pratt and Doc Lavan, of not playing their best or even of losing on purpose, they sued him.

The manager of Ball's Terriers, Fielder Jones, took over as skipper of the club late in 1914, when Ball replaced Mordecai Brown and gave Jones an ownership interest in the struggling Federal League club. Jones had been the respected player-manager of the 1906 world champion Chicago White Sox. He was familiar with spitball pitchers; he had perhaps the greatest ever, Ed Walsh, on his staff. Jones had left baseball two years later to tend to his timber holdings in Oregon.

In 1916 he had a merged club of Browns and Terriers, with more than fifty men under contract.[11] He was faced with the challenge of melding two cultures: that of his hard-nosed Terriers and that of the Browns of Rickey, a college man with a more patient and empathetic style.

Jones had a reputation as an innovative tactician who knew the game inside and out. He was tough. Just a year earlier, *Baseball Magazine* had described him as "cool, calm, calculating; mercilessly sarcastic."[12]

For the second straight year, Jones produced significant improvement. His 1915 Terriers had won 25 more games than they had the year before, and his 1916 Browns picked up 16 games on the 1915 club.[13] But like the Yankees, and to an even greater extent, the 1917 club fell far short of expectations. The Browns fell to a 57-97 record. And as odd as it may have seemed to many observers, Phil Ball criticized his manager for being too lenient and called for an "iron fist" in 1918.[14] Clearly Jones was on the "hot seat."

Jones called Shocker, his new acquisition, one of the best natural athletes

14. Urban Shocker's first St. Louis manager was the dour but brilliant baseball man Fielder Jones. He had led the 1906 Chicago White Sox to a World Series upset of the Cubs. But he took losses very hard and simply walked away from baseball after a particularly tough defeat during the 1918 season. *Walter P. Reuther Library, Archives of Labor and Urban Affairs, Wayne State University.*

he had ever seen.[15] He also said Shocker had the rarest of pitches, an up-curve, which only Al Orth, a submarine pitcher of the early Yankees, had thrown.[16] This is a puzzling comment because Shocker threw overhand. From a standpoint of pure physics, an up-curve can be thrown only with an underhand delivery.[17]

Once again Shocker sustained a significant injury. In his first start, on April 18, a line drive off the bat of Chicago's Happy Felsch broke a finger on his pitching hand as he tried to snare the ball. It laid him up for three weeks. His next start was against his former team, and he beat his drinking buddy, Ray Caldwell, in 12 innings. Shocker's performance was a messy one; he walked 10 men. Veteran New York sportswriter Sam Crane noted that Shocker still had that ability to bear down when in trouble and limit the damage. He called Shocker's game "splendidly heady."[18] Caldwell, who many were surprised was still a Yankee, had announced to the New York press that spring, "Just put it in the book that I will win 30 games this year."[19] He would fall 21 games short of his goal.

Shocker faced the Yankees four times between mid-May and early June. He insisted on pitching against them twice in any four-game series. After losing a 1–0 decision to New York in June, he came back to beat them with 4⅓ innings of relief work on one day's rest.

The big baseball news early that season was surrounding the Red Sox's slugging pitcher, Babe Ruth. Damon Runyon seemed to have a special ability to size up a player early in his career. On May 6, when Ruth was hitting .438 and had not yet started a game in the field that season, Runyon wrote, "He is undoubtedly that rare bird of baseball, the natural hitter. They are born, not made. Furthermore, he is undoubtedly one of the most powerful hitters the game has seen in a long time."[20]

Whether Runyon was a seer is unknown. But it is possible Red Sox manager Ed Barrow read Runyon's column that day; Boston was in New York to play the Yankees. Barrow started Ruth at first base that afternoon and then continued to do so. The Babe hit home runs on May 6 and 7 and pushed his batting average up to .500 on May 9. The *New York World*'s George Daley, not known for hyperbole, called Ruth "the seventh wonder of the world" that summer.[21] In late July Jack Dunn, Ruth's manager of his first professional team, in Baltimore, told Runyon's paper that if Ruth plays as a regular, "he will prove to be the most sensational player in the game."[22]

Shocker got a chance to face the Babe in one of his last games before he entered the army. He beat the Red Sox with a 2–1 five-hitter. Ruth was playing first base, and interim manager Jimmy Austin directed Shocker to walk him three times, which he did.[23]

Austin, the club's thirty-eight-year-old infielder and still a starter, had taken over for Jones on June 13, and Shocker had an indirect role in Jones's departure. Just a day earlier, he took a 4–0 lead over Washington into the ninth inning. The Senators then rallied for six runs, as Shocker and his teammates were overrun. After the game, Jones quickly departed without saying a word to anyone. He never returned—not to the Browns and not to baseball.

While an old-school baseball man, Jones found the game very stressful, and he took losses hard. Not known to the public at the time was that he had a serious heart ailment; it had played a role in his quitting the White Sox a decade earlier. When Jones died of heart disease in 1934, his *New York Times* obituary stated that he was one of baseball's three greatest managers, along with Connie Mack and John McGraw.[24]

Shocker reported for his army physical in Detroit on May 27 and was inducted on June 25. His last two games that season were against the Tigers; the schedule happened to have the Browns in Detroit, where he was preparing to enter the service. He finished his abbreviated season with a 6-5 record. While he tossed only 94 ⅔ innings, his 1.81 earned run average was second only to Walter Johnson's, among pitchers who qualified in that category.

Shocker joined the 340th Regiment of the 85th Infantry Division, activated at Camp Custer, at Battle Creek, Michigan, and deployed to France that August. The 340th did not fight as an intact force and instead supplied replacements for other units.[25] And the war ended quite suddenly, before many American troops reached the front. The mere fact that hundreds of thousands of them were about to do so proved a decisive Allied advantage in a war that had devastated both sides with casualties.

New York Daily Mirror sportswriter Dan Parker, who was stationed with Shocker's 85th Division in Clemency, France, told a strange war story. One night the men in the barracks were awakened by exploding shells that seemed to be coming from all directions. It turned out that Shocker had tossed his cartridge belt into the pot-bellied stove.[26] Whether or not he was reprimanded for the practical joke, Parker did not say. But when the young ballplayer was mustered out of the army in the spring of 1919, it was with the rank of corporal.[27]

Newspapers carried an account that year in which Shocker said he had escaped death in a hand-to-hand fight with a German soldier, whom he killed with his bayonet.[28] This seems unlikely; he probably saw no action. A catastrophic 1973 fire in St. Louis destroyed at least sixteen million military records, including Shocker's.[29] But Parker later confirmed their division did not see combat in the war.[30] It is possible Shocker was having fun with reporters, spinning a melodramatic war story. He had

15. Urban Shocker had a tumultuous year in 1918. He was furious that the Yankees had traded him, he entered into a marriage that would not last, and he went overseas as part of the U.S. war effort in France. *Private collection of Dennis Goldstein.*

a wry sense of humor, which may have been evidenced here as well as with his cartridge belt.

In March Shocker wrote the Browns that he would arrive stateside on the *Leviathan* in early April and that he had been working out in France.[31] It may have been a blessing that he did not muster out sooner: the influenza pandemic that claimed millions of lives worldwide was at its peak in late 1918. The ships with thousands of returning solders in close quarters became, in the words of historian John Barry, "death ships" and "floating caskets."[32] Shocker was discharged from Camp Upton on Long Island in late April 1919 and returned to St. Louis.[33]

On May 12 Shocker filed for divorce from Minerva, with whom he had lived for only a few weeks, on grounds of "extreme cruelty."[34] She filed a crossbill, contesting what appears to have been a bitter divorce. He claimed that she was suspicious and spread stories about him to baseball managers, and he said she threw dishes while he was throwing pitches. She in turn claimed he was so suspicious, he insisted she travel with him on road trips. They met in court in the summer of 1919 over an alimony hearing.[35] The divorce was not finalized until June 29, 1920.

Shocker appears twice in the 1920 Detroit census. He is listed as living with his wife (information she likely provided). He is also listed as living with his sister Cora Nieman and her husband, Fred, with whom he had been enumerated as residing in the 1910 census. The full story of Shocker's marriage and divorce is a puzzle that does not lend itself to easy explanation. But with the war over, he was ready to focus once again on his first love, baseball.

12

A Summer to Remember

Here comes a kid out of nowhere;
Millions soon leap to his name.
There goes a star who is fading,
Hurled from his summit of fame.
Going and coming they travel,
Like ships that pass in the dark,
One who is fading to ashes,
One who has just caught the spark.
—from "What Is Sport?" by Grantland Rice

In his first five weeks back with the Browns, starting on May 11, 1919, Urban Shocker tossed four shutouts, and the last was the sweetest, a 1–0 win over the Yankees in the Polo Grounds.[1] His rancor toward his former team was becoming well known, especially in New York. George Underwood called that 1–0 game a little skit that could have been called "Revenge of the Outcast's Triumph."[2] Monitor (the pen name of George Daley) wrote in the *World* that Shocker was still angry at his old club and "swore he'd make the Yanks regret it."[3] The headline in the *St. Louis Times* was blunt: "Shocker Avenges Exile by Yankees."[4]

Another thing was becoming well known throughout the baseball world: Urban Shocker had a devastating slow ball, perhaps the best in the game. Monitor said he struck out Frank Baker on "a slow, twisting floater that just lazily spun over the plate."[5] And Underwood wrote that "with his spitter working like a charm," Shocker had the ball "writhing and twisting across the plate until the Yankees threatened to dislocate their backbones trying to connect safely."[6]

Underwood was not the only observer who thought Shocker's slow ball was a spitter. The best explanation came from the purveyor of the pitch himself. "I can get a slow ball to drop just like a spitter," Shocker said. "You will find players all over the league talking about my slow spitter, which isn't a spitter at all, but a slow ball with a freak break."[7] He always credited that broken middle finger, which had healed badly and left a crook.

Harry Schumacher called Shocker's change of pace "as pretty a slow ball as ever was thrown."[8] George Moriarty never had to hit that pitch as a player just before Shocker's era, but he did have to call it during his long career as an umpire. "His slow ball tantalized the batsmen," Moriarty explained. "The umpires found it troublesome to gauge, as he contrived to keep it high. Ten feet in front of the plate, it looked as if it would be shoulder-high, but it invariably dropped low enough to be called a strike if the batsman passed it up."[9]

Since Shocker's pitch was not preserved on film, we will never know just how slow and dynamic it was. But a question emerges: was Urban Shocker a spitball pitcher? He himself admitted that batters mistook his slow ball for a spitter.

The answer is both yes and no. He did indeed throw the spitter, but used it less and less frequently as his career progressed. Shocker did not say he never threw the spitter; he merely said that batters often mistook his slow ball for a spitter. Whereas some spitball pitchers used the wet delivery almost exclusively, as did the Indians' Stan Coveleski, Shocker resorted to it only a few times each game.

Perhaps because he did not throw the spitball often, there are few descriptions of it. One comment on how he prepared it came from Damon Runyon in 1919. Shocker was "one of those slobbery spit-ballers," he wrote. "He almost eats the old apple when he is wetting it up and is very deliberate."[10] He bluffed it frequently, bringing his glove and ball to his mouth and suggesting he was "loading up."

This decoy maneuver was just one weapon in Shocker's chess match with hitters. And he had been developing and refining a number of weapons. Schumacher had noted Shocker's progress as a pitcher two years earlier, at the start of the 1917 season. He pointed out that Shocker had come to the Yankees in 1916 "as a spitballist pure and simple, but is now equipped with as extensive a repertoire as almost any member of his staff."[11]

The Browns had won about half their games in 1918, after Shocker entered the service. They finished in fifth place, with Jimmy Austin and then Jimmy Burke as acting managers after Fielder Jones had resigned. The club then brought Burke back for 1919. "Goose Hill" Jimmy had grown up on the sandlots of that St. Louis neighborhood and had managed the Cardinals for a good part of the 1905 season.[12] Like Jimmy Austin, the man he followed, his life had revolved around baseball for decades.

Burke, also known as "Sunset Jimmy," played for five Major League teams over seven seasons and managed in the Minors. Known as an aggressive, hustling guy, he told Fred Lieb, "I had to be a fighting ball player. That's how I got by. I wasn't a great ball player, so I made the best of such assets as I possessed."[13] He became an assistant coach for the Browns in 1918, where he operated as a buffer between the dour Fielder Jones and his players.

While he and Jones were both scrappy, Burke was an outgoing, smiling, rah-rah guy. Baby Doll Jacobson, who would emerge as a hitting star for the Browns in the 1920s, credited Burke with saving his career. Jacobson had five brief Major League tryouts, including three with John McGraw's Giants, starting back in 1912. Veteran New York sportswriter Sam Crane was impressed with his potential as early as 1913, because of his "pluck, gameness, and stamina."[14] But he lacked confidence and kept being sent to the Minors for more seasoning.

In the spring of 1919, Burke let Jacobson know he would be a starting outfielder. When Burke told him, "Send for your wife," Jacobson said, those four words "made me a success where I had been one of the most pitiable failures in baseball."[15] Jacobson relaxed and responded with a .323 batting average. He would follow 1919 with batting averages of more than .350 the following two seasons, on his way to a career .311 mark.

After leading the American League with 11 home runs in 1918, Babe Ruth was on a pace to hit more than twice that number in 1919.[16] Fans

16. Jimmy Burke was almost the polar opposite of Fielder Jones. He was a "rah-rah" manager who led by positive reinforcement. But he did not get the results that management wanted. The Browns had losing records in both 1919 and 1920, and Burke was not brought back for 1921. *From the collections of the St. Louis Mercantile Library at the University of Missouri–St. Louis.*

were turning out in enormous numbers to see him, and pitchers were taking notice. Shocker had a great hitter as a teammate, George Sisler, but Sisler was cool and detached, understated in his greatness. He was one of the league's top three hitters for the third season in a row. He again had a batting average above .340 and would finish at .352.

Unlike Ruth and Ty Cobb, Sisler lacked what sportswriters called "color."[17] As Christy Mathewson said, "He is every bit as valuable a player as Ruth, some people think more valuable. But he has another temperament. When he makes a great hit or a great play and the crowd is ready to idolize him, he modestly touches his cap and fades out of sight."[18]

The Babe was more of a Shocker kind of guy, nervy and audacious. Shocker relished facing the best, and Ruth filled that role.

Four days after shutting out the Yankees, the Browns went into Fenway Park. Boston's starting pitcher was one of the game's best, Carl Mays. He was also one of the least-liked players and had developed a reputation as a headhunter, one who used the beanball as a weapon to intimidate hitters.[19] In 1917 he had hit Buck Thrasher of the Athletics in the head, and he had knocked his own former teammate, Tris Speaker, unconscious the following year.[20] Mays came out on top against Shocker, 2–1, and Ruth got the better of this matchup with the Browns' pitcher with a couple of hits, but no home run.

On July 10, the Babe hit his tenth home run of the season off Shocker. Ray Caldwell was the opposing pitcher. Huggins had gotten tired of his act and traded him the previous winter.[21] In August, when Shocker again beat Boston, he did what few pitchers were doing this season: pitched to Ruth with men on base. The Fenway fans responded with cheers when he struck out the Babe with two men on base.[22]

One reporter wrote, "Five times the colossus faced the cool St. Louis hurler and not once did he reach the initial sack on a pass."[23] Shocker told *Baseball Magazine*, "There's one thing Babe Ruth can be counted on to supply. He gives the opposing pitcher a thrill."[24] The Ruth-Shocker confrontations would become some of the game's best in the coming years.

Sid Keener pointed out that Shocker not only had a great slow ball but he also mixed up his pitches and kept the batters guessing. It was what he had "under his cap" as well as "in his right arm," he said. When

Shocker again shut out the Yankees on July 16, he "worked the corners, he tossed his spitter around their knees and the fast one around the caps."[25] Jimmy Burke soon realized what hitters would find out repeatedly in the 1920s, that "No player ever gets a ball just to his liking with Shocker on the firing line."[26]

On August 7 the Browns came to New York for a series that had pennant ramifications. The two teams were clustered in a close race for second place, still within striking distance of the league-leading White Sox.[27] Shocker beat the Yankees for the fourth time in 1919, in the first game of a doubleheader, but he was not the center of attention on this day. Carl Mays was.

In their quest to build a winner, the Yankees had acquired Mays from the Red Sox, a controversial move that Ban Johnson, the league's president, opposed and tried to stop.[28] But the New York owners had gone to court, and before the start of the second game, the umpires were served with an injunction requiring them to let Mays pitch. He did so and won, and Colonels Ruppert and Huston soon secured a permanent injunction.[29] Mays would win 53 games for the Yankees in 1920–21 and 80 between 1919 and 1923.

The reaction around the league to the Mays deal was mostly unfavorable. Typical was this comment from Ed Wray, sports editor of the *St. Louis Post-Dispatch*: "The public will resent one-town domination of the game, and the club owners will become discouraged trying to compete against almost unlimited bankrolls, umpire bullying, and dictated rulings."[30]

Two weeks later, when the Browns faced Mays again, he managed to do something rare. He turned George Sisler, "that gentlemanly graduate of college circles, into a rampant belligerent."[31] In the first inning, the Browns' first baseman felt that Mays was trying to bean him. He also complained to umpire Moriarty that Mays was tampering with the ball.[32] Moriarty spent ten minutes checking the pitcher's glove, belt, cap, shirt, and pants for a possible foreign substance he was hiding. When none was found, Mays and Sisler had words and squared off to fight. Moriarty, a scrappy six-footer, stepped between them.

Sparks continued to fly throughout the game. Moriarty warned the Yankees on the bench to stop "riding" Sisler and ejected New York pitcher

17. The 6'6" Davenport was one of the tallest men in the game. His raw talent was undermined by his drinking. His fight with his club's manager and business manager late in the 1919 season ended his Major League career at age twenty-nine. Davenport was the second hard-drinking player with whom Urban Shocker had hung around. *Walter P. Reuther Library, Archives of Labor and Urban Affairs, Wayne State University.*

Bob Shawkey for excessive bench-jockeying. Mays hit two St. Louis players in the fourth inning, and the Browns took advantage of the beanings to score twice and tie the game. But the Yankees won, 5–2.[33]

Shocker's teammate, pitcher Dave Davenport, was a towering man for his day at 6'6". He won 22 games for the 1915 St. Louis Terriers of the Federal League, and he enjoyed moderate success with the Browns the next three seasons. In 1917 H. R. Hoefer described him in *Baseball Magazine* as "a man of few words, and between moody, taciturn, and glum most people would call him on a casual acquaintance."[34]

Davenport's performance had been in decline this season. There were hints in the press that he had a drinking problem. Even *Baseball Magazine* weighed in during the 1919 season that he would be released if he did not show "some energy in the right direction."[35]

With a 2-11 record for the season, Davenport did not show up for his scheduled start on September 2. He was suspended for the rest of the season without pay. The club was so short on pitchers that Shocker, who had suffered a shoulder injury a few days earlier, volunteered to pitch and was quickly "plastered up."[36] He managed to go eight innings in a 4–3 loss to Cleveland and Ray Caldwell, his old friend, who had resurfaced on the Indians.[37]

When Davenport heard that he had been shut down for the year, he attacked Burke and business manager Bob Quinn after the game, and there were reports he pulled a knife on them.[38] He never played another game for the Browns or any professional team, finished at the age of twenty-nine. The *Sporting News* later reported that the Browns wished Davenport, the Fred Fulton of baseball, "all the luck in the world, mostly bad."[39]

Perhaps it was just a coincidence, but right after the Browns' scrap with Davenport, the club left by train for Detroit, and Urban Shocker was nowhere to be found. Unable to pitch and needing to rest his arm, he stayed in St. Louis and apparently did not ask for permission or even inform management. Burke suspended him on September 4, and people were puzzled as to his whereabouts.

The *St. Louis Star* reporter wrote that the club needed Shocker badly, and noted, "The absent boxman is not the type who will quit without some fair reason. He has never been a disturber and has always proved loyal and faithful to Burke."[40] The *Sporting News* was less forgiving; their St. Louis correspondent wrote that Shocker "seems to have quit cold" and "sulked the last part of the season."[41] His season was shortened on both ends, yet he still managed to win 13 games. Only Walter Johnson had more shutouts in the American League.

On September 15, more than ten days later, Shocker sent a telegram to Burke explaining that his arm was lame and he needed an operation. The suspension was rescinded, with business manager Quinn smoothing things over. A few days later, Doc Lavan, now a member of the Cardinals and a practicing physician, performed the successful operation for removal of a "tumor."[42]

There may have been more to the Browns' concern and Shocker's suspension. Once again he was enjoying the nightlife and associating with a ballplayer who was not the best influence. The *Sporting News* reporter noted that Shocker had been "chumming together around Grand and Olive" (in downtown St. Louis) with Dave Davenport, who was also his roommate on the road. The report tried to minimize Shocker's behavior, saying it was temporary because he "fell in with bad company."[43] Yet once again Shocker had become close to a player who drank himself off his team.

13

The End of an Era

The Deadball Era (1901–19) was coming to an end, and the Lively Ball Era was about to begin. "The fight against the predominance of the pitcher is almost as ancient as baseball itself," wrote sportswriter Irving Sanborn in September 1920.[1] Baseball is cyclical in nature, and events were transpiring to give the hitter the upper hand in his struggle with the pitcher.

Starting in 1920, trick pitches, also known as "freak" pitches, were banned, and the spitball was among them. A decade earlier, *Spalding's Official Baseball Guide, 1909*, had a symposium on the spitball. Most of the sportswriters favored banning "the wet one." Typical was this comment: "We must look for some legislation before long in regard to the pitcher. We are all willing to concede that he is a plucky, determined Base Ball character, and the very fact that he is so persistent and combative makes it necessary now and then to subordinate him a little to the other men who are part of the game."[2]

Yet even then, there was concern that a ban would be difficult to enforce. "While the spit ball is sloppy, dirty, and disgusting," wrote W. A. Phelon of the *Chicago Journal*, "it is, I fear, impossible to get rid of."[3]

The discussion on banning the pitch went dormant for a number of years. When the two masters of the pitch passed from the scene, Jack Chesbro (last season as a regular, 1908) and Ed Walsh (last effective season, 1912), it would have been easy to ban the pitch: there were no star pitchers who would be driven out of the game. Now, as 1920 approached, there were many good ones, and Urban Shocker was one of them.[4]

The debate was rekindled in the second decade of the century because pitchers had resorted to extreme measures of "doctoring" the ball to affect its flight: the emery ball, the mud ball, the paraffin ball, the shine ball, and other "freaks." They had simply taken it too far. At the same time, baseball's owners saw the crowds Babe Ruth was drawing. Bringing more hitting into the game would bring more fans into the ballparks. It would also attract more casual fans, including immigrants, who could more easily relate to a high-scoring game than to a low-scoring one dominated by pitching.[5]

Baseball Magazine had a two-part series on the subject in the summer of 1919, and the publication's editor went to the heart of the matter. "The spit ball hurts batting and therefore strikes straight at the heart of the game's popularity," wrote F. C. Lane. "The game has become one-sided; too much of a mere pitchers' duel. Something should be done for the downtrodden batter. One of the simplest and easiest ways to lighten the batter's load is to throw out the spitball."[6]

Baseball's winter meetings in December 1919 took place against the backdrop of widespread rumors of a "fix" of the 1919 World Series.[7] The owners' concerns could have added impetus to clean up the game and generate more hitting as a bulwark against a possible scandal. And Sanborn made an interesting observation in his article. He suggested the game was becoming too vulnerable to gamblers because one player—the pitcher—had so much control over the outcome. Simply put, a low-scoring game was more vulnerable to a fix.[8]

In February 1920, the Joint Rules Committee enacted regulations that banned pitches such as the shine ball and the mud ball.[9] There was a fierce debate on the spitter. Was spit a "foreign substance" on the ball? Ultimately they decided to ban that pitch, too.[10] As a concession to the spitball pitchers, as well as the owners of teams with spitballers, they were given one year, 1920, to continue throwing that pitch while they developed a replacement. By 1921 the spitter would be illegal for all pitchers.

How did the ban on trick pitches increase hitting? There were a couple of ways. Doctored balls had erratic movement as they approached the plate. Shocker's spitter, for example, broke straight down, as if it had fallen off a table. F. C. Lane said of the spitter, "It is a tricky and dangerous ball to control. But once mastered as only a few have been able to master it, it is all but unhittable."[11]

Also, many of the trick pitches were hard to control and potentially dangerous to a hitter. Now that they were banned, the batter could get comfortable and settle in at the plate.

Organized Baseball introduced one more change at this time. They instructed umpires to keep fresh white balls in play. In the Deadball Era, a game might be played with just two or three baseballs. Even foul balls had to be returned by the fans; after all, they were the property of the home team. The ball quickly became dirty (hard to see) and mushy (hard to hit very well or far), yet it stayed in the game.

During the 1920 season, the owners felt they were spending too much money on balls, so umpires were instructed to keep balls in play longer.[12] They did so until August 1920, when Carl Mays pitched a ball that struck Ray Chapman, fracturing his skull. He died twelve hours later. The dirty ball may have played a role in his not seeing it until it was too late. After that tragedy, the umpires replaced dirty and scuffed balls regularly. "Pitchers will tell you," wrote Lane in 1929, looking back at the 1920s, "that the lively ball troubles them much less than the everlasting 'new' ball."[13]

There was one last contributing factor to the emergence of the Lively Ball Era, starting in 1920: Babe Ruth. Not simply for what he did with the bat, but for what he showed other hitters to do—drive the ball farther by swinging from the end of the bat. Others soon started to copy him.

A few years later, New York sportswriter Ford Frick wrote a verse that reflected his preference for the new era of long-ball hitting: "I like the new days better—when they hit 'em far and handsome, when the pitchers shake and shiver at the Babe's unseemly pranks. Oh, the spitball served its purpose, but the home-run ball's much nicer; it's so helpful to the hitters—and especially to the Yanks."[14]

In 1929 Ruth looked back at the fortuitous timing of his move from pitcher to everyday player. "I've been a pretty lucky fellow. . . . In the old days when defense was the big thing I was a pitcher. . . . And when things switched over and hitting became the rage, Ed Barrow, then managing

18. Urban Shocker was one of seventeen pitchers who were allowed to throw the spitball after it was banned, prior to the 1920 season. In actuality, he threw the pitch only sparingly, but bluffed it often, by bringing his glove and the ball to his mouth. His "dry spitter" was actually a devastating change of pace. *SABR–Ottoson Photo Archive.*

the Red Sox, turned me into an outfielder and gave me a chance to 'take my cut' with the rest of the sluggers. So I got a break going and coming. You can't beat that!"[15]

From 1919 to 1921, earned run averages climbed by almost one full run. By the summer of 1920, shine ball master Hod Eller of the Cincinnati Reds was grumbling, "The world has gone mad over freak deliveries."[16]

Umpire Billy Evans commented on the ban's impact on the spitball pitchers. He felt the two Urbans, Shocker of the Browns and Faber of the White Sox, would be impacted the least. Shocker, he wrote, "has a good fast ball and a pretty fair curve. His change of pace is well-nigh perfect, and he knows how to pitch. Shocker's ability, plus his gray matter, should enable him to weather the storm."[17]

Shocker was not the least bit perturbed about the ban. "I am candid in saying that I will not throw 25 spitballs in an entire game. . . . The spitter is used by me only in the pinches. . . . I bluff it frequently, and I'll have something for the batters this summer that will be more valuable than the spitter."[18] Shocker was working on his slow ball (what today is called a change-up), which was already very good, to make it even better.

And while he could not showcase his performance with the Yankees, many of Shocker's battles with Babe Ruth would be on the nation's biggest stage, in New York City. The Yankees had just purchased the Babe from the Red Sox. Shocker's goals of beating the Yankees and besting the Babe had just morphed into one big challenge.

14

Challenging the Great One

Sad as the wind through the cedars at dusk;
Drear as the masterpiece Chopin arranged;
Sadder than memories lifted from musk,
Aye, even sadder than lovers estranged;
Where with a sudden intaking of breath
Just as some pitcher decides he has won,
Far rings the monody reeking with death—
Ruth hits another home run.

—"The Pitcher's Requiem, Part I" by Grantland Rice

The Babe was turning the baseball world upside down. After hitting an astounding 29 home runs for Boston in 1919, he came to New York and continued his assault on pitchers on the bigger stage. Before Ruth, the home run had been a rare and heralded event. Typical was this quote from Walter Trumbull in 1917, after a ninth-inning Wally Schang home run beat the Yankees: "There is nothing more extraordinary than a home run. No scene in melodrama can so grip the chords that thrill. No orator with silver tongue [can] so sway an audience to rapture or despair. A Circuit Clout is the greatest transmutter [*sic*] of emotions. It makes smiles grow where none grew before, or smothers laughter beneath a pall of gloom."[1]

The accolades Ruth got early in the 1920 season were emphatic. Typical are these two from the New York press corps, a group not easily impressed.

"Ruth is absolutely the last word—the ultimate consonant and vowel. Beside him all the great sluggers of history are overshadowed. The baseball world is witnessing the most extraordinary exhibition of batting of all time."[2] Another appeared the same day, June 3, less than two months into Ruth's New York career, a day after he hit three home runs in a doubleheader. "The Master Mauler has become the outstanding figure in the world of sport. He has become a national institution, has taken hold of the popular imagination."[3] Ruth had hit 13 home runs in the space of just 16 games.

Urban Shocker started against New York for the first time this season on May 22.[4] After he beat them, 2–1, George Daley wrote in the *World*, "In the breast of this young Wolverine, the insult Huggins gave him when he tossed him in 'to boot' in the Pratt deal in 1918 is still rankling. Col. Jacob Ruppert and Col. Til Huston hummed in unison last night after the latest beating: 'Far be it for me to be a knocker, but WHY did Huggins trade Urban Shocker?'"[5]

Sometime during this season, the Yankees made a desperate attempt to get Shocker back. "Two years later [after the trade]," revealed Browns business manager Bob Quinn in 1945, "Ruppert offered me $100,000 for Shocker."[6] Quinn was not interested.

On June 20, the Yankees came to St. Louis. With an 8-3 record, Shocker seemed on his way to that signature of pitching success, a 20-win season. Browns fans turned out the largest crowd in the city's baseball history, 27,526.[7] A New York writer, Arthur Robinson, described the crowd on the field that day. The mob prevented the players from taking warm-ups, and the scene seemed like a giant picnic, with soda vendors putting their empty crates on the infield. By the time the police got the crowd under control for the 3:30 start, the fans were ten deep behind the outfield ropes.[8]

A reporter once asked Ruth why he did not go for "a fat average" by hitting more singles—though his batting average was not bad: he would hit .376 in 1920. His reply was, "My job is to knock 'em a mile, and that's what the fans expect."[9] In this game, Shocker whiffed the Babe, who was trying to please the crowd, on "a ludicrously wide pitch," but the Yankees beat him, 4–3.[10]

The Browns' first baseman, George Sisler, had three hits in the game and raised his batting average to .419. Unlike Ruth, he was satisfied with spraying hits all over the ballpark and did not swing for the fences. Yet he hit 19 home runs this season, an impressive number and second only to Ruth's 54. Branch Rickey, his coach at the University of Michigan and his manager for his 1915 rookie season with the Browns, said, "George Sisler was the smartest hitter who ever lived. He was a professional with that bat in his hands. He never stopped thinking. . . . In the field, he was the acme of grace and fluency."[11] Shocker said that having Sisler in the field was like having a fourth outfielder, one who covered the shallow right side of the outfield.

Ruth got revenge against the Browns' ace just three days later. Shocker returned to the mound on two days' rest, so he could face New York a second time in the four-game series. The Babe hit home run number 20 off him, and the Yankees won for the second time in the series. Shocker's volatile temper was on display in this game. While he protested a balls-and-strikes call with the umpire, Del Pratt scored from third base. Shocker felt time should have been called and threw down his glove and started stomping on it in anger.[12]

Shocker's reputation for pugnacity was growing. Harry Pierce of the *St. Louis Star* noted that he "enjoys a scrap as much as Jack Dempsey."[13] Sam Murphy, the sports editor of the *New York Evening Mail*, said that Shocker was a hard loser. "He fights for everything and never seems happy, even when he has a game by a wide margin."[14] Shocker had thrown a tantrum on the mound the previous year when arguing balls and strikes, as well as the call at the plate on a squeeze play, with umpire George Hildebrand. He was so upset that he threw his glove at the umpire.[15] Fred Lieb said Shocker almost threw a punch at Hildebrand, and the writer was surprised he was not ejected.[16] The New York fans booed Shocker the entire game.

While his temper tantrum was not surprising, Shocker's mistreatment of his glove was. He usually took good care of it and took pride in his fielding.[17] Ballplayers in that era left their mitts on the field when their team went to bat. Players from the opposing team knew Shocker would have a fit if they touched his glove. Athletics pitcher Ed Rommel said that Shocker was extremely superstitious. "If you got hold of his glove between innings, he was licked."[18] Shocker soon began taking his mitt with him into the dugout.

On July 13 the Browns came into New York as the Yankees were just percentage points behind the first-place Cleveland Indians. The doubleheader, played on a stifling 88° day, drew 38,823 fans to the Polo Grounds, the biggest crowd in Major League history.[19] Fred Lieb wrote that the city had gone "baseball dippy" over Ruth and the Yankees, with "dementia baseballicana in its worst stage and is reveling in the malady."[20]

They came to see Ruth, but Shocker had plans of his own. He loved the noisy fans in an opponent's park; they energized him. The *New York Times* usually gave straightforward accounts of ballgames and left the colorful language to the Hearst papers. But not today. "The former Yankee flinger, Urban Shocker, came back to worry his old teammates with his tantalizing spit ball, which was never working with more oily smoothness. . . . The slippery ball never cut such frivolous capers at Shocker's command before. The ball jumped away from the Yankee bats like a grasshopper."[21]

After striking out the Babe one time, Shocker decided to have some fun at the slugger's expense, an event the *Sporting News* featured along with a picture of Shocker, "some psychologist as well as a pitcher."[22] The next time the Babe came up, the Browns pitcher turned his back on the Babe and waved his outfielders in. All three took a few hesitating steps forward. He appeared to be taunting Ruth, who pounded his bat on the plate, demanding the pitch. He swung at a slow ball that handcuffed him so much that he almost toppled over.

Once again, Shocker turned to outfielders Tobin, Williams, and Jacobson and waved them in even more. Once again they stepped forward. By now the Babe was getting angry, and the fans were howling. Shocker once again got him to swing early and miss badly. Now, for the third time, the pitcher waved his outfielders in. He kept on motioning them forward until they stood on the back edge of the infield.

Once again, after setting up the Babe with a fastball that was far from the strike zone, Shocker delivered a teasingly slow ball that Ruth missed for strike three. The New York crowd erupted with tremendous applause. Shocker probably figured that if Ruth had gotten hold of one of those pitches, it would not have mattered if his outfielders were standing against the outfield walls.

Baseball Magazine took note of what had occurred. "No slugger ever smote the empty atmosphere with more force or persistence. Unfortunately, he [Ruth] confined his attention pretty largely to the air. When he swung at Mr. Shocker's offerings, the ball was no longer there. It had moved on somewhere else. . . . No Bush League batter was ever more thoroughly or hopelessly discomfited than the powerful home run king on that occasion."[23]

James Sinnott wrote that Ruth did not even manage a foul. "Shocker mixed them up beautifully for Babe Ruth. First he would serve him a curve, then a slow one, then a fast one, and then perhaps a spitter. He had Ruth completely baffled."[24] One of the balls "fell dead at [catcher Hank] Severeid's feet," in the words of Frank O'Neill.[25]

By the end of the game, Shocker had the victory with 14 strikeouts, one of the highest totals in a game in baseball history and his career high.[26] Babe Ruth was the victim three times. After striking out twice in the second game and cursing loudly, Babe Ruth took his favorite bat and smashed it against the concrete steps of the dugout.

Reporters called Shocker's win "revenge of a lifetime."[27] For him, it was simply another slap in the face of Miller Huggins and his damn Yankees. The game had cost them more than Ruth's bat. They had fallen a half-game behind Cleveland.

Shocker notwithstanding, pitchers around the league were walking Ruth intentionally, giving him one base rather than four bases from a home run. When the Yankees were on the road, such a strategy helped the home teams compete, but it disappointed their fans. One St. Louis paper's headline sarcastically read, "Pay a Dollar at Sportsman's Park to See Babe Ruth Walk."[28]

The issue generated a lot of discussion; there was concern that the intentional walk was undermining the game. A number of proposals were put forward to penalize such a move.[29] John B. Sheridan noted that no other baseball question had generated so much debate. "I seriously question the strategy of the cinch base on balls," he wrote. "It savors too

19. Urban Shocker emerged as a star in 1920. Nothing established his reputation more than his showdowns with Babe Ruth, who hit 54 home runs in his first season with the Yankees. Shocker's dramatic performance on July 13, when he struck out 14 Yankees, including Ruth three times, drew attention across the baseball world. *Private collection of Michael Mumby.*

much of timidity, fear, and of the sure thing." Sheridan felt a good hitter should have a chance to hit.[30]

Shocker sometimes exhibited selective memory when he spoke of his battles with the Babe. He once told a Philadelphia sportswriter, Stoney McLinn, "In the eight seasons I have faced Ruth I have not walked him intentionally one time. . . . I don't care what the situation may be—the winning run may be on a base when Ruth comes up. . . . The [fans] want to see one of us win our little battle, and I enjoy that contest with Babe as much as anybody in the ball park."[31]

On July 28 Shocker beat Bob Shawkey and the Yankees, 1–0, and he gave the Babe three passes; at least one was intentional. In his previous game, Ruth had been walked by the Red Sox all four times he came to the plate. Boston won easily.[32] Shawkey's loss was his first after 11 straight wins.

The Babe had not totally lost his sense of the strike zone or his sense of humor. "It is pretty tough for me to be doing so much walking when I have a fine automobile rusting in the garage," he said. "If they won't let me use base hits as a means of transportation, they ought to furnish me with at least a bicycle."[33]

One of the more vivid accounts of Shocker's slow ball came from a writer for the *New York Graphic*. He said it drifted by the Yankees "as mist drifts past a street lamp on a foggy night."[34] Sam Crane described it a little differently. He said that batters, including the Babe, fell for Shocker's "little dinky linky slow-drop teasers. They looked too good to let go by."[35]

Shocker beat New York again three days later, though he was not nearly so sharp. Ruth, Wally Pipp, and Bob Meusel all homered for the Yankees, who still lost, 13–8. Shocker gave up 10 home runs in 1920—and 6 of them were to Yankees.[36] Shocker did have bad games; every pitcher has them. One of his worst came on July 25 in Detroit. The Browns were beaten, 21–8, and Shocker retired only one man and gave up five runs.

On August 23 Shocker won his 20th game, a four-hitter against Washington. It would be his last win of the year. On August 29 he was injured in a game against the Yankees that was delayed and then resumed in a steady rain. Twice Shocker slid into home plate and was tagged out; the Yankees scored the winning run off him with one out in the ninth inning.

While he went the distance, Shocker was injured in one of those contact plays at the plate and continued to pitch with a noticeable limp. W. O. McGeehan of the *New York Tribune* wrote that Shocker was "a little peevish about everything" during the game. He also wrote that Shocker was hurt when he tried to collide with Yankees catcher Muddy Ruel to dislodge the ball.[37] One report said he strained a knee tendon; Dr. Robert Hyland put his leg in a plaster cast. Shocker did not pitch again that year and was on crutches for an extended period of time.[38]

The game was significant for a couple of other reasons. Carl Mays pitched in relief. Just two weeks earlier, one of his pitches had hit and killed Cleveland's popular shortstop, Ray Chapman. The Browns were merciless in taunting Mays during this game. The usually unflappable pitcher even complained to the umpire about the slurs, which "provided a touch of slime which adheres to those whose tongues provided it," in the words of the *Times* reporter.[39] While the paper did not cite names of those tongues, surely Shocker's was one of them. He disliked Mays intensely and would not have passed up the opportunity to add his voice.

Also, the win moved the Yankees into second place, a game ahead of the Indians and 1½ games behind the White Sox. Chicago would fall by the wayside when the Black Sox scandal broke in late September. But the Yankees were unable to edge out Cleveland, who played inspired ball while wearing black armbands in memory of their fallen teammate, Chapman.

Shocker was saluted by New York sportswriters for "being game enough" to pitch to the Babe and for believing "he can cope with the greatest stickers in the world."[40] And he got the ultimate compliment from the Babe himself. Ruth spoke to a St. Louis paper about "the Missouri Moisture Mixer," as the *Globe-Democrat* called Shocker. "He is one of the best pitchers I have ever faced, and he knows how to pitch," said Ruth. "He keeps you guessing all the time and never gives you a good ball. His control is perfect, and he has a wonderful 'spitter.' He is a great pitcher and is one of the best in baseball."[41]

Shocker was laid up and immobile in his cast for much of the off-season. When he was confined to his bed, he "called for a ball and amused himself by lying flat on his back and bouncing it against the ceiling," in the words of a *Sporting News* writer.[42] This seemingly impossible exercise made both his doctor and business manager Quinn nervous.

Shocker could not wait to face the Babe again in 1921. He explained to *Baseball Magazine*, "He gives the opposing pitcher a thrill no matter what happens. . . . Why do cowboys ride wild steers and risk their necks on bucking broncos? It's a dangerous sport, but it gives them a thrill, I suppose, to think they have conquered something which was strong and reckless and hard to handle."[43]

15

The Showdowns Continue

On August 12, 1920, a little over a month after Urban Shocker's divorce was granted, a wedding took place in Edwardsville, Illinois, about thirty miles northeast of St. Louis. Elizabeth Kamp of St. Louis and James U. Shockcor of Cleveland were married that day. James listed his occupation as baseball player and his age at his next birthday as thirty. It was the second marriage for both; Elizabeth listed herself as a widow. Why one of the best-known athletes of St. Louis chose to go to such lengths for a clandestine wedding is not known, but the couple wanted their privacy.

Shocker accurately listed his parents' names and provided his correct age, not his younger baseball one. He signed with his distinctive and bold signature. Elizabeth Kamp was Irene Elizabeth Owen, whose first husband, Arthur Kamp, lived in St. Louis.[1] They had divorced years earlier, and he was still very much alive. Born on November 21, 1890, she was just a couple months younger than Shocker. Also attending the ceremony was her son, Cletus, who was ten years old. Irene was a strong-willed and fairly large woman who went by the name of Rene to those with whom she was close.[2]

While she was a Catholic and raised her son as such, Rene's 1920 wedding had to be a civil ceremony because she had divorced and her first marriage had not been annulled. Urban may have converted to Catholicism during his marriage to Rene.

A debate surrounding the spitball had been swirling for months and came to a head before the start of the 1921 season. The spitballers, led by Dana Fillingim of the Braves and Bill Doak of the Cardinals, two of the lesser names among the group, had organized a lobbying effort during the 1920 season to exempt them from the ban and "grandfather" them for the balance of their careers. Keep the rule against the spitter in effect for new pitchers, they argued, but let the seventeen veterans who had registered for the 1920 one-year exemption continue to throw it.

They based their appeal on two arguments, with a subtle threat added to the discussion. The first argument revolved around fairness. The Yankees' veteran spitballer, Jack Quinn, put it quite simply. "Cutting out the spitball after permitting me to pitch it all my life," he said, "is like reaching into my pocket and taking money from me."[3] The injustice of depriving men of their livelihood gradually won over a lot of people, including prominent sportswriters such as Fred Lieb and Sid Mercer and umpires such as Billy Evans and Bill Klem. The latter said after the 1920 season, "Let the delivery pass out of existence as those who use it drop out of the league."[4]

The second argument was their appeal to the owners' pocketbooks, not simply the spitballers'. The pitchers took every opportunity to talk to owners before ballgames. Why should the owners sacrifice their property rights, which these pitchers represented? And the timing was fortuitous: some of the biggest pitching stars of 1920 were spitball pitchers. Stan Coveleski won three games for the Indians in the 1920 World Series, and Brooklyn's losing Series team was led by another spitballer, Burleigh Grimes. They had won 47 games between them during the regular season. Shocker, Quinn, and the White Sox's Red Faber won a combined 63 games that year. Each of these men represented real value to their owners and terrific appeal to the fans.

The editorial writers of the *Sporting News* were not swayed. In late October, an editorial stated that the owners were selfish in never wanting to give anything up, even if it was worth only a nickel, though they clothed their arguments in terms of fairness for the players.[5] And a month later, a biting editorial entitled "Unmoved by Slippery Sobs" stated that the "piteous pleas of the spitballers" rang false, since they never tried to develop alternate pitches.[6]

Late that year and early in 1921, the owners had the real concern that if these pitchers' pleas were rejected, they would take the matter to the game's new commissioner, Judge Kenesaw Landis, who had a reputation of standing up for the little guy as well as for unpredictability. At the winter meetings, the joint Rules Committee agreed to extend the exemption to these pitchers until the end of their baseball days.[7]

Shocker had been saying that he was not particularly worried about the ban, but now the spitball kept one more weapon in his arsenal. He jokingly told *Baseball Magazine* after the 1920 season, "Perhaps if I broke some of my other fingers, I could get the ball to roll over sideways, or maybe even jump into the air."[8]

Since 1920, many pitchers have thrown the spitter—and other trick pitches—illegally. It raises the question: Did Shocker, a crafty student of the game, throw freaks other than the spitter? Using the "Where there's smoke, there's fire" guideline, there was virtually no smoke of illegality around Shocker's pitching. But there were a couple of later accounts—much later. In Waite Hoyt's 1976 interview with Eugene Murdock, he said Shocker used to suck the seams of the ball to raise them, and then packed them with tobacco or dirt. The result, said Hoyt, was that the ball "sailed like hell."[9]

In a 1950 article in *Sport* magazine, Yankees broadcaster Mel Allen recounted a story by umpire George Hildebrand. The arbiter said that Shocker once cut thirteen stitches of a ball with a razor blade, and the cover came off the ball when a Cleveland batter drove what appeared to be a home run.[10] The Hoyt story seems more credible, although I have not come across accounts of Shocker being accused of hurling a "sailer." The Hildebrand story seems hard to believe: if it had occurred, surely it would have been a headline everywhere. I have not seen it.

Hildebrand was not Shocker's favorite umpire. Later in the 1920s, the pitcher said that he had been tossed out of games by only one umpire—twice by Hildebrand.[11]

I have found only one contemporary account of Shocker being suspected of throwing other trick pitches. It came from a Cleveland sportswriter in 1921, looking back at the Indians' championship season of 1920. Francis Powers wrote, "Urban Shocker, the erudite and astute pitching star of the

St. Louis Browns, also was under fire on numerous occasions, but in his case, the talk died out as the season progressed. Any man that can pitch the sort of ball thrown last summer by Shocker does not need artificial aids."[12]

In 1920 Shocker and other designated pitchers were allowed to throw the spitter; after that season, they were allowed to continue using it for the rest of their careers. For this reason, Powers is likely referring to "artificial aids" other than the basic ingredient in the spitter, saliva. These include pitches like the emery ball and the mud ball, as well as the tampering Hoyt and Hildebrand mention. Powers is not weighing in on whether he thinks Shocker threw a spitter, which he did and which Powers probably knew he did. It should be noted that the fact a pitcher can win without trick pitches does not ipso facto mean that he would never add such weapons to enhance his arsenal.

Perhaps the last word on Shocker's spitball should go to Burleigh Grimes, the last legal spitball pitcher, whose final game was in 1934. Thirty years later, when Grimes was elected to the Baseball Hall of Fame, he was asked who was the best ever spitball pitcher. Urban Shocker was the best he ever saw, said Grimes, "because he had everything else to go with it."[13]

Shocker would be playing for his third manager in 1921. The impatient Phil Ball did not re-sign Jimmy Burke, and the Browns promoted their coach, Lee Fohl, to the position. He had managed the Cleveland Indians for four years. A cup-of-coffee player in the Majors (he had appeared in five games), Fohl had a long career as a Minor League catcher and manager before Cleveland. He managed the Akron Champs of the Ohio-Pennsylvania League in 1910, with whom the teenaged George Sisler had signed. Sisler never played for them and instead went to college at Michigan.

Ironically, in the spring of 1916, Fohl's Indians had claimed Shocker when the Yankees put him on waivers. New York pulled Shocker back, and a dispute broke out whether they had done so in a timely manner. The league's president had ruled in favor of the Yankees. Now, five years later, Fohl had Shocker—in St. Louis.

Quiet and unassuming, Fohl was a soft-spoken man who knew a lot about pitching. He led the Indians to a surprising second-place finish in 1918 and quit under fire the following year. Many blamed Babe Ruth for his firing, though the story is a bit more complicated.

On July 18, 1919, Fohl's relief pitcher gave up a two-out ninth-inning home run to the Babe (his second of the day) to win the game. Fohl was blamed for bringing that reliever, Fritz Coumbe, into the game in the first place and for not having Ruth walked intentionally. The Indians' star outfielder, Tris Speaker, had been the fans' choice to manage the club for some time. After this game, Fohl decided to step aside.[14]

Fohl had joined the Browns' staff primarily because of the Bob Quinn connection. Quinn had become the business manager of the Browns after Branch Rickey left for the crosstown Cardinals and was perhaps Phil Ball's best hire. Quinn quickly learned that his boss "roared a great deal, and some people were intimidated. They tried to avoid crossing him. They yessed him to death."[15]

Quinn discovered that when he spoke frankly with Ball, even disagreeing with him, the owner appreciated the straight talk. Ray Gillespie, a young reporter at the time, later recalled, "Bob Quinn was one of the finest men I ever met. He served as a buffer between Phil Ball and the press and the outside world in general. He and he alone could handle Phil Ball during his cranky spells."[16]

Quinn had been a longtime general manager of the Columbus Minor League team, where he developed a farm system for his club.[17] In 1907 he had signed Fohl as a catcher; Fohl soon became his trusted right-hand man as the manager of Ohio clubs that Columbus controlled in Lima and Akron.

Quinn was the man who negotiated the Shocker trade. He was quietly building a rising baseball power in St. Louis. "When I took over the Browns in 1917," he told a *Sporting News* reporter years later, "they were the worst club I ever saw."[18] Quinn built around George Sisler and Hank Severeid, a tough and smart catcher. Among his best signings was Ken Williams, a slender power hitter who would average .345 from 1921 to 1923. Williams would team up with Baby Doll Jacobson and Jack Tobin in a fearsome-hitting outfield. Between 1919 and 1925, they would all have batting averages of at least .300 every year, except in 1924, when Tobin's .299 missed by one hit.[19] In 1921, they had a combined batting average of .351.

Tobin was a product of St. Louis's sandlots and one of the original Federal League players.[20] He was gaining the reputation as the best drag

20. Bob Quinn was the Browns' business manager who assembled the powerful club of 1922. A shrewd evaluator of talent, he was also a man of impeccable integrity. When he died in 1954, John Kieran wrote in the *New York Times*, "If Diogenes encountered Bob Quinn, he'd have thrown away his lantern and ended successfully his search for an honest man." *Private collection of Margo Quinn Hemond.*

bunter in the game. "Nobody wanted to work too hard at bunting, and if you're going to be good at it, you really have to work," he explained. "And another thing, everybody wanted to swing for the fences."[21] By working hard at it, he said, he could easily bunt the ball just beyond the pitcher and short of the second baseman.

As the Browns' lead-off hitter, Tobin scored 132 runs in 1921, second only to Babe Ruth, who set the still-standing American League record with 177. Tobin explained that hitting first was not always an advantage for rounding the bases—because he often had the slow pitcher on base ahead of him. When Urban Shocker was on second base, and "I'm on first," explained Tobin, "he often says, 'Now don't step on me, if somebody else slaps it out.'"[22]

The Browns led the American League in batting average in 1920, but their earned run average was one of the league's worst. In 1921 their batting average fell slightly, but their pitching remained weak.

A sad note hung over the Browns' spring training camp of 1921. Pitcher Carl Weilman, an anchor of the club's pitching staff in the mid-1910s, was forced to retire because of recurring health problems. He lost a kidney in 1917 and missed most of that season and all of the next. While he made a stirring comeback in 1919, he was not as good in 1920 and was near collapse after many of his games. He stayed on with Bob Quinn and the Browns as both a scout and coach.[23] His slow ball was said to be terrific, and surely he and Shocker compared notes on their change-of-pace pitches.[24]

On May 5 Shocker faced the Tigers. Ty Cobb was now both Detroit's manager and star outfielder, having taken over for Hughie Jennings in the former role. Shocker loved to challenge Cobb, and a Detroit reporter wrote of the pitcher's "running fare of repartee" with Cobb. In the sixth inning, Shocker "invited him to hit a slow ball."[25] "Taunted" might be the more accurate word. Cobb did hit it—he knocked it into the bleachers. By the end of the inning the Browns were down 9–0, and Shocker was done for the day. Cobb was not a home run hitter; he hit 117 in his long career. But he hit more off Shocker—5—than off any other pitcher.

In his syndicated life story, serialized and published in newspapers in 1926, Cobb explained how he hit Shocker's floater. He would move up in the batter's box, and the pitch would be called a ball. Then Shocker would bring the pitch down and, in Cobb's words, "we'd sock it."[26] This is quite different from the account Hughie Jennings gave in his life story, published a year earlier.[27]

A month into the 1921 season, it was clear the Yankees would challenge the world champion Indians for the pennant. When they came to St. Louis to meet the Browns for the first time, New York was just a game behind Cleveland. The Babe already had 12 home runs, ahead of his 1920 pace, when he finished with 54. The Browns, however, were still a team hovering around the .500 mark.

The Yankees edged Shocker in 10 innings in their first meeting of the season. He struck Ruth out twice and walked him twice. Three days later, Shocker took to the mound against the Yankees again. Ruth won the individual battle, with a double and a home run. In the seventh inning, with the Browns clinging to a 4–3 lead, the Babe came up with two men on base. Lee Fohl wanted his pitcher to walk the slugger, but Shocker insisted on pitching to him. He won the debate with his manager, but lost the battle when Ruth hit the ball into the center-field bleachers. The blast went more than 500 feet and was the longest drive ever hit in Sportsman's Park; the *New York Times* said it traveled 200 yards.[28] The Browns pulled out the game with a dramatic two-out rally in the ninth.

> It was impossible to watch him at bat without experiencing an emotion. I have seen hundreds of ball-players at the plate, and none of them managed to convey the message of impending doom to a pitcher that Babe Ruth did with the cock of his head, the position of his legs, and the little gentle waving of the bat, feathered in his two big paws.[29]

Shocker commented on something that must have weighed on pitchers' minds: just how hard Ruth hit the ball back up the middle. "That bird is going to perforate a moundsman some day. . . . Just an inch or so saved me that day from having my head driven in sections to the outfield."[30] No wonder W. O. McGeehan called Ruth's bat "the modern hammer of Thor and the club of Hercules."[31]

Syndicated columnist Davis Walsh wrote in early June that Shocker "continues to live only that he may annoy the good Mr. Huggins."[32] But the Yankees beat him twice that week in the Polo Grounds, led by two

Ruth triples and a double. One New York writer said the Yankees were treating him as a "sub-urban."[33]

The Yankees appeared to be taking the measure of the Browns' pitcher. Perhaps his insisting on facing them twice in every four-game series was giving them plenty of chances to observe him and time their swings. In four games against Shocker this season, they had scored 24 runs off him (20 were earned runs) in 32 innings. Was it finally time for New York to call him their "erstwhile jinx"?

A month later, on the anniversary of Ruth's smashed-bat and five-strikeout afternoon, the Yankees beat Shocker and the Browns, 11–1. When Wally Pipp and then Carl Mays, of all people, hit home runs in the fourth inning, Shocker got so upset that he hit both Chick Fewster and Ruth with pitches. One report said he challenged the entire Yankees bench to a fight in their six-run inning.[34] Lee Fohl pulled him before the end of that fourth inning, after he had given up seven runs. Shocker's record dropped to 10-9, with a bloated earned run average of 4.56 for the season. The Browns had fallen 12 games below .500, barely holding on to sixth place.

What was happening to the man *Baseball Magazine* had recently called "one of the great pitchers of 1920"?[35] The July 13 performance was explained away by a bad blister on Shocker's throwing hand, which made him unable to grip the ball properly, but that begs the question of why he insisted on pitching that day.

Shocker had been struggling for a while. Three weeks earlier, on June 22, after he was beaten in Detroit, 7–6, he simply disappeared. There was a vague report that he had twisted his knee in that game and was being treated by a Detroit doctor. Bob Quinn naturally wanted him to join the team and have the Browns' doctor attend to him. When Shocker refused to report, Quinn suspended him.[36]

He missed more than two weeks, and St. Louis papers started to leak hints of just how bad the matter had become. Shocker had received "bitter criticism" from his teammates, who did not "feel too kindly to him" when he finally did show up, according to St. Louis reporters.[37] Martin Haley of the *Globe-Democrat* was blunter, writing that there was no use "beating around the bush." Shocker was "at loggerheads with his teammates, not just management." The pitcher might be traded.[38]

A subtle pattern was beginning to emerge, one that would continue for the next three years. Shocker usually disappeared in Detroit (and sometimes to Detroit), where his sister Cora and her husband lived. If he did go off on occasional benders, perhaps triggered by his own bad performances, it was a safe and convenient hideaway, where he would not even have to be around his wife.

It is hard to get precise information on this issue. Spink Award–winning sportswriter Bob Broeg told me a number of times about Shocker's drinking problem, which he heard secondhand from his mentor, J. Roy Stockton, who covered baseball in the 1920s in St. Louis.[39] When Roger Godin was researching his book on the 1922 Browns in the late 1980s, he interviewed Jack Tobin's brother. James Tobin recalled, "I think he flew pretty high every once in a while. . . . Urban Shocker used to be pretty well-faced [flushed] all the time. I don't know what it was from, but it would flush up real red."[40] And perhaps coincidentally and oddly, one New York paper reported that an abusive fan kept yelling "Urban Shicker!" at Shocker during a game. "Shicker" is the Yiddish word for drunk or alcoholic.

On July 27 Shocker went back to New York and beat Carl Mays, 7–5, not an overpowering performance, but one that was good enough. Damon Runyon described Shocker's slow ball, which was working very well that game. "He had the so-called Murderers' Row spellbound with a sling so slow you could almost see the elastic in the ball as it gradually eased its way over the plate."[41] One New York writer saluted Shocker for his work at a key point in the game. "Matty [Christy Mathewson] never pitched with any more skill than Shocker did in the eighth."[42]

Ruth came into the game batting .360, with 36 home runs; his nearest competitor, the Browns' Ken Williams, had 16. Fohl instructed Shocker to walk the Babe at a key time in the game and later explained, "Of course the crowd wants to see Ruth win, but we are fighting for place. . . . Any time you give the big fellow a good ball, he is going to knock it out of the park. . . . You can't play your outfielders in the middle of the next block."[43]

Shocker hit his stride in August. Between August 4 and 21, he won six straight games, all complete games. The last of those wins brought the Browns back to the .500 mark. It came in New York, and Shocker again had an outburst for which he was becoming known. Only this time it provoked a wild response from the Yankees' little manager, Miller Huggins. Hug had been under enormous pressure all season, second-guessed by the press, co-owner Til Huston, the fans, and even a number of his players.[44]

As this series began, the Yankees were only one game out of first place. With the Browns clinging to a one-run lead in the game, umpire Tommy Connolly ruled that Shocker's pitch had grazed Yankees catcher Wally Shang and awarded him first base. Shocker disagreed—and not respectfully. One New York account said he "became enraged" and "frothered [*sic*] like an enraged bull."[45] He hurled the ball against the ground, and the Yankees' Aaron Ward scampered home all the way from second base. Shocker grabbed the ball and thought he tagged him on a close play at the plate.

After a long argument, Connolly sent Ward back to third, ruling he should be awarded just one base. This angered Huggins, who thought Ward had scored and the Yankees had tied the game. The crowd of more than twenty-five thousand howled when Shocker "playfully jabbed and slapped little Hug with his glove."[46] Those were the words of a St. Louis reporter; a New York one said that Shocker punched him.[47] Huggins had to be restrained, and some accounts described the almost amusing scene in which a big policeman lifted the Yankees' manager and dragged him back to the dugout.[48] The Browns held on to win the game, 5–4, and Shocker had his 19th win.

Shocker showed no favorites in the Cleveland-New York pennant race, at least not until the end of the season drew closer. He shut out fellow spitball pitcher Stan Coveleski of Cleveland on September 10, 2–0, on a three-hitter. Just six days later, Shocker knocked the Yankees out of first when he beat them, 10–3. The Babe hit home run number 56 and struck out three times in the game.

Heywood Broun painted a picture of those whiffs, writing that Shocker's slow balls "loitered and dawdled" before "a sudden decision to swoop downward."[49] Shocker's "stuff" was not all slow; so much was being written about it that it is easy to forget he had a good fastball. Broun noted that after setting up the Babe with "dawdling" pitches, he struck him out with a fast one. With his seven strikeouts that day, Shocker took over the league lead from Walter Johnson.[50] Fred Lieb moaned after the game that

21. Urban Shocker's "slow ball," his change of pace, often fooled the Babe and made him awkwardly swing and miss. This image of Ruth on the receiving end of such a Shocker pitch was typical, but not the only result. Ruth also homered off Shocker four times in 1920–21. *St. Louis Post-Dispatch.*

every time Shocker faced New York, "the trade" looked a little worse.[51] Another New York paper noted that St. Louis fans had raised thousands of dollars for Shocker for his 25th win of the year, which this was.[52]

The following week, the Yankees hosted the Indians for a four-game set that would probably determine the pennant. The teams came into the series in a virtual tie for first place.[53] After taking two of the first three games, a New York win in the final game would give them close to a lock on the pennant, a two-game lead with just a handful left to play.

The key Yankees pitcher that day was Waite Hoyt, who had just turned twenty-two. He had come to New York as part of a blockbuster eight-player trade with the Red Sox after the 1920 season, in which the two teams swapped catchers and back-of-the-rotation pitchers. The biggest name in the deal was Del Pratt, the man New York had paid so dearly for in 1918.[54] Pratt played well in his three seasons in New York, but was one of the leaders of an anti-Huggins faction in the clubhouse. Sportswriter John Kieran later called Pratt "the greatest clubhouse lawyer baseball ever knew."[55]

Hoyt had been overlooked by most observers who weighed in on the trade. He had only 10 career wins and a reputation for stubbornness. Yet Huggins, a shrewd appraiser of talent, said during spring training of 1921, "Young Hoyt is a pitcher of infinite promise."[56]

The Yankees were wondering who would start for the Indians. When they looked over to the Cleveland sidelines, they could not believe who was warming up: it was Urban Shocker, for a full half-hour before the game.[57] What was he doing there? Had he been sold or traded to the Indians?

No, Shocker was still a member of the Browns. He was just having some fun with the Yankees and probably with Miller Huggins in particular. Besides the history between the two men, a lot of midwesterners were rooting for the midwestern team to win the pennant over the hated rich East Coast team. Back in 1920, the Yankees and their supporters felt that midwestern teams might have been showing favoritism toward Cleveland; even Jacob Ruppert had raised the subject.[58] For the Indians, letting Shocker warm up by their dugout was not illegal and might give them a psychological edge. They ended up starting their ace, Stan Coveleski.

Hoyt had won the first game of the series for his 18th win of the year and was rushed in as a reliever in this final game, with the Yankees down 3–0 in the first inning. He would have to prevent the game from getting more out-of-hand. The Yankees prevailed, 8–7, with the Indians' potential tying run on second base when the game ended. Hoyt had won his second game in the series. The infinite promise was starting to flourish. Heywood Broun called this "the greatest baseball game ever played."[59]

Earlier in the season, a Yankees-Browns game had been rained out. New York had insisted on making up the game; they figured on another easy win against a .500 club, at best. The Browns now had an opening in their schedule, as did the Yankees, the day after the Cleveland series. The New Yorkers were upset; now they did not want to make up the game, for an obvious reason.

The Browns would start Shocker, of course. The Yankees had taken a two-game lead in the pennant race, and they again had to face the man who had taken a "Kiplingized oath" against them.[60] While the Yankees had some success with him in 1921—they beat him in four of nine decisions—they knew how tough he could be. Shocker reassured the Indians after their heartbreaking loss that they should have a good night's sleep and not worry. He would take care of New York for them the next day.[61]

New York sportswriter Robert Boyd set the ominous stage as Shocker warmed up for the game he indeed was going to pitch. "His hat tilted rakishly to one side and chewing slippery elm to induce saliva, his air of confidence cast shadows of defeat long before the start of the game. . . . Confidence personified and with a touch of the sublime egotist, Shocker's own concept of conquering the slugging Yankees was 'easy.'"[62] Damon Runyon noted that the Babe (who was coaching third base) and Shocker engaged in a running verbal duel during the game.[63]

New York sportswriter Frank O'Neill wrote after the game, "Shocker never was greater in all his career, and his performance was worthy of the masters."[64] He tossed a five-hitter; only three men got on base in the first eight innings, and two were erased by double plays. The Yankees mounted a mini-rally in the ninth. With two men on base and two outs, Babe Ruth came to the plate. Shocker gave him a free pass and then retired Bob Meusel to nail down the 2–0 win. After the game, in an era when players were so accessible to fans, many followed Shocker into the clubhouse; they berated him for walking the Babe.[65] Shocker just smiled; he knew he had made the right move. In an editorial the previous year, the *Sporting News* had stated the obvious. "It is often good strategy to walk the big fellow. And a pitcher cannot be blamed for using his head."[66]

Shocker had his 27th win of the season, one in which he "quaffed deeply of the joyous cup of revenge," in Sid Mercer's words.[67] The Yankees did hold on to capture their first American League pennant, but it would have been a lot easier had Shocker not been on "the other side." George Daley, the sports editor of the *New York World*, wished the Yankees had Shocker, even though he brought flamboyance, swagger, and temperament along. "The Yankees call him [Shocker] a gallery player. Be that as it may, he seems to thrive on hard knocks. Feed the Yankee pitchers the same kind of meat."[68]

16

The Underdog Arises

Hell hath no fury like a cast-off scorned
Who, coming back to face his old-time team,
Shows that his salary whip is still adorned
With all its pristine power, curves and steam.
"So I've been chucked out by this bunch of mutts;
I'll show these dumbbells just where I belong"—
And as he backs them into deeper ruts,
His savage growl becomes a battle song.
—"The Cast-Off's Revenge" by Grantland Rice

Bob Quinn knew that his club needed more pitching if it was going to seriously compete for the 1922 American League pennant. The Browns were an offensive powerhouse (they had a team batting average of .303 in 1921), and one more arm might push them over the top.[1] So Quinn made a headline-grabbing deal when he acquired Minor League pitching star Dave Danforth from the Columbus Senators of the American Association for eleven men. "These players aren't worth a nickel to us, and Danforth may 'make' us," said Quinn.[2] While the Browns were training in Mobile, Alabama, a local reporter declared, "If he [Danforth] flashes, it means the flag."[3] For once, the Browns had won a major battle with the Yankees, who also wanted Danforth and offered Columbus $25,000. It was players and not money that Columbus manager Pants Rowland wanted in return.

Danforth had won 25 games for a bad Columbus club in 1921; they won only 66 that year. He was no youngster. The thirty-one-year-old had two earlier stints in the Majors and brought some baggage with him.[4] He had long been suspected of tampering with the ball and throwing trick pitches. He was the acknowledged father of the shine ball and was accused by Hughie Jennings and Ty Cobb, among others, of throwing the emery ball and the paraffin ball.[5] But respected umpire Billy Evans told Quinn he thought Danforth was "clean."[6]

The Browns picked up another edge on the Yankees before the 1922 season began. Baseball's commissioner, Kenesaw Landis, had suspended Yankees stars Babe Ruth and Bob Meusel for going on postseason barnstorming tours without permission.[7] Ruth had openly defied Landis, who had warned the slugger not to challenge him. He framed the issue as "a mutinous defiance intended by the players to present this question: which is the bigger—baseball, or any individual in baseball?"[8] Even Colonels Ruppert and Huston understood that the judge who had stared down John D. Rockefeller and Standard Oil in the famous 1907 antitrust court ruling would not back down from a ballplayer, no matter how big a star.

Landis suspended them until late May and forfeited their World Series checks of $3,306. The Yankees purchased outfielder Whitey Witt from the Athletics to cover during their absence. New York had fortified their pitching, too, with another big winter trade with the Red Sox. They picked up veteran hurlers Joe Bush and Sam Jones and swapped shortstops with Boston.[9] They also paid Red Sox owner Harry Frazee $100,000. The close relationship between Frazee and the Yankees' owners proved to be a far richer source of talent than just Babe Ruth. Many observers felt the deal did not favor the Yankees because Bush and Jones were both approaching thirty, and the shortstops—Roger Peckinpaugh for Everett Scott—seemed to be an even swap.

Urban Shocker could not wait for the season to begin. He once again worked in the off-season in a St. Louis department store and had recovered from a broken wrist he suffered in December while he was moving furniture.[10] At spring training in Mobile, he shared his training regimen. "I found that 100 throws, just light tosses, hardened my arm and prepared it best for the strain of pitching. I would work until my muscles were good

22. In 1922 the combination of Ken Williams (*right*), who led the league with 39 home runs, and George Sisler, who hit .420 despite a late-season shoulder injury, brought the Browns to the cusp of the 1922 American League pennant. They are seen here in late August 1922 with batboy Joe Ryan. *Private collection of Steve Steinberg*.

and tired, but I never put any great effort into one pitch. The result was that my arm hardened gradually, and there never was a chance to get the arm sore."[11]

He was so confident about the Browns winning the pennant that he offered to bet half his salary on it.[12] St. Louis reporter Martin Haley wrote at the start of the season, "Urban is a changed man entirely. He has cut out all the rough stuff. He has mapped out a straight and narrow path for the season."[13]

In one of baseball's wonderful little coincidences, the Browns opened a series in the Polo Grounds on May 20, the very day that Ruth and Meusel were returning. The Yankees had to feel good; they had a two-game lead over the second-place Browns. They had managed a 22-11 record while the two powerful bats were missing from their lineup. For St. Louis, Shocker was carrying even more of the pitching load than usual. This would be the Browns' 32nd game. Shocker had started 10 of them and relieved in 4 others.

Ken Williams, who hit 24 home runs in 1921 (a distant second to the Babe's 59) already had 11 by the time Ruth returned. He hit 3 on April 22 and would hit 2 in one inning on August 7, feats even the Yankees slugger had not accomplished. While he had a great jump on the Babe for the home run title, Williams told *Baseball Magazine* around this time, "I have never made any claim that I could equal Babe Ruth as a home run hitter. . . . I know I am not his equal."[14] There was another home run hitter on the Browns that spring. On April 28 Shocker's home run helped beat the Indians. It was his only career home run.

If there is a criticism of Lee Fohl as a manager, it is that he overworked his pitchers. Yet the reality is that Shocker demanded the ball, and Fohl did not refuse him. Hugh Fullerton felt that was a mistake because Shocker wanted to pitch all 22 games against the Yankees.[15] A reporter of the *St. Louis Star* had a different view. He described the St. Louis pitching star in larger-than-life terms that sounded like a portrayal of Babe Ruth:

> He is a man of naturally extravagant and exaggerated powers in almost every way. He might be called an extremist. He dines like Gargantua. He has the strength of Samson, and the fighting talent, nervous energy,

> and tremendous driving force of Achilles. When he moves, it is with a child's ease and, if necessary, he could hit with a giant's force. And all these qualities are contained in a figure so compact and balanced that it impresses the eye more with its symmetry than its power. If anyone thinks that the physique of the human race is degenerating, let him consider Urban Shocker. He should be reassured.[16]

While Shocker commanded plenty of attention from the New York press, one can only wonder how big a figure he would have become had he been pitching for the Yankees, in the nation's biggest city, at the peak of his career.

The May 20 game brought out an enormous crowd, and Ruth was honored with many gifts, including a silver bat, in pregame festivities. The headline of Heywood Broun's article in the *World* conveyed how Ruth did: "38,000 Hail Ruth from Elbe [*sic*] with a Puny Bat; Gifts by Truckload Symbolize a Fatted Calf; Event a Memorable One, Despite the Churlish Mr. Shocker."

In three at-bats against Shocker, Ruth failed to get the ball out of the infield. "Shocker was not touched by the spirit of the day," Broun wrote, and then continued in language only he could have penned. "In the old days it was customary to have a fatted calf killed when a prodigal returned, but he was not expected to do it himself, much less bring it down upon the wing."[17]

Shocker was his usual argumentative self, disputing balls and strikes, for which he drew hisses and boos. He gave up only three hits, but appeared to be on the losing end of a heartbreaker, 2–1, as Yankees pitcher Sam Jones took a toss and stepped onto first base to end the game. Umpire Oliver Chill's arm went up signaling the final out, the Yankees ran into their clubhouse, and their fans poured onto the field in celebration.

But the Browns did not leave the field. Lee Fohl argued that Jones had juggled the ball as the runner crossed the base and therefore never got the final out. After a conference, the umpires agreed. Jones was charged with an error, and the Browns had tied the game on the play. The stunned Yankees players—many of them in the showers—had to come back on the field, which had to be cleared of fans.

Jones became unnerved, walking in a run and then giving up a bases-loaded home run to Baby Doll Jacobson. The Browns had an improbable 7–2 win and closed to within a game of New York. Jones then lost seven straight games and did not win again for more than a month.

The Yankees gave a hint of what lay ahead when they took the next two games over the Browns, both in extra innings. Then, on two days' rest, Shocker beat New York again. On May 27 he took a perfect game into the 8th inning against Urban "Red" Faber of the White Sox, who was also a spitballer. Shocker lost the no-hitter in the 8th and the game in the 10th, 2–1, on an unearned run. Just three days later, Shocker pitched into the 15th inning against Detroit before being ejected by umpire Brick Owens for arguing balls and strikes. The Tigers scored the winning run in the 16th, and the result was another 2–1 loss.

By the end of May, Shocker had pitched 128 innings and was on pace to close in on Ed Walsh's twentieth-century mark of 464, set in 1908. Was the pace too much for the man the *Star*'s reporter had called "the most remarkable specimen of pitching humanity"?[18] Umpire Billy Evans weighed in on the man he called "one of the greatest pitchers of the game" that season. "Shocker is a glutton for work. No task is too great," he wrote. "No situation is too rough for him to face. The harder the going, the more important the series, the better he likes it."[19]

The *Sporting News* had an editorial in early June saluting Ruth, even though he was only slowly regaining his batting eye and swing. "Babe Ruth can't hit a low one on the inside. Like hell he can't. Ask Urban Shocker. . . . Babe can hit anything he can time."[20]

The Yankees came into St. Louis on June 10 with a 2½-game lead over the Browns. Shocker, of course, took the mound; he had a 12-5 record, and the season was not two months old. He did not seem "right" in this game. Wally Pipp homered off him in the second inning. The third was a total meltdown: Babe Ruth connected for a two-run home run, and an angry Shocker then drilled Frank "Home Run" Baker in the side of the ribs. Baker left the game and went to the hospital for X-rays. They were negative, at least initially. While he came back for a week, he then sat out more than a month, and the blow he took from Shocker probably was a factor.[21] It was the last time the slugger played regularly; he would retire at the end of the season, this time for good.

The Yankees bench was now razzing Shocker fiercely, and he told umpire Dick Nallin that he would "knock 'em down," without specifying who he would target. Later that inning, everyone found out. One of Shocker's least favorite players, Carl Mays, on his way to a big win, stepped up to the plate. Mays would hit Shocker well in their match-ups.[22] The Browns pitcher was upset with Mays's sneer of ridicule, as well as the Yankees' success against him in this game.

Shocker's first pitch was high and tight. Had Mays not dove from the box, he would have been hit in the head. The second pitch came to the same spot, and down went Mays again. He said something to Shocker when he got up, and Shocker nodded to whatever Mays had suggested. Shocker then went into a slow windup, but instead of an expected slow ball, another pitch almost hit Mays in the head.

J. Roy Stockton described the action. "Mays figured one ball near his head might be an accident and that the second might be a coincidence, but, by George, when a third one sailed at his head, it looked too much like a habit."[23] Mays charged to the mound, bat in hand. Umpire Billy Evans, who was stationed at second base, jumped between the men, and a fight—if not a riot—was averted.

After Shocker walked Mays, he hit the next man, leadoff hitter Whitey Witt. Once again the batter rushed to the mound, players poured out of the dugout, and the umpires had to prevent a war. By the end of the inning, Shocker's last on this day, all that was left of him, wrote the reporter of the *American*, was "a spark of glowing anger."[24] The Yankees went on to win, 14–5.

Despite the mutual animosity between Mays and Shocker, Mays spoke highly of Shocker when he looked back at their careers. "He was the best pitcher in the game against dangerous batsmen," said Mays. "He didn't fear the dangerous, the big hitters. That's when he was at his best."[25]

The next day Shocker insisted on taking on the Yankees again, and Fohl let him do so. Frank O'Neill wrote that a pitcher with less of an ego than Shocker would have accepted the shelling he took and left it at that for this series. "Shocker cannot lose with the same grace with which he wins," wrote O'Neill.[26] And Shocker was beaten badly yet again, going seven innings and giving up eight runs.

One New York writer reported that Shocker's behavior was particularly egregious, though the details remain a mystery. "He was guilty of conduct which was a disgrace to baseball, if all that the Yankees' players say is true."[27] The Yankees had stretched their lead to 4½ games.

Shocker went to the hospital soon after the game and stayed there for the rest of June. Many commentators were not surprised that his body had simply broken down from too many innings and too many pitches. The *Sporting News* account noted that while Shocker's workload was admirable, "there is a limit to what the flesh can endure."[28]

Shocker's leg had given out to the strain of too many innings. A pitcher may deliver the ball with his arm, but his legs give him the stability and push to deliver each pitch. He had strained a ligament and ruptured a blood vessel in his leg. He had surgery and missed more than three weeks in the heart of the season.[29] His next start would not come until almost a month later, July 7. The Browns would have to manage without their workhorse, who was reduced to the role of a spectator.

17

Good but Not Lucky

When the Yankees beat Shocker in back-to-back games, they extended their lead over the Browns to 4½ games. With the pressure of a pennant race that seemed to be slipping away from the Browns, Lee Fohl started Hub Pruett, a rookie, the next day, June 12. The twenty-one-year-old struck out Babe Ruth three times and beat New York, 7–1.

Pruett had been recruited by the St. Louis Cardinals. When he went to Sportsman's Park to sign with the National League club, the Cardinals were out of town, and the Browns' Bob Quinn inked his name on a contract instead. Pruett had a screwball, similar to the fadeaway of the great Christy Mathewson. Pruett explained that when he was a child, Mathewson had been his idol. If a right-handed pitcher like the Giants star could throw the pitch, "Why couldn't a lefty like myself do it?"[1]

The pitch was a reverse curve and required a twist of the wrist. Babe Ruth simply could not lay off it; it was too tempting. It also befuddled him. On July 12, exactly a month after his big win against the Yankees, Pruett again struck out the Babe three times. The first ten times he faced Pruett, Ruth struck out seven times and did not get a hit. "He has fooled me into swinging at bad balls," said Ruth. "The next time I bat against him, I shall make a point of waiting for a good one, and then, perhaps, I'll break the charm that he appears to have cast over me."[2]

Just as the Yankees rallied during the absence of Ruth and Meusel, so

23. Urban Shocker's third St. Louis manager, Lee Fohl (*right*), was a former catcher who knew pitching and deferred to Shocker's desire to start an inordinate number of games. In 1922 the Browns pitching staff was bolstered by the addition of screwball pitcher Hub Pruett, who was a spot starter and dependable reliever. He also had Babe Ruth's "number" and made the Babe chase his signature pitch repeatedly. *St. Louis Post-Dispatch.*

now did the Browns while Shocker was out. Pruett was just one of the pitchers who stepped up. On July 7, when Shocker started for the first time in almost a month after his leg injury, the Browns were one game ahead of the Yankees, a 5½-game swing in the race.[3] They posted a 15-7 record in their ace's absence. Equally significant, the Yankees had stumbled badly, winning fewer than half their games and losing eight in a row at one point. The Browns had taken over first place.

Now Shocker was back, and he looked very good. His second start came against the Yankees. The reporter for the *New York Times* marveled at his game. Shocker "rose to magnificent heights in the pinches. His control was perfect. The spitball broke across the corners, and a puzzling slow ball floated past Yankees' bats. It was a great exhibition of pitching, of coolness and skill and perfect confidence."[4]

One St. Louis sportswriter was already conceding the pennant to the Yankees (and to the New York Giants in the National League) because they had the pitching depth, and pitching was "the backbone of all baseball."[5] On the surface it seemed like the Browns pitching staff consisted of Shocker and a few other nameless guys. Even Babe Ruth wondered how St. Louis stayed in the pennant race with only one dependable pitcher.[6]

But something surprising was occurring with the Browns. The taciturn old catcher Lee Fohl was making an impact. He was not generating the newspaper copy that Branch Rickey, manager of the crosstown Cardinals, was. Roy Stockton noted that the two managers were "no more alike than a pterodactyl is like an ice cream freezer."[7] While Rickey was very public in instructing his players, Fohl was doing so behind the scenes.

The Browns' pitching was improving—a lot. They would lead the league in earned run average this season, something that many followers of baseball history find surprising. The team's earned run average dropped from 4.61 in 1921 to 3.38, well below the league average of 4.03. And the club cut back its number of walks by almost 25 percent, a stunning reduction. Elam Vangilder, a journeyman pitcher who won 99 games in an 11-year career, reduced his walks per nine innings from 3.3 in 1921 to 1.8 in 1922. Vangilder also won 19 games for the 1922 Browns.[8]

Shocker tossed a 1–0 shutout over the weak Red Sox in his first start and beat the one good pitcher they had not sent to the Yankees, Herb Pennock. Just four days later came the start against New York in the Polo Grounds. Shocker pitched well, but once again was involved in a 2–1 game; he was on the losing end to Joe Bush. Arthur Robinson described the Browns pitcher that day as "a livid statue of revenge."[9]

They lost on a freak play and a bad break. The box score shows that Aaron Ward homered. In the second inning, his two-out drive hit Ken Williams's mitt and fell into the bleachers. Four innings later, Ruth scored after reaching on an error. The *New York Times* reporter who had raved about Shocker's performance noted that it wasn't enough. "It couldn't avail against the Yanks and their carload of horseshoes."[10]

This was only a three-game series, and Shocker was not going to start another game against New York on only one day's rest. But after the final game was postponed a day by rain, there he was on the mound for the last game of the series. Bob Shawkey shut out the Browns that day, 4–0. After posting a 17-9 record against New York, Shocker had now lost four straight to them. The *New York Times* even joked that it was too bad Shocker could not pitch every game against the Yankees.[11] The Browns' lead over New York had been cut to just a half-game.

On July 23 the Yankees used the Boston connection to shore up a glaring weakness. With the aging Home Run Baker hobbled, they needed a third baseman. For some time they had been eyeing the talented Joe Dugan of the Athletics. But his manager, Connie Mack, did not want to make the strong even stronger and traded the unhappy Dugan to Washington. When the Senators turned around and sent him to Boston that same day, Dugan had become much more accessible to the Yankees. Now he was one. As with the Bush-Jones deal, Harry Frazee got a sizable cash payment as well as players, $50,000 this time.[12]

There was a public outcry from fans and teams across the country. Even the *Sporting News* weighed in. The "Scribbled by Scribes" columnist wrote, "There are only two big league ball clubs any more, and they both play at the Polo Grounds in New York." The other clubs, he wrote, are "either pawns or farms or foils for these two."[13] But the biggest outcry came from St. Louis, where even the chamber of commerce got involved and formally protested the late trade deadline of July 31.[14] One St. Louis sports editor groaned, "Alas, we have no Frazee," referring to the Red Sox owner, Harry Frazee.[15] His close relationship with the Yankees' owners and his financial difficulties had led to his sending much of Boston's talent to the Yankees the past four years.

Two days after the Dugan acquisition, the Yankees came to St. Louis, and Shocker was on top of his game as he shut them out and beat Carl Mays. Before the game, Shocker told Harry Schumacher that the Yankees might have his goat, "but they haven't got my number, and I can prove it."[16] And he did. Ken Williams hit his 22nd home run and maintained a decent lead over Ruth with 15, but Tilly Walker had taken over the league lead with 24. Williams would soon seize it back. Starting on July 28, he hit home runs in a record six straight games. Then, on August 7, he hit his 29th and 30th, both in one inning. George Sisler also lost his lead in the batting race in late July to Ty Cobb. But by August 7, he had climbed into a tie with Cobb. Both were hitting .409.

It was an eventful week for the Browns. On July 27, in a game against New York, Dave Danforth was ejected by umpire Brick Owens for throwing a doctored ball after a pitch sailed, a move that came with an automatic 10-game suspension. Danforth had been a disappointment for the Browns; he had won only 5 games.[17] Fohl suspected he was tampering with the ball and did not use him regularly, in part because every time he did pitch, opposing hitters complained, and controversy brewed.

When Danforth had beaten the Yankees in mid-June, they repeatedly demanded to inspect the balls he threw. They felt he was either loading the seams with mud or roughing up one side of the ball—not with emery paper but with an abrasive fingernail. Billy Evans was the umpire behind the plate and said Danforth had pitched a clean game.[18] New York sportswriter Tom Meany observed, "It seemed that Danforth was not only a pitcher but a practical psychologist as well. Nobody ever saw the left hand which was supposed to be so ruinous to the surface of a baseball."[19]

If true, he certainly was getting hitters worked up and distracted. Danforth once said he considered the great Philadelphia Athletics southpaw Eddie Plank as his model. Plank was almost legendary for fidgeting on the mound and driving batters to distraction. "Get the batter nervous, and you have him down," Danforth explained.[20] Bob Quinn, as well as Fohl, suspected otherwise and warned Danforth to cut out the funny stuff.

In early August the Browns put Danforth on waivers; not a single team claimed him. Ed Wray wrote, "Dave was either unanimously voted of little value, or a tacit agreement to 'railroad' him for the good of the game had taken effect."[21] He publicly proclaimed his innocence, but the Browns optioned him to the Tulsa Oilers of the Western League. New York writer Frank O'Neill may have been exaggerating somewhat, but perhaps not by much, when he said that the Browns' pennant chances depended "entirely on the durability of the good right arm of Urban Shocker."[22]

After Shocker trimmed the Yankees, 3–1, on August 25, he was ecstatic. "Gee, it feels good to be back in the game with everything," he told reporters. "For a while I thought I was losing my stuff, but now I realize that the trouble was in my leg and not my arm. I'm ready to go every other day for the balance of the season if I'm needed." He then added, talking about the Yankees, "They're easy for me."[23]

He struck Ruth out twice and pushed his record to 21-12. Heywood Broun noted that the Shocker of old was on the mound that day. "Shocker grinned and swaggered," he wrote.[24] But the Yankees had gotten hot in August. When they won the second game of a doubleheader that day, they closed to within a half-game of St. Louis.

Three days later, Shocker and Bob Shawkey faced off in a game that Fred Lieb called "a thrilling throbbing struggle between two pitching titans."[25] He compared it to the classic Christy Mathewson–Mordecai Brown duels of fifteen years earlier. He noted that the "burly" St. Louis pitcher, going on two days' rest, could come back quicker than any other pitcher.

But even Shocker had limitations, and when the game went into extra innings tied 1–1, the better-rested Shawkey had the edge. In the 10th inning, a drive down the line by the Browns' Eddie Foster that would have scored the winning run was called foul. Foster then fouled out. Years later, Sisler closed his eyes and sighed, "I can still see in my mind where the ball hit. It was a fair ball.[26] When Joe Dugan scored the winning run in the 11th inning, Shocker had lost another 2–1 game to the Yankees. And they now had a 1½-game lead on the Browns.[27]

The schedule now favored St. Louis. They would play their last 23 games at home, while the Yankees would be on the road for their final 18. On September 11, the Browns beat the Tigers, and Sisler hit safely in his 39th consecutive game, just one short of the modern record, Ty Cobb's 40. But Sisler injured his shoulder reaching for an errant throw. He did not play the following day; Dr. Hyland called it a "severe strain of the deltoid muscle."[28] The first baseman could not even raise his arm above his shoulder.

Newspapers reported that Sisler would probably be out for the rest of the year. Lee Fohl said, "It's tough, tough, I tell you. In my entire life in baseball, this is the hardest blow I have ever encountered."[29] A year earlier, Cleveland star Tris Speaker had injured his leg shortly before the crucial late September series with the Yankees. He played hobbled and had only one hit in 13 at-bats. It appeared that the Yankees would again benefit from such an injury to an opponent's leading hitter.

On September 13 Babe Ruth's column appeared in the *New York American*, and he talked about what Shocker, "one of the greatest pitchers of his time," was capable of doing. "One truly great pitcher could win in a seven-game series. . . . He could pitch every other day in such a series and might even establish a World Series record by winning four games."

One distraction the Browns had to deal with—and Lee Fohl was concerned about—was the ceremonies St. Louis fans were organizing for the players before the season was over. The city had not had a pennant winner in this century, and the Browns did not want to discourage supporters. But these events made it hard to stay focused on the job at hand. In mid-September, Shocker was honored at the New Grand Central Theatre the night before he was to pitch in a big game.[30]

Just three days after Ruth's column appeared, the Yankees came to St. Louis for a three-game series with the Browns, what soon became known as the "Little World Series."[31] They had a half-game lead on the Browns, and the opening game matchup was Shocker against Shawkey once again. St. Louis had a reputation for rowdy fans, and one New York paper wanted to make sure the Yankees had protection from cushion- and bottle-throwers.[32] Almost thirty thousand fans turned out for the game, including more than ten thousand on the field, behind ropes in the outfield.[33]

Sisler played for the first time since the injury; he had been getting electric treatments for his shoulder. He got a double to tie Ty Cobb's record, but he was not close to his usual form. With two runners on base and only one out in the sixth inning, he grounded into a double play, and the Yankees clung to a 2–1 lead.

In the ninth, with the score unchanged, New York center fielder Whitey Witt was knocked unconscious and suffered a severe laceration from a soda bottle a fan threw at him. It was a tense scene, with Yankees charging out of their dugout, many with bats in hand, and the fans on the field pushing the ropes forward.

24. Bob Shawkey joined the Yankees in 1915 and won 20 games for the fourth time in 1922. He started the first game in Yankee Stadium on Opening Day 1923. Here he is seen (*left*) on the 50th anniversary of the stadium in 1973, with Mrs. Babe Ruth and Whitey Witt, the Yankee who had broken the hearts of St. Louis fans with his key hit in the 1922 "Little World Series." *Diamond Images, Bob Olen Collection.*

The police and umpires regained control. Home plate umpire Billy Evans had been knocked unconscious on this very field back in 1907 and needed six weeks in the hospital to recover.[34] The Browns were retired quietly in the bottom of the ninth, with many of the fans—disgusted with the violence—rooting for Shawkey to retire the Browns. The perpetrator in the bleachers was not identified, let alone apprehended. Rewards were offered by both the Browns and the league for his capture.[35] For the third time this season, Shocker had lost to the Yankees by the score of 2–1.

The following day Hub Pruett once again followed a Shocker loss in a crucial game for the Browns' pennant hopes. And once again he responded with a gem, a five-hitter. While Babe Ruth finally hit a home run off him, it was New York's lone run in a 5–1 loss. George Sisler hit safely to break the Cobb record, and the Browns were again just a half-game behind the Yankees. For the final game of the series, Joe Bush would shoot for his 25th win of the year, and the Browns would send Dixie Davis to the mound. One of Bob Quinn's acquisitions, Davis had won 34 games for St. Louis the previous two seasons but had fallen off this year. He had won but 10 times.

What followed was one of the most famous games in St. Louis baseball history. When Davis died in 1944, the *Sporting News* declared it had received more telephone inquiries over the years about this game than any other St. Louis sporting event, including Game Seven of the 1926 World Series, when the Cardinals' Grover Alexander struck out Tony Lazzeri with the bases loaded.[36]

Davis pitched the game of his life, helped by some breaks the Browns got. Both Baby Doll Jacobson and Ken Williams scored after hitting ground-rule doubles into the crowd.[37] After seven innings, the Browns had a 2–0 lead, and Davis had given up only two infield hits, both to Witt. He had missed the second game, but had recovered from the head injury enough to play; he looked like a wounded soldier, with a big bandage wrapped around his head.

In the eighth inning, the breaks went the other way. After Dugan doubled for the only solid hit off Davis all afternoon, an infield hit by Wally Pipp bounced off Davis's glove, and a throwing error cut the lead to 2–1. Perhaps Shocker felt it was time for the Browns to beat the Yankees by that score and take over first place.

The Yankees led off the ninth with another infield hit off Davis's glove, this one by Wally Schang. The two managers, Miller Huggins and Fohl, then entered into a chess match. Huggins sent up Elmer Smith, a dangerous power hitter, to pinch hit for Aaron Ward.[38] A passed ball sent Schang to second base. Fohl then made the decision to pull Davis from the game, for which he later was harshly criticized. He explained that the move was not because Davis had weakened but rather "to win with the shift." Platooning was not common in this era; Cleveland manager Tris Speaker used it more than anyone.[39] It didn't even have a name yet; Fohl called it "the shift." He knew if he brought in a left-handed pitcher, Huggins would pull Smith, also a lefty, which he did.

25. A journeyman pitcher with a career record of 75–71, Dixie Davis pitched the game of his life in the rubber-match showdown with the Yankees in the "Little World Series" of September 1922. Despite pitching brilliantly for eight innings, he was pulled in the ninth. The Yankees rallied for a come-from-behind win with the help of a series of breaks and a hit off Urban Shocker in relief. *Private collection of Steve Steinberg.*

Fohl brought in Pruett, who had pitched the previous day. The new pinch-hitter, Mike McNally, laid down a bunt, and catcher Hank Severeid went for the lead runner at third base and threw wide. Pruett then walked the next batter on four pitches. Fohl brought in Shocker, who had saved a number of games for the Browns in relief in recent years. He induced the next Yankee to hit the ball on the ground to the shortstop, who threw home to retire Schang.

Shocker was just two outs away from saving a 2–1 game. Up came Whitey Witt, with his bandage still wrapped around his head. In what Harry Schumacher called "divine retribution," Witt hit the ball up the middle, scoring two runs.[40] Shocker then got Dugan to hit into a double play. But the damage had been done. When Joe Bush retired the heart of the Browns' order in their last at-bat, he had his 25th win. New York had a 3–2 victory and took a crucial 1½-game lead over the Browns.

Frustrated St. Louis fans quietly threw an avalanche of leather seat cushions onto the New York press corps sitting below. They had been stunned into silence. Sportsman's Park had turned "sepulchral," in the description of one New York reporter.[41] John Sheridan wrote, "Just like the old-time story books in which we used to read about fairies vanishing, so did a one-run lead the Brownies held going into the final inning waft into oblivion."[42] As had a two-run lead going into the final two innings.

It was really less a fairy tale gone badly than a horrible dream. Martin Haley provided a more apt postscript. "That one inning will remain indelible in the memory of the fans who witnessed it to the grave. It was a nightmare."[43]

George Sisler managed just two hits in 11 at-bats in the showdown series. "I should never have played against the Yankees. The arm was so badly crippled that I had to lift my gloved hand with my left hand in order to catch balls at first base," he said. "At bat, I was swinging with one hand."[44] Nevertheless, with those two hits, he had tied and then broken Cobb's record.[45]

A heartbreaking loss can take the spirit out of the losing team and propel the winning one forward. And that is precisely what occurred. The Browns dropped their next two games to the sixth-place Senators and fell 3½ games behind New York. After they blew a lead and lost the first game to Walter Johnson, one St. Louis sportswriter noted that St. Louis fans were still stunned. "A cemetery could not have been shrouded with more gloom than was Sportsman's Park yesterday. . . . The stands, almost deserted, indicated that the fans were in mourning."[46]

The second loss was a shutout: Shocker lost his fourth straight game. More surprising was his performance and his behavior. He allowed 15 hits in eight innings and lost his composure after the 7th. An abusive fan had been jeering and taunting him during the game. Shocker asked two friends who were sitting behind the Browns dugout to get rid of the fan. They went to the upper deck and got in a shouting match with him before police intervened. The fan left the ballpark before blows were exchanged. Sid Keener was moved to write, "It was the first time I've ever seen a home player call upon personal friends to eject a fan who did not meet with his approval."[47]

St. Louis did salvage the final game of the series, barely. They almost blew a 7–0 lead but held on to win, 7–6.

The Yankees went from St. Louis to Detroit and swept the third-place Tigers in dramatic fashion. They rallied from behind in all three games; all were one-run wins. They had now opened up a 3½-game lead over the Browns.

The race got interesting at the end. The Yankees lost two straight games to the last-place Red Sox, while the Browns twice beat the White Sox. Shocker got his 24th win but again was not sharp; he gave up 15 hits in the 11–7 victory. The Yankees then expected to face Herb Pennock in their final game with Boston; he had already beaten them three times in 1922.

Pennock was brilliant against them again, scattering two hits over seven innings. However, the Red Sox mysteriously started Alex Ferguson instead. The journeyman gave up three runs in the first inning and retired no one. Pennock came in, but it was too late. New York won, 3–1, and with an insurmountable two-game lead they clinched the pennant. The Browns closed to within one game on the season's final day.

Did the close relationship Red Sox owner Harry Frazee had with the Yankees' owners play a role in Boston's starting Ferguson and not Pennock? That will probably never be known. But the Yankees were impressed with the lefty, Pennock. They had no southpaw on their staff. Exactly four months later, they sent three prospects to Boston in exchange for Pennock.

Both the 1922 Browns and their individual performances stand out statistically. They are the only team in the half century of sixteen Major League teams to lead the league in both batting average (.310) and earned run average (3.38)—yet not win the pennant. Ken Williams led the league in home runs with 39 (Ruth finished with 35). Despite his injury, George Sisler hit .420 with 246 hits. And he stole a career-high and league-leading 51 bases that season.

Urban Shocker's season is one of but a handful in baseball history in which a pitcher led his league in strikeouts and fewest walks per nine innings,[48] and 1922 was his only season in St. Louis where his winning percentage lagged behind that of his team.[49] After gaining wins in his first two decisions against the Yankees, he lost seven of the next nine. Despite missing a month of the season, he won 24 games and was involved in 41 decisions.

The Browns won only 8 of 22 games against the Yankees in 1922. New York sportswriter Tom Meany summed up the Browns' season this way: "It was a great team, that '22 bunch, great but not lucky. And in baseball as in life, you often have to have both."[50]

18

A Lost Season

Phil Ball was generous with his 1922 team. With the profits he made that season, he could afford to be generous.[1] The players split $5,000 he gave them midseason and $20,000 he bestowed at the end of the campaign.[2] Ball did have to be prodded, though. When Quinn told him he wanted to give Shocker a $2,000 bonus, the owner said, "What are you trying to be, generous?" "No, not generous," replied Quinn. "Just honest."[3] Whether Ball was generous or honest with his star pitcher at contract time, Shocker signed for a 1923 salary of $9,000, a huge increase over the $5,000 he had earned each of the previous two seasons. Quinn continued to be a masterful broker between Ball and his players and manager.

Shocker also received an auto from the fans at the end of the 1922 season.[4] His sister, Cora, said that whenever he was approaching her Sylvan Lake, Michigan, home for a visit, he would blast the loud horn of his red Marmon convertible to announce his arrival.[5]

Shocker had a new approach to rounding into form, drawing on the experience of his monthlong injury the previous season. Rather than concluding he had overworked his arm, he decided he had not prepared the rest of his body sufficiently. "I'm going to work slowly this year. I'm going to get my body in condition and forget my arm," he told Roy Stockton. "I'm not going to be as soft as I was last year."[6]

A pall was cast over the Browns' spring training camp when George Sisler did not appear in Mobile. Initial reports said he was in the final stages

26. St. Louis fans awarded Urban Shocker with a convertible, in recognition of his yeoman's work during the 1922 season. He enjoyed driving to his sister's home in the outskirts of Detroit and announcing his arrival with a blast from the horn of his auto. *Private collection of Joan Willenbrock (granddaughter of Urban Shocker).*

of recovering from his shoulder injury. But what gradually emerged was more serious. He had developed a sinus infection that damaged his optic nerve, which resulted in his seeing everything in duplicate. Hitting a baseball is not easy, and hitting one when the batter sees two is impossible.[7]

Martin Haley wrote of the Browns that spring, "Their enthusiasm has waned, their confidence has withered, their aggressiveness has lost its luster."[8] Ken Williams was more explicit. "If Sisler can't play," he told Stockton, "we're ruined."[9] Sisler would miss the entire 1923 season.

On April 18 Shocker ruined the Tigers' home opener when he beat Detroit, 4–3. The next day Shocker and Ty Cobb got into a fight after the two had a "fire of verbal running banter" during the game. Cobb swung first and missed; Shocker then landed a solid blow to the chin.[10]

Shocker recognized Cobb's greatness; he just enjoyed rankling him. He said that what made Cobb so challenging was that opponents never knew quite what he was going to do. In this way, "he always establishes a mental hazard." The good pitcher, explained Shocker, needs to do the same thing to the batter—keep him guessing. "If you can contrive to give him something he isn't looking for, you have him."[11]

Shocker's first six starts of the season were complete games; by May 13 his record stood at 5-1. He continued to argue the strike zone with umpires. "The squawking ability of Shocker is well known," wrote one New York reporter, after Shocker was tossed from a June 13 game in which he was pitching well.[12] It was his first game in the new Yankee Stadium. The Yankees won and maintained their American League lead of three games. The Browns were unable to get any traction in the pennant race. Without Sisler, they fell four games under .500.

Shocker tended to lose his temper more quickly when he was pitching poorly. In early August, when the Senators scored four runs off him in the third inning, he argued so vehemently that their catcher, Muddy Ruel, had not touched second base on his way to a triple that umpire and former manager Pants Rowland ejected him.[13]

Two weeks later, when he beat the Tigers, 5–2, a St. Louis writer described Shocker as "slow, tantalizing, deliberate," probably referring to both his slow ball and his pace on the mound.[14] John Foster had called that pitch "a drop or duck ball." As the batter starts to swing at it, he explained, "the ball dives like a man taking a running plunge from a float. It is a mighty tough ball to hit."[15]

As for his spitball, George Moriarty compared it to that of the master, the White Sox's Ed Walsh, early in the century. But he added that Shocker depended more upon "his wits" than that pitch.[16] And during this season, Walsh himself, who was an American League umpire in 1922, was asked about Shocker's spitter after calling one of his games. "Shocker is a great pitcher," Walsh said. "But, honestly, I don't know whether he is a great spitball pitcher. In nine innings today, he threw exactly four 'spitballs.' I was surprised. I expected a flock of them. But he came up with everything a good pitcher should have."[17]

Shocker pushed his record to 15-5 when he beat the Athletics on July 18. A 30-win season seemed a possibility. That month John McGraw called him the smartest pitcher in the American League, pointing out Shocker's ability to win a lot of games for a weak team.[18]

Roy Stockton had a graphic column the next day about the Browns' star pitcher.

> It's worth the price of admission to watch Urban Shocker pitch. . . . Every time he works, he shows something new. Every time you watch him you note little things he does that make him a great pitcher. . . . Shocker's keen mind, his ability to outguess, outsmart the enemy enables him to fool batter after batter. . . . Shocker was as much master as is the cat with the half-dead mouse, which it permits to run so far and no farther. . . . Shocker has a most remarkable baseball brain. He lays plans and meets situations instantly, without a bit of hesitation."[19]

A few days later, Shocker's friend and former Cleveland sandlot star George Uhle beat him, 9–2. Uhle was on his way to a 26-win season in 1923. Back in 1920, he was struggling after a promising rookie season the year before.[20] More than a half century later, in 1973, Uhle credited Shocker with identifying his problem. "I found out myself through my real good friend Urban Shocker. . . . I asked Urban if I wasn't . . . tipping off my pitches. . . . He said, 'Yes, and everyone in the league knows it.'"[21]

Dave Danforth had rejoined the Browns for the season, at the insistence of Phil Ball. Both Bob Quinn and Lee Fohl would have preferred that he not return, but they had no choice. Ball had wanted to fire Fohl at the end of the 1922 campaign, blaming him for the club's falling short of the pennant. Quinn had talked the impulsive owner out of that move, but was tiring of dealing with Ball. When the Boston Red Sox were sold by Harry Frazee that spring, the new owners offered Quinn a stake in ownership and the role of president. He jumped at the opportunity.

Joe Vila noted that Quinn had hired Fohl in 1921 even though there were better-known managerial candidates available. "When Quinn left for Boston, Fohl lost his most loyal supporter."[22] He was now directly in the line of supervision—and the line of fire—of Phil Ball.

Opposing teams had been complaining about Danforth's pitching all season (Ty Cobb was the most outspoken), and matters came to a head on August 1. In the ninth inning, he was about to gain his sixth straight win, a 2–0 two-hitter over the Athletics, when umpire (and columnist) George Moriarty tossed him for throwing a ball with rough spots. Again,

27. Lee Fohl had two veteran players as his coaches: Jimmy Austin (*left*), the Browns' third baseman for more than a decade, and Lefty Leifield (*center*), a star pitcher for the Pittsburgh Pirates from 1906 to 1909, including his 19-8 season for the world champions of 1909. Both men reflected Fohl's subdued personality. *St. Louis Post-Dispatch.*

the ejection was accompanied by a 10-game suspension. (Shocker nailed down the shutout win in relief.) Danforth's teammates rallied behind him this time and signed a petition to the league's president, Ban Johnson. They noted the pitcher's powerful grip and maintained that Danforth had done nothing illegal. Even the straight-laced George Sisler signed the letter.

But Lee Fohl refused to sign. And he had a prominent supporter in the press. Sid Keener wrote, "I have talked with almost every umpire in the American League on the charge against Danforth. The report from them is unanimous—that Dave applies a foreign substance or otherwise tampers with the ball."[23] Keener was passionate in his defense of the now-beleaguered Fohl. "I know the character of Lee Fohl. He would give a friend the last dime he had in the world. . . . If Lee wouldn't sign [the petition], there must be some black smoke in the air."[24]

A writer for the *St. Louis Star* noted of Ball that summer, "There is no taffy and saccharine about him. He would not flatter Neptune for his trident. . . . His head at a challenge is wont to rear itself amazingly like that of a gamecock. He is given to swift red spurts of explosion. He flares until he turns himself into a conflagration. At times he looks like he is running to his own fire."[25]

A few days later, Lee Fohl was on the receiving end of that personality when Phil Ball fired him. In his press release, Ball said that he had terminated Fohl "for the good of the game."

Ball had blamed Fohl for a lot of things, especially the Browns not winning the pennant the previous season. In particular, he felt that the team's letdown after the "Little World Series" would have been avoided by a more inspiring leader. After St. Louis dropped those two games at home to the weak Senators, even the *New York Times* noted the club's drooping morale. "The struggle is rapidly assuming the aspects of a rout, with Lee Fohl playing the role of Napoleon just after he left Moscow."[26]

Fohl did have a parting statement, and the classy, soft-spoken man had words, not about his owner, but about his workhorse pitcher. "One more word before I depart—when pitching is discussed, don't overlook Urban Shocker. He is my idea of one of the greatest pitchers the game has produced."[27]

But Fohl was troubled by Ball's wording of his termination; he felt it impugned his reputation. "I stand upon my record in baseball. . . . I have always played my cards on the table. The man who says Lee Fohl ever did a dishonest trick in baseball lies to [*sic*] his teeth. This is not something that a private apology will satisfy. I want complete vindication."[28] I. E. Sanborn wrote that Fohl "has been a great credit to the sport in his quiet way and has an enviable reputation for squareness. He has not decreased his renown for honesty, if it is true that he sacrificed his job, rather than back up a player who he thought was breaking the rules."[29]

When Fohl said he would take his case to Commissioner Landis, he prompted Ban Johnson, the league's president, to get involved.[30] Johnson did not want Landis to expand his power by intruding into a club's business. He persuaded the stubborn Ball to reword the release. Ball issued a correction, that Fohl had been let go "for the good of the game as played by the Browns." Fohl appreciated and accepted the revision. For the third time, the popular Jimmy Austin became the club's interim manager; most people expected George Sisler to lead the team in 1924.

There is no record of Shocker's position on the Danforth controversy; apparently all the players signed the petition. Surely Shocker had admiration for a pitcher who, in Tom Meany's words, got hitters "so engrossed in looking for illegal pitches that they forget to hit the legal ones."[31] But Shocker had praise for Fohl as his manager was leaving. "Fohl was the best manager I ever worked for," he said. "I believe that he was both a good general and an excellent handler of men."[32]

On August 16 Danforth returned to the mound, under the close scrutiny of the umpires (Billy Evans was behind the plate), as well as league president Ban Johnson. Danforth lost that game to the Yankees, 3–1, but gained a lot of admirers. He constantly asked for new baseballs (58 were used in the game) and tossed a three-hitter. Even Sid Keener was moved to write, "It was a game that only a steel heart and a concrete spine could have pitched. Considering all events in the case I have never seen its equal on the ball field."[33]

The disruption in the Browns' clubhouse can only be imagined. The loss of their star player—there was still no word on when, or even if, Sisler would return—the firing of their manager, and the Danforth controversy were only some of the challenges the team faced. Dixie Davis suffered from neuritis for much of the season and won only four games. And Hub Pruett's arm problems severely limited his effectiveness. He too won only four games; his earned run average rose by almost two runs from 1922.

Pruett was looking like a one-year wonder, and Ty Cobb was not surprised. "No arm can stand such punishment," he said in 1922, referring to the strain the screwball generated. "He's throwing away his arm trying to win a pennant for the Browns. He'll have no arm next year. Mark my words."[34] And Cobb seemed to be right. Pruett maintained that his problem was overwork, not the strain that the screwball put on his elbow.[35] He had already missed three weeks of the 1922 season with arm trouble.

Danforth joined Shocker and Vangilder as the anchors of the pitching staff. The three of them posted 52 of the club's 74 wins in 1923. One thing Shocker could not reverse this season was his difficulty in beating

28. Dave Danforth was a storm center for the Browns in 1922 and 1923. Suspended both seasons for throwing pitches that sailed, he made an impressive return on August 16, 1923. Here he shows his grip shortly after that game. He always professed his innocence, and it was never proven he did anything illegal to the ball. *St. Louis Post-Dispatch.*

the Yankees for the second year in a row. When he lost to Joe Bush on August 6, for the third time in 1923, the Yankees had beaten him in all four starts against them this season. The New York press had fun talking about Shocker no longer "shocking" or "nemesising" the Yankees, now that the jinx had been "decapitated."[36]

This early August game was a classic. Shocker was in total command through seven innings, holding a 3–1 lead. The *New York Times* reported that three times in the game the Babe was so off-balance and swung so hard at slow balls and spitters that he tumbled out of the batter's box.

In the eighth inning, Shocker faltered, and Ruth came up with the bases loaded. The *New York American* set the scene. "Here was King Babe in gripping, dramatic conflict with King Shock."[37] Two papers reported that Shocker pointedly ignored the Browns' dugout, which was trying to get his attention. With a two-run lead, did Fohl want him to walk Ruth intentionally, walking in a run, yet maintaining the lead?[38] The Babe won the battle, clearing the bases with a double and giving New York a 5–3 victory. Miller Huggins saluted the man he had traded away. "We beat one of the best pitchers in the American League, and one of the best in baseball. We beat him when he was at his best."[39] The next day, Shocker preserved a win over the Yankees. A month later, in his column in the *New York American*, the Babe called Shocker the league's "craftiest pitcher."[40]

The rivalry between the Babe and Ken Williams was a natural outgrowth of their 1922 home run race. Late that season, the respected sports editor of the *New York Evening Mail*, Hugh Fullerton, fed that rivalry with a column favorable to Williams. "In every style of attack, he is better than the plumpened Bambino, and his superiority as a base runner is so great that it gives him a safe lead in the figures."[41]

Williams became the founding member of baseball's "30–30 club" in 1922, when he stole 37 bases, to go with his 39 home runs. Ruth, who stole only 2 bases that year, "used to be daring, resourceful, speedy and dangerous in sliding," wrote Fullerton, and now "has lost much of his speed and skill and can no longer stretch hits."[42]

In a late spring 1923 column, the Babe pointed out that Williams had an advantage hitting in his home ballpark, Sportsman's Park, which had a short right-field fence.[43] Williams did hit 32 of his 39 home runs the previous year at home, while the Babe hit only 14 of his 35 at home. However, Lee Fohl pointed out that the right-field bleachers in the Polo Grounds were even closer to home plate than those in Sportsman's Park. Fohl suggested that if Williams played in New York, he would hit 75 home runs in a season.[44] While the two men were neck-and-neck early in the 1923 season, Ruth recaptured the home run crown with 41, to Williams's 29.

There was an ongoing debate in the 1920s about the increase in offense and whether the balance between hitting and pitching had swung too far in the direction of the batter. But strong attendance figures overruled any preference of baseball purists. W. R. Hoefer summed this up in an article entitled "The Reign of the Wallop" that summer. "Batting is king. All other departments of the game are now subordinate subjects. The increased crowds at the present games strongly indicate that the public likes the present era of free and fancy swatting. . . . And if the public prefers the new game, the magnates prefer it."[45]

A related debate revolved around the reasons for the increase in hitting. Was the ball livelier, or were other factors involved? For one thing, Babe Ruth was showing a new way of hitting, swinging for the fences from the end of the bat, rather than choking up. "He has not only slugged his way to fame," wrote F. C. Lane, "but he has got everybody doing it."[46]

On August 5 Fred Lieb expressed his view. "We are still convinced that a low grade of pitching is more responsible for the hard hitting of today than the make of the ball. When a real pitcher gets hold of the present ball, he can do as many things with it as any of the former twirling greats of the game."[47] Just ten days later, Shocker gave additional support to Lieb's argument when he easily beat the Yankees. While he gave up a home run to Ruth late in the game, Shocker "never looked better in his interesting and colorful career," wrote one New York reporter.[48]

By the end of August, the pennant race had been settled. The Yankees had a 12½-game lead, and the Browns were 16 games back, struggling to stay above .500. They scored 686 runs this season, a steep decline from the 868 they had pushed across the plate in 1922.

Jack Tobin had a significant milestone this year: 1923 was the fourth consecutive season he had at least 200 hits. No one in the modern era had done so, not even Ty Cobb or Rogers Hornsby.[49] John Sheridan felt that Tobin was the closest player to Willie Keeler's style of place hitting, the ability to put the ball in a certain spot, where there was no fielder. "If Johnny ever gave hitting a thought, he would be one of the greatest hitters of all time," Sheridan wrote. "He just goes up there and takes a crack."[50]

Shocker still had personal targets, and on August 30 he reached one of them. He won his 20th game, the third straight season he reached that benchmark. He had given up only two runs in his last three games, all complete games. And he had a good chance to win at least 24 games for the third year in a row.

Shocker would again lead the American League in fewest walks per nine innings in 1923. He spoke about his approach to control with Frank Graham. "Pitching is just this and that," he said as he held his fingers an inch apart. "For every hitter there is a spot where he can't hit the ball—and by that I mean he can't hit it good. The idea is to find each man's spot and drop the ball into it."[51] "Hitting at bad balls," Shocker told F. C. Lane, "is the greatest favor the batter can do the pitcher."[52]

A few days earlier, Shocker started against Philadelphia, and Commissioner Landis was in attendance. Before the game, he asked the Browns pitcher how he felt. "Never better, your honor," replied Shocker, adding, "I want you to be the judge."[53] He then held the Athletics to one hit in the first seven innings, on his way to a three-hit win.

19

Free Agency in 1924?

So long as there's a dream to dream—
So long as there's a song to sing;
So long as coming dawns shall gleam
Upon our boundless wandering;
So long as there's a road that leads
Out and afar—through mile on mile—
Beyond life's narrow faiths and creeds,
So shall the game be worth the while.
—from "Song of the Off-Trail" by Grantland Rice

After completing their series in Chicago on September 9, 1923, the Browns boarded a train for Philadelphia and their final eastern road trip. Urban Shocker was not on that train. Phil Ball and new business manager Billy Friel had refused his request to bring his wife along on the trip, something Bob Quinn had permitted in the past.[1]

A few years later, Ford Frick would note that Shocker's wife never missed a game played by her husband's team.[2] The Browns soon suspended Shocker and fined him $1,000, more than 10 percent of his annual salary. Those penalties only hardened his resolve, and the two sides prepared for a protracted dispute. Shocker's season was done.

Some teams forbade spouses to travel with the team.[3] They subscribed to the "old school" view expressed by I. E. Sanborn in *Sporting Life* a few years earlier. "Woman is, always has been, and probably always will be the primary cause of much of the discord, dissension, petty jealousy, and other disruptive elements in a baseball team. . . . Teams have been broken up and pennants lost—by women, who never have the slightest suspicion of the damage they have done."[4] Westbrook Pegler had a more pithy description of Phil Ball's philosophy: "Women in baseball are like gun play in a crowded streetcar."[5]

Bob Quinn had felt that Rene Shocker was a positive influence on her husband. And one St. Louis sports editor felt the Browns had made a "tactical blunder," because a wife's presence can keep a player from "waywardness."[6]

It was becoming evident Ball wanted to rid himself of his prima donna pitcher. Harry Schumacher gave the countervailing opinion. While Shocker could be difficult, he wrote, his pitching record shows why a club "can afford to overlook an occasional peccadillo by the red-necked star."[7]

On September 27 Shocker dropped a bombshell on Organized Baseball. He appealed directly to Commissioner Landis. He claimed he had been deprived of his personal liberty and asked that he be declared a free agent, able to negotiate with any and all teams. What became known as "the Shocker case" quickly became baseball's cause célèbre.

When Landis had assumed power almost three years earlier, at the height of the Black Sox scandal, he had secured enormous power from the owners. One clause in the National Agreement granted him the authority to hear disputes between clubs and players in which a suspension was longer than ten days. Landis told a St. Louis reporter, "There is absolutely no question as to this point [jurisdiction]. . . . He [the player] sometimes is not adequately represented. I hold his case, as I did on the bench."[8]

Landis introduced a wild card into what seemed to have been a straightforward matter: a player had not obeyed team rules, which he had agreed to do when he signed his contract. Landis was known to be mercurial on the bench, and he had recently shocked the owners when he permitted Rube Benton, who had been banned by the National League's president, to return to baseball. Benton was a pitcher whose activities, in the words of baseball historians Harold and Dorothy Seymour Mills, "combined pitching, boozing, wenching, and gambling, and who was accused of

29. Commissioner Kenesaw Mountain Landis ruled baseball with an iron hand after assuming his position in early 1921. He had an unpredictable streak and enjoyed standing up for the underdog. When Urban Shocker took his quest for free agency to Landis in the fall of 1923, Organized Baseball's owners and American League president Ban Johnson shuddered. Ultimately Johnson engineered a settlement to avoid a ruling by Landis that could have set a dangerous precedent. *Private collection of Steve Steinberg.*

perjury and possession of 'guilty knowledge' of the 1919 World Series plot."[9] Yet Landis had let him back in the game.

Moreover, Ball was the only Major League owner to abstain from the unanimous vote to hire Landis.[10] Would Landis factor that animosity into his ruling on the Browns star? John Sheridan of the *Sporting News* boldly wrote of Landis's "erratic actions," and a *New York Sun* reporter spoke of "a new point of law" Landis might discover.[11]

As the December owners' meetings approached, Fred Lieb wrote, "There is a stick of dynamite in the Shocker case. . . . It is fraught with danger."[12] A man "high in the councils of Organized Baseball"—likely Ban Johnson—told one newspaper man that if Shocker were ruled a free agent, the American League would simply not accept the decision. It would break away from the National Agreement with the National League. The result would be chaos, with a possible return to the player raids of 1901–2 between the two leagues.[13]

A group of owners, led by Ball and working with American League president Ban Johnson, planned to clip Landis's wings at those winter meetings. But they unwisely dropped so many hints in the press that Landis got wind of their pending action and preempted it. First, he deferred his ruling on the Shocker case. Then he made a dramatic offer—or threat—at the meetings to tear up his contract and resign if he did not have the owners' full support. Not wanting to lose this important symbol of the game's integrity, the owners meekly fell into line, and Landis had secured a resounding victory. Eugene Murdock, Johnson's biographer, called this meeting "the critical point in Landis's leadership."[14]

A couple of weeks later, Ed Wray was sounding more ominous. If Shocker is declared a free agent, he wrote, "The fireworks that will follow should make the last days of Pompeii look like a wet match."[15] Fuel was added to the fire from reports, probably emanating from Johnson, that no team would sign Shocker (not a conspiracy, but a gentlemen's agreement), effectively ending his career.[16] To further complicate matters, Shocker was strongly intimating that if he did not get a ruling in his favor from Landis, he would take the matter into the civil courts.[17] That move, said a *Sporting News* reporter, would trigger a legal battle that would shake the National Pastime "to its foundation."[18]

Ban Johnson, as well as many of the club owners, felt the risks of a Landis ruling were simply too great. The case had to be settled. Of course, he had to persuade Ball to pursue a negotiated settlement. That would be no easy matter. When Phil Ball got into baseball in St. Louis in 1914, *Reedy's Mirror*, the city's new literary journal, wrote of the ice magnate, "He has not the polished mien. . . . He is no merchant of conversation. . . . He does not affect a great softness of manner, unruffled evenness of temper."[19] In the intervening decade, Ball had not mellowed.

The private correspondence on the Shocker case between the two men, close friends, is both explosive and revealing. Ball wrote Johnson on January 12, "You know I am not keen to compromise any kind of a proposition, when I think I am absolutely right, as I think I am in the Shocker

30. Phil Ball was a gruff and unpolished man who loved baseball and owning the Browns. But his autocratic style combined with Urban Shocker's stubbornness and temperament led to their almost inevitable falling out, which captured headlines in the off-season of 1923–24. *Missouri History Museum, St. Louis.*

case."[20] A few days later, Ball wrote him, "He [Quinn] and I were both fully convinced that he [Shocker] had thrown a ball game or two, but we could not prove it. But if I ever could prove it, he would go the same route that Gideon [*sic*] went."[21] Ball went on to say that discipline had to be maintained and added that if Landis were to rule Shocker a free agent, he would sue Landis personally for $100,000.

Johnson prevailed upon Ball to let him act as his agent in negotiating with Shocker. The league president then called on Quinn, the former Browns executive and now the president of the Red Sox, who had good relations with Shocker in St. Louis, to join him in meeting with Shocker. Quinn already had suggested to Ball that he negotiate a settlement. He told Ball that "sometimes we have to swallow our pride" and that a compromise would make Shocker "just twice as good a pitcher for the Browns in 1924."[22]

Shocker met with Johnson and Quinn and decided to settle. With Johnson acting as Phil Ball's proxy, the pitcher signed for a salary of $12,000 for 1924, a big increase. Quinn realized that Ball's ego would make him hesitant to rescind the $1,000 fine. So the fine remained and was taken into account when the salary was set.

Johnson wrote to Ball after the settlement, "Mr. Shocker related his side of the story in a quiet way and evidenced no resentment. . . . This was the second time I ever met Shocker, and I am frank to confer, his conversation impressed me. . . . I gave him the contract, with the full thought he was entitled to that much money. He is one of the greatest pitchers in the American League."[23]

Ball was still bitter and wrote back, "I do not quite understand how Shocker 'sold' himself to you so thoroughly. Of all the dirty, contemptible, game-throwing rats in the business, Shocker is the one, and his wife ten times worse. Mr. Quinn is the greatest settler on earth."[24] Ball added that Sisler also thought Shocker was "crooked," and Ball was relying on Sisler "knocking his head off if he does not go straight."

The final word in their exchange came from Johnson, and one can only wonder whether it gave pause to the Browns owner. "The real motive and desire of Shocker to take his wife east was to consult a specialist in Philadelphia. She is afflicted with cancer in the right breast, and it seriously affected the use of her arm."[25] Irene Shocker would die of uterine cancer in early 1933 at the age of forty-two.

What is to be made of Ball's charges about Shocker throwing games? There is no evidence suggesting this. With the exception of 1922, when Shocker lost a number of heartbreaking 2–1 games, his winning percentage was considerably better than that of his team. Had Sisler thought Shocker was dishonest, he would not have fought to keep him.[26] Had Quinn thought Shocker was dishonest, he would not have gone to such lengths to help settle the case and keep Shocker in St. Louis. None of Quinn's correspondence suggests he suspected Shocker was crooked.

Ball had a track record of making wild charges. A few years earlier, he had accused two of his players, Del Pratt and Doc Lavan, of throwing games. Branch Rickey, a man of unquestionable character, later recommended Pratt as the baseball coach to the University of Michigan and acquired Lavan, who played six years for Rickey's St. Louis Cardinals.

Ultimately Ball may have signed off on the deal because he recognized Shocker's ability to help his team win. There may not have been a baseball owner who wanted to win more than Phil Ball. He once told Dan Daniel, "I'd give anything to win with the Browns. Well, money is no object. . . . That's why I stay young. I sit behind the screen, right behind the plate, and I hope and hope."[27]

All parties were probably relieved the Shocker case was resolved with a negotiated settlement. Francis Richter wrote in his *Sporting News* column, "The temperamental and probably ill-advised player had refused to admit the errors of his ways, to take his punishment. . . . [Shocker] escaped the full consequences of his rank insubordination, but better than the possible—nay probable—consequences of a decision by Commissioner Landis subversive of club rights and league sovereignty."[28]

Shocker notified Landis he was withdrawing his appeal. The price of fighting on was too high; the risk of being locked out of the game by a "gentlemen's agreement" was too great. Even if he won the battle for free agency, he might lose the war and be blackballed. Shocker said he looked forward to pitching for his new manager, Sisler. "I'm going to try my upmost to have the greatest season of my career," he told reporters. "Manager Sisler can count on me to be ready to pitch my head off."[29]

Shocker had just completed four very good seasons. From 1920 to 1923, he won more games than any other pitcher, 91. What is even more striking is that, because of injuries and suspensions, he had missed more than fourteen weeks during that time span.[30]

20

The Temperamental Spitballist

The Yankees won their first World Series in October 1923, finally beating the Giants, whom they met in the fall classic for the third straight year. But Miller Huggins believed that winning teams tended to get stale and complacent, and the intense Shocker would be an effective antidote.[1] Despite the difficulties Shocker had caused his club—or perhaps because of them—Huggins wanted the fierce competitor on his club.

Phil Ball wanted New York pitcher Sam Jones in return, but Huggins resisted. "Why should I give up Jones, who was the best pitcher in the American League last season?"[2] Huggins did say that he offered a couple of other experienced pitchers for Ball to choose from. One was Carl Mays, whom Huggins had soured on and used only sparingly in 1923.[3]

The other was Waite Hoyt, winner of 55 games over the past three seasons.[4] Hoyt continued to be headstrong and difficult to manage; Fred Lieb confirmed that Hoyt was indeed offered to the Browns.[5] Disciplinarian that he was, Ball did not want to exchange one prima donna for another, and he turned down that deal with New York. The Yankees soon sold Mays to Cincinnati of the National League and held onto Hoyt, with whom Huggins ultimately ironed out their differences.

There were also reports the Red Sox wanted Shocker; Bob Quinn had hired Lee Fohl to manage the club in 1924, and acquiring Shocker would reunite the two men who had worked well together in St. Louis.

George Sisler was indeed signed to manage the Browns; this would get him back in the game, even if his eye injury were to persist. Reports said that Shocker could bring the Browns $100,000 to $150,000 from potential suitors. But Sisler did not want to lose his best pitcher before he had managed his first game. "It would be hard to arrange any trade which would give the Browns the value that Shocker represents to the team," he said.[6] He prevailed upon Ball—no easy feat—not to deal Shocker, at least not yet.

After beating the White Sox on Opening Day 1924, Shocker was hit hard in Detroit. He gave up seven earned runs in fewer than five innings and took the loss. He then simply disappeared. A few days passed before he made contact with the Browns. He attributed his poor outing to tonsillitis. He had since lost fourteen pounds and said his condition was "near diphtheria." Shocker went on to explain that he had told the team's trainer to inform manager Sisler that he would stay behind in Detroit to recover. The trainer, he went on, apparently forgot to deliver the message.[7]

Shocker spoke more dismissively of his club to another reporter, declaring, "If they don't know where I am, it's probably because I didn't tell them." That writer noted that Shocker was "a temperamental star" who did "just about as he pleases, whether it pleases anyone else or not."[8] When the Shocker case had been before Commissioner Landis, the *Sporting News* hinted at Shocker's personal problems. "There is a lot to the Shocker case that cannot be told and will not be told." The paper's reporter went on to say that St. Louis fans had analyzed Shocker's temperament and associations and were ready to part company with him.[9]

It is possible Shocker was being affected by the impending loss of his parents, who both were seriously ill. His father died of stomach cancer on April 24, and his mother passed away just four weeks later. They were survived by all nine of their children and were buried in Cleveland's Brooklyn Heights cemetery.[10] Whether their illnesses and deaths contributed to Urban's stress and led to his "disappearance" and possibly going on a drinking spree is not known. But reports said his father died before Urban reached his bedside.

When Shocker returned to action on May 7, the Indians knocked him out of the game in the second inning. He faced the Yankees a week later, the day they raised their world championship flag and honored Babe Ruth

31. Urban Shocker projected supreme confidence and sardonic arrogance during his years with the Browns. He strutted on the mound, and his performances backed up his attitude. His notoriety was limited because the peak of his career was in St. Louis, away from the big stage of New York City. *Private collection of Steve Steinberg.*

for his 1923 American League Award, a precursor to the Most Valuable Player Award. Shocker raised his game against New York, "literally toying with the home batters," in the words of a St. Louis reporter. He beat them, 11–1.[11] Shocker made Murderers' Row look like they had been struck by "a stroke of paralysis," in the words of the *Sporting News* writer.[12]

Joe Vila, a critical observer who was stingy with praise, was moved to salute Shocker after watching this game.

> Shocker is a smart pitcher, no mistake. He's a master of control, uses a change of pace and frequently bluffs with his spitball. . . . He served up curves, speeders or floaters, mixing in a wet ball now and then with the desired results. The Yankees, always expecting the damp fling, were mystified to such an extent that their vain efforts to hit the ball safely were distressing, to say the least. Shocker proved conclusively that a pitcher who uses his head and keeps the enemy guessing as to the kind of ball that is coming with each delivery can subdue the hardest hitters.[13]

While Shocker did make four more starts in May, he did not show up for all of the Browns' games and arrived late for others. His manager, George Sisler, "covered" for him a few times, but by the end of May he had given up and fined his pitcher. Sisler had turned down an offer to manage the club back in 1921 because he wanted to focus exclusively on his hitting. Now as manager, he had a major distraction, and it was not his style to act as disciplinarian. But now he felt he had no choice. "A man must keep in condition, fit to play, and if he doesn't, something must be done," he told reporters.[14]

When Sisler was announced as the club's new manager, most of the reaction was positive. Joe Vila wrote, before the selection was finalized, "Sisler, in the opinion of the sharps, is a born leader."[15] He also said that Shocker "worships" Sisler and would do his best for him.[16] Ken Williams appreciated the fact that Sisler asked for players' input during spring training and said, "He is the best man I ever worked for."[17] In *Baseball Magazine*, W. F. Hoefer did not question Sisler's baseball knowledge, but wondered about his personality. "Whether he possesses the vital spark of leadership is, of course, another matter, and only time can tell as to that."[18] He did note that Sisler's apparent lack of aggressiveness may be nothing more than a lack of bluster.

Then there was the question of Sisler's playing ability and the extent to which he would regain his old form. Before spring training, Vila reported Sisler was considering returning to his original position of pitching, where sharp eyesight was less crucial.[19] While many reports of his recovery were positive, they may have been based more on hope than reality. A *Post-Dispatch* photographer bluntly wrote that Sisler looked terrible and that people who said otherwise were "spoofing themselves."[20]

Later that spring Ford Frick wrote of telltale signs from Sisler: "A slight twist to his head, a shade of anxiety that shows in his eyes, a bit of a squint." Pitchers told Frick that Sisler was "missing balls he used to murder."[21] The most telling evidence came from Sisler himself. He told *Baseball Magazine* that year that he used to focus on "place hitting," driving the ball between fielders. Now he was concentrating simply on what he called "meeting the ball, in other words, hit it."[22] And then there were the numbers. When Frick's article appeared on June 9, Sisler was batting .317. When the August issue of *Baseball Magazine* hit the newsstands on the first of that month, his batting average was .298. Back in 1922, those figures were .424 and .403, respectively.

Sisler had wanted to shield Shocker from the press and therefore kept details of his behavior private. Some writers felt the fans should know the full story, that it was the public's business. A *Sporting News* columnist bemoaned "the wall of secrecy" that teams maintained while they coddled their star players.[23] Vila described Shocker as "erratic" and an "in-and-outer" that summer, words that he had used for Ray Caldwell years earlier.[24]

Shocker did not take kindly to what he felt was excessive attention. "I have never seen any of the other players placed under such close surveillance as myself, and it gives me the impression that I am being railroaded. . . . They cannot forget the trouble that came up between the club and myself last fall."[25] After calling the shots during his battle for free agency a few months earlier, he was once again at the mercy of Phil Ball.

League president Ban Johnson felt particularly responsible for Shocker's behavior; he had been instrumental in signing him to the lucrative contract. On June 7 Johnson wrote Sisler that the pitcher's "recent dissipation" was destroying team morale. "Shocker will run his course very speedily as a professional player, if he persists in his present conduct."[26]

Johnson was also still concerned about Dave Danforth and what he might be doing with the ball. The league's president wrote Sisler that if Danforth was defacing the ball with his rough hand, he should desist immediately.[27] The pitcher was getting fewer complaints than in the previous two years, but Ty Cobb was still outspoken and heckled Danforth constantly when the Tigers faced him.[28] And when Danforth shut out the Yankees in early June, their manager, Miller Huggins, protested that the pitcher was loosening the ball's cover with his rough thumbnail.

For the second straight season, Danforth was a key member of the Browns rotation. After winning 16 games in 1923, he won 15 this season. No one ever figured out what—if anything—he was doing to the ball. "His work on the pitching mound," wrote F. C. Lane in *Baseball Magazine*, "has been more carefully scrutinized and more universally criticized than that of any pitcher on record, not excepting the ill-omened [Carl] Mays."[29]

Elam Vangilder was available to the Browns only intermittently and usually only for short stints as a reliever. He had developed a blister on a pitching finger while hitting balls in practice, and the finger became stiff after becoming infected.[30] He won only five games all season.

In early June, Shocker beat the Yankees in St. Louis. He gave up two runs in the first inning, and the fans booed and taunted him, with cries for Sisler to take him out. Ford Frick had been critical of St. Louis fans a few weeks earlier, when he wrote that their favorite word was "boo." Sisler kept Shocker in, and he limited New York the rest of the way, for a 6–3 victory.

Ruth nicked him for a triple, but Shocker in turn struck out the Babe twice. "He pitched as though the very pennant depended on that game," wrote a *Sporting News* reporter. "When Urban is right, there is not a more competent right-hander in the league."[31] Just a week earlier, the same reporter had written that Shocker was "a bad boy . . . cutting up."[32]

Sid Keener met the rumors of Shocker's drinking head-on that June. "Perhaps Urban did take a few sips of something with foam on the top,

32. Urban Shocker, seen leaving the batter's box for first base, was as aware of the strike zone as hitter as he was as a pitcher. He had a remarkably high on-base percentage and was also a skilled bunter. This is at Sportsman's Park, before the 1926 remodel. *Private collection of Steve Steinberg.*

but what of it?" he wrote. "His pleasures have never interfered with his work in the uniform."[33]

But in 1924 those "pleasures" were interfering with his work. If ever there was a season during which Shocker's demons seemed to gain the upper hand, it was 1924. He had seven starts in which he gave up four or more runs in short outings, five innings or less. His earned run average was above 5.00 through July; he managed to bring it down to 4.20 by season's end, still far higher than any other year.

Despite his struggles on the mound, Shocker's control did not desert him; his walks per nine innings was third lowest in the league.[34] Earlier in the year, umpire Billy Evans wrote, "I know of no other pitcher in the American League who works with greater care on his batters than Urban Shocker of the Browns."[35] That summer Evans wrote a column on the smartest pitchers in the game, not factoring in their natural ability. His "all-star gray matter" pitching staff included Shocker.[36]

Shocker's understanding of control and pinpoint location extended beyond his role as a pitcher. He had a remarkable eye for the strike zone when he was at the plate. This season he walked 22 times, with only 67 at-bats and 99 plate appearances. His batting average was .239, and his on-base percentage was almost 200 points higher, .433. For his career, Shocker's relative walk rate was one of the highest in history for a pitcher.[37] He drew walks in 13.3 percent of his plate appearances; since 1901, no pitcher has had a higher rate.[38]

He benefited greatly from the play of one of the league's best catchers, the durable Hank Severeid. F. C. Lane called him "a catching Hercules" in 1924, his fifth straight season of catching more than 115 games and his fourth in a row with a batting average of more than .300. "Severeid's prodigious strength is linked with an endurance quite as extraordinary," wrote Lane.[39]

When the Red Sox won their game on June 7, the day Shocker beat New York, they moved into a first-place tie with the Yankees, both with records of 24-16. Lee Fohl was managing the most surprising team in years. The previous two seasons Boston had lost more than 90 games. Now, almost two months into the 1924 season, they seemed to be contenders for real.

A month later, history had dictated reality, and patterns had been reset. The Yankees were in first place; the Red Sox had tumbled to sixth and were still falling. The Browns were in the middle of the pack, winning about half of their games.

Sportswriters had used many words to describe the talented yet petulant Shocker of the early 1920s. One of the most appropriate phrases was that of an unnamed Cleveland newspaperman, who called him "the temperamental spitballist."[40] That temperament—and temper—erupted again in the July 15 game against the Yankees.

New York was rallying from behind in the eighth inning when the Yankees' Bob Meusel hit a line drive that umpire Billy Evans thought was caught, whereas umpire Brick Owens felt the ball had been trapped. Then, "after taking nearly as many ballots as the late Democratic convention," with the teams and the umpires going back and forth, the latter ruled the ball had been trapped, and the Yankees had tied the score.[41]

Shocker exploded in rage, directing most of his epithets at Babe Ruth on third base as he stormed off the field, with umpire Owens alongside him. The *New York Times* reporter wrote of the mystery of that inning: "It was impossible to tell whether Umpire Owens chased Shocker or Urban left of his own free will. The first anyone knew of his going he was waving [pitcher Billy] Bayne from the bullpen and hurling repartee at Ruth as he walked away."[42] The Babe soon scored, and the Yankees had rallied for a 5–4 win. Shocker took the loss; his record fell to 7-8.

Baby Doll Jacobson hit a home run in the game, his 13th of the season, en route to his most productive long-ball season, when he hit 19.[43] He was one of the largest men in the game, at 6'3" and 215 pounds, but he did not swing for the fences. John Sheridan felt Jacobson could hit the ball farther than Ruth did, "if he ever did really step into it right."[44] But Jacobson explained, "By trying to murder the ball, I missed many a hit I would otherwise have made, and my batting average suffered. It is all a question of mathematics."[45] He added that he was a "wrist hitter," whereas the Babe was a "shoulder hitter."

Jacobson was also one of the best fielders in the game. As Shocker approached his mid-thirties, he was striking out fewer batters and allowing more balls to be put in play.[46] Jacobson provided a safety net, playing the outfield behind him. He covered a tremendous amount of ground in center field; he was often one of the leaders in putouts at that position. Jacobson said that his secret was not speed, which he lacked, but his knowledge of hitters. "Play the batter, and you have the secret," he said.[47] When he left the Majors, he owned a number of fielding records.

Jacobson had one of baseball's more unusual nicknames. When he came to bat with the Mobile Sea Gulls in 1912, the band was playing the popular song "Oh, You Beautiful Doll." He hit a home run and, as he told the story, a female fan sitting behind the plate exclaimed that he must be that beautiful doll. Then a reporter used the nickname for him in a story, and it stuck.[48]

Long before computers and Sabermetrics, some ballplayers looked for patterns and predictors by observation. Jacobson did so with his positioning in the field, based on where batters tended to hit the ball. Shocker did so with batters' weaknesses, pitches and locations they did not like to hit. Sid Keener wrote, "I doubt there is another pitcher in the game who studies his batters as carefully as Shocker and gives them just what they don't want."[49]

Shocker made a fascinating observation about pitchers' preparations just before games. Pitchers always warmed up before games they were starting. But on the road, he observed, they had to sit while their teams batted first. By the time they went to the mound, they had cooled off and were not "loose" with all of their "stuff," he explained. Because of that, Shocker never warmed up on the road until just before he took the mound after the top of the first, and not before the game.[50]

At the 2015 SABR national convention in Chicago, David Smith, founder of Retrosheet, presented a paper that expounded on this very hypothesis. "Throughout baseball history, the home team has scored significantly more runs in the bottom of the first inning than either team does in any other inning," Smith noted. He explored possible explanations for this phenomenon, including the visiting team's travels, and came up with only one hypothesis that correlated (and correlated strongly) with this first-inning edge for the home team: after warming up, the visiting team's pitchers had to sit through the top of the first and were not warmed up when they finally took the mound. "Greater length of top of first offers the best explanation for increased scoring in bottom of first."[51]

On August 1 St. Louis fans hounded Shocker again when he walked Ruth a couple of times. The Babe had hits in his other three at-bats, and the Yankees edged the Browns, 3–2. Fans shouted "yellow" at Shocker, and even a New York reporter was critical of the city's "notorious sportsmen."[52] Shocker himself had told *Baseball Magazine* there were times that walking the Babe was the sensible action. He also explained that not all of the free passes Ruth got were totally intentional. "Two or three years ago, the Babe would hit anything he could reach," said Shocker. The slugger was now more selective and therefore a better hitter.[53]

On September 6 Shocker pitched and won both ends of a doubleheader against the White Sox, both complete-game victories by the score of 6–2. It was a rare achievement of both ability and durability.[54] The following week he gained his 16th and last win of the season, a four-hitter, completed in just 78 minutes.

The Yankees were denied their fourth straight pennant by the Washington Senators. That left St. Louis as the only Major League city not to have won a pennant in the new century. The Browns finished the season in fourth place, even with the return of Sisler to the playing field. He hit .305, not terrible but almost 100 points below his combined average of 1920 to 1922.[55] The Browns also lost Ken Williams for more than three weeks due to a midseason ankle fracture.

Damon Runyon had written of Shocker, "Only a little carelessness in his make-up keeps him from being one of the greatest the game has ever known."[56] It remained to be seen which pitcher would emerge in the coming seasons: one who was careless or one who was great.

21

Back Where I Belong

Some time, amid the tumult and the throng,
We hear an old, lost song;
A broken strain from one we used to hear
Back in some vanished year;
A melody, borne through the drifting haze
Of life's forgotten days;
The tumult dies around us, strangely thrilled,
With roar of traffic stilled;
Our eyes now mist—our hearts torn back—and then
We dream old dreams again.

—from "Over Lost Trails" by Grantland Rice

In 1985 baseball historian Norman Macht interviewed eighty-nine-year-old Milt Gaston and asked the former pitcher why the Yankees had traded him in December 1924. "They wanted to get Shocker back. He was a star at that time," Gaston replied. "They had to have Shocker back. Ruppert and him [Huggins] wanted Shocker."[1]

Despite Shocker's less-than-stellar 1924 season, Miller Huggins still wanted to bring him back to New York—even more so now, after the complacent Yankees had fallen just short of the 1924 pennant. Shocker, having "never tasted world series money," would provide the Yankees' pitching staff with "a mental stimulus," said Huggins.[2] And now Browns manager

George Sisler, as well as owner Phil Ball, wanted to deal Shocker. Roy Stockton admitted Shocker would probably do better in another uniform.[3]

Huggins again offered Waite Hoyt to the Browns; Ball still did not want to exchange one headstrong pitcher for another.[4] And while the Yankees were now willing to trade Sam Jones, his star had fallen after a disappointing 1924 season.[5] The Browns had expressed interest in the Yankees' young first baseman, Lou Gehrig, who appeared in only 23 games that season.[6]

In 1934 Gehrig recalled Huggins telling him, "I'm going to fight hard, but I can't win without Shocker. And if you go, don't forget, it isn't because I want you to go."[7] Shortly after Gehrig's death, Dan Daniel confirmed that Huggins had once told Gehrig, "I hate to think of the terrible mistake I would have made had I sent you to the Browns for Urban Shocker. If they had insisted, you would have gone."[8]

In 1924 Shocker appeared in court for two separate cases. In June Shocker settled a $10,000 lawsuit between Cletus Kamp, his fourteen-year-old stepson, and United Railways. The boy's father, Arthur Kamp, had been struck and killed by a St. Louis streetcar a year earlier. At the time, Shocker notified the court that he intended to adopt Cletus.[9] Almost six months later, Shocker was back in court to finalize the adoption. The judge jokingly said that he would issue an injunction to keep the Browns pitcher in St. Louis.[10]

Shocker was traded to New York on December 17, 1924. In the end, the Browns decided they needed pitching.[11] The Yankees sent Gaston, veteran Joe Bush, and southpaw Joe Giard to St. Louis. Huggins saw Gaston as one of the best young pitchers in the game, but was guided by a "win now" philosophy, which New York's impatient fans demanded. The inclusion of Giard, a promising Minor League pitcher with Toledo, was a complex part of the deal.[12]

Then there was Bush. If Shocker had been a Yankees jinx, at least in his early St. Louis years, Bush had been unbeatable against the Browns for some time. Papers reported he had won 17 straight decisions against them; a review of the baseball database Retrosheet shows the streak was 14 since the Browns had last beaten him in June 1922, still an impressive run. And if his pitching were to deteriorate, Bush was one of the best-hitting pitchers in baseball and could be used as a pinch hitter.[13]

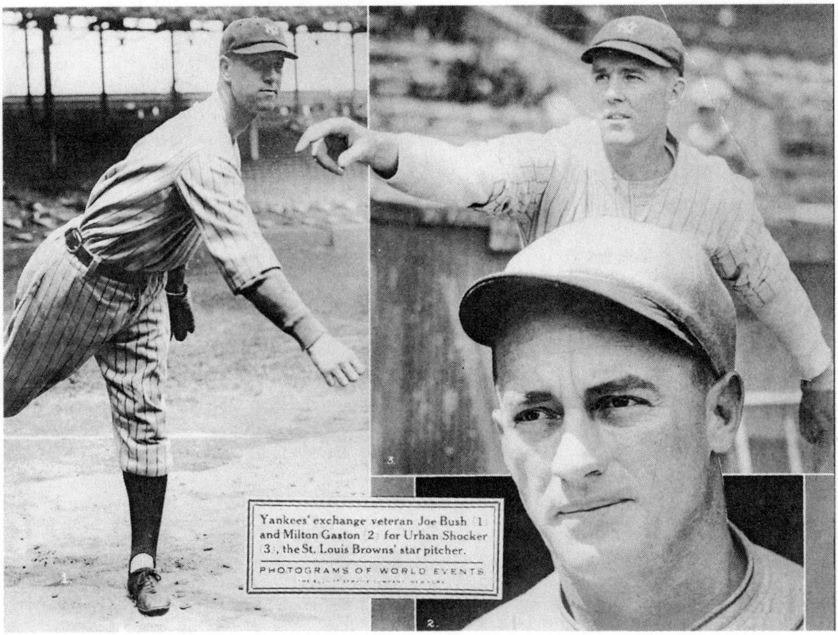

33. In an age when ballplayers had no say in where they played, Urban Shocker had his dream come true after the 1924 season: he was returning to the Yankees. Despite Shocker's scrapping with the New York club for years, their manager, Miller Huggins, wanted him for his fierce desire to win and yearning to reach the World Series. *Private collection of Steve Steinberg.*

Shocker's reputation preceded him. A *Sporting News* columnist wrote in November, "Shocker is a trifle temperamental—headstrong, it might more aptly be called. Like all stars, he wants his way. A Bolshevik? Well, no. It's not that bad."[14] Joseph Gordon went further in the *New York Daily Mirror*, writing that Huggins had "colossal nerve" to take such a "tough customer."[15]

The Yankees' owner, Jacob Ruppert, did not want his manager to bring aggravation upon himself and raised this concern to him. But Huggins wanted the fierce competitiveness and pitching skill Shocker would bring to the club. Had he not traded Shocker in 1918, perhaps the Yankees would have won the five pennants in a row that he believed the club "could have, should have won," from 1920 to 1924.[16] "You get him, Colonel, and I'll handle him," Huggins told his boss.[17] As with most of their deals, business manager Ed Barrow worked closely with Huggins to finalize the trade.

Shocker thanked St. Louis fans, saying, "I feel I have done my duty for the St. Louis club" and added that he would keep his home in that city, which he did.[18] In January Huggins made a special trip to St. Louis to meet with Shocker. They got together in the hospital, where the pitcher was recovering from two minor surgeries: one to remove his tonsils and the other to remove a "fibrous tumor" on his pitching shoulder.[19]

Huggins was frank and raised the issue of his new pitcher's reputation for being a challenge to handle. "I told him the fans of New York would not stand for the temperamental stuff," Huggins said. "Shocker assured me with all sincerity that he was so tickled with his transfer to the Yanks that he would be a model ball player." "I don't know what kind of winning ball I'll pitch," he replied. "But I do know that it will be the best ball I can pitch."[20] He then became the first Yankee to sign his 1925 contract, which called for a salary of $12,500, $500 higher than his 1924 earnings.

Observers were divided as to which team got the better part of the deal. Supporters of the Yankees' side of the ledger noted that while Shocker and Bush were the same age, Bush had more wear and tear on his arm, having pitched in the big leagues for three full seasons before Shocker started in 1916.[21]

One thing Shocker had going for his career longevity was his method of and approach to pitching. George Sisler noted, "Urb Shocker is the most cunning pitcher in the American League. All he needs is control. That's why he'll be pitching long after a lot of other fellows who have more real 'stuff' are forgotten."[22] Umpire Billy Evans explained it a little differently. "Shocker is a pitcher who performs without a bit of wasted effort. There is no wasted effort because it is only in the pinch that he puts everything on the ball."[23]

Perhaps thinking of Shocker's inconsistent performance in 1924, W. O. McGeehan of the *Herald Tribune* wondered just what pitcher Huggins was getting. "It looks as though the Yanks bought a brick without testing it with the acid," he wrote, "but only a season will show how much Shocker will assay to the ton of ivory."[24]

It was no secret around the American League that Huggins wanted

Shocker. One New York writer described him as "jubilant" over the deal and declaring, "He'll just about make our pitching staff."[25] There was another Yankee who was very pleased and confident the man he was getting had indeed been "tested with acid," and that was Jacob Ruppert. As he told *New York World* sports editor George Daley, "Frankly, I believe that Shocker is the best pitcher in baseball today. I have seen him in action against us so often, when so much was at stake for us and when so little was at stake for the St. Louis club, when he fought us so desperately that he really made our pulses stop, that I have decided that he can pitch for all of the millions piled up in the Yankee Stadium. He is a money pitcher if ever there was one."[26]

Back in 1921, after Shocker had beaten the Yankees in the late September game that almost cost them their first pennant, the *New York Tribune* reporter wrote, "Hell hath no fury like a pitcher scorned."[27] Now that rage had been neutralized; Huggins had brought Shocker back to New York.

In February 1925 syndicated columnist Henry Farrell wrote a column on the importance of "heart" in making an athlete great. Among his examples was what Ruppert told him of Shocker. "If a game should be played for a million dollars, I wouldn't want to see any better pitcher on the mound for me than Shocker."[28]

22

Clouds Approaching

Give me but room to fight my way,
I ask no other gift from Fate;
Though it should crowd on me at bay,
Where only ghosts and shadows wait.
Shadows of old defeats blown by.
Ghosts of old dreams drawn from life's pit;
Yet all I ask is room to try
And prove Fate cannot make me quit.
No glint of glory from the height,
No flare of fame to call me far;
Merely the ground to make my fight
Against whatever odds there are.
—"Song of the Stalwart" by Grantland Rice

Urban Shocker had always wanted to return to the Yankees. His 1918 trade had cost him the thousands of dollars that three World Series checks would have generated. It also had removed him from baseball's biggest stage and from the emerging dynasty Jacob Ruppert was building with the help of Miller Huggins, Babe Ruth, and business manager Ed Barrow. While he reveled in beating his old team and "took the greatest delight in pitching to Babe Ruth," his longing was to return to the Yankees.[1] But it did no good for him to express his wishes; a player had no control over where he played.

Now his dream had come true. Fred Lieb, who described Shocker as "elated," quoted the pitcher. "How does it feel being back on the Yanks? Say, it feels like getting back home or returning from the minors to the majors."[2] Another New York reporter wrote, "The old Yankee jinx was just bubbling over with joy at the thought of his transfer."[3]

Yet at this time of enormous satisfaction and peace of mind for the pitcher, something did not feel right. He recognized that he was no longer young; he was paying increased attention to pacing himself during a game, something that observers such as Billy Evans had noticed. Shocker was surely facing the realization that "today's rookie is tomorrow's champion, and today's champion is tomorrow's also-ran," as Ford Frick put it. "Whatever else may be said of professional sport, it makes philosophers of the men who play it. It teaches them to accept the inevitable."[4]

But something else was happening. Shocker was very ill in Hot Springs, Arkansas, in late February. He and his wife stopped there on their way to the Yankees' training facility in St. Petersburg, Florida. A number of players made the annual Arkansas visit, where they worked off excess winter weight in the resort town's baths, fed by natural springs.

Slivers of information appeared in New York newspapers at this time. Shocker had "a severe cold" and was told to refrain from strenuous exercise and taking steam baths.[5] In early March, another report said his "cold had lasted 10 days and resulted in weight loss of 10 pounds." Moreover, Shocker had trouble breathing.[6]

This "cold" and congestion may have been the early signs of a heart condition, most likely mitral valve prolapse. A century ago, it was often caused by childhood rheumatic fever. The valve can become inflamed, and "over the ensuing two to four decades, there is gradual scarring and calcification of the valves and eventually becomes severe enough to cause symptoms," cardiac physician Dr. Ronald Siegel explained to me. When the scarring causes the valve to seal improperly, it does not open fully (valve stenosis) or not properly close, "resulting in a 'leaky' valve (such as mitral insufficiency/regurgitation or aortic insufficiency/regurgitation) or both," continued Dr. Siegel. The heart becomes enlarged and weakened to compensate for the volume of leaked blood. "The malfunctioning valve results in excessive work for the heart muscle, which tries to compensate by stretching (cardiac dilation) and becoming thicker (hypertrophy), analogous to a weight lifter's physique. This process staves off symptoms until a time is reached when the compensatory mechanisms fail and symptoms ensue."[7]

Shocker's doctor was Robert Hyland, the team physician of the Browns and Cardinals and later known as "the Surgeon General of baseball."[8] Just when Hyland first suspected and later confirmed Shocker's condition is not known.[9] And neither is when—or how—Shocker accepted the diagnosis and grim prognosis. When enough blood leaked back into the heart's atrium to cause a heart murmur that could be heard through a stethoscope, Hyland would have started to monitor the condition.

Mitral valve failure was not treatable in the 1920s. It has been correctable since around 1960, with surgery that repairs or replaces the defective valve with an artificial one. Gradually Shocker would become increasingly fatigued from physical activity, and eventually his heart would fail. "Fluid retention in the lungs is what leads to the shortness of breath," wrote Dr. Siegel. "Fluid retention in the lungs also predisposes to bacterial lung infection (pneumonia)."[10] Pneumonia is often the secondary cause of death, resulting from that lung congestion.

With his mitral valve not sealing properly, Shocker would have experienced congestion when lying in bed, the result of the congestion in his lungs (orthopnea). As his condition worsened, he would have been unable to sleep in a horizontal position. Instead, he would have slept in a partially reclining position, probably with the help of pillows, so he could breathe more comfortably.

In 1957 sportswriter Bill Corum revealed a story he had been sitting on for almost thirty years. Shocker had told him in the summer of 1928 that he had "a bum heart for some time. . . . I've slept sitting up for three years now."[11]

Eddie Bennett, the little batboy and mascot of the Yankees since 1921, became Shocker's roommate on the road.[12] It was a convenient pairing: the batboy with a back deformity that left him hunched over and the athlete who could not lie in a flat position in bed. They were kindred

34. Upon his return to the Yankees in 1925, Urban Shocker roomed with the club's mascot and batboy, Eddie Bennett. Bennett's deformity and Shocker's secret (that he could not sleep lying down) made for a complementary pairing. Bennett is seen here (*left, in uniform*) about to carry equipment in 1926 spring training. *Private collection of Steve Steinberg.*

spirits, both suffering from debilitating diseases.[13] Shocker did not mind rooming with Bennett, whom he knew would not make an issue of the pitcher's style of sleeping. He would keep it to himself.

There may have been another reason why Shocker chose the club's mascot as his roommate. In the early twentieth century, hunchbacks were believed to bring good luck, and many ballplayers would rub the hump of such a mascot before going up to hit. The most famous was Louis Van Zelst, the mascot of Connie Mack's Athletics from 1910 to 1914.[14] Shocker was extremely superstitious, more so than any other player in the game, according to Yankees pitcher Bob Shawkey. He said Shocker was superstitious about everything. As an example, he said that when Shocker did leave his glove on the field, it had to be palm up, with the fingers pointing to his dugout.[15] Ford Frick devoted an article—some of it tongue-in-cheek—to Shocker's superstitious nature.[16] Is it possible that Shocker believed that rooming with a good-luck "charm" would cure him or at least slow the progression of his heart disease?

Shocker decided to keep his condition a secret from all but his wife and son. Why share it with others? It certainly would not help him keep an edge on opposing batters if they knew he was ailing. Nor would it help his salary negotiations with Yankees management. Most of all, his teammates and the fans would not have understood this illness. Ballplayers just weren't supposed to get very sick.

Shocker could do nothing about his heart, but he could still do plenty on the baseball diamond, and that was what he intended to do. At some point, he would have the challenge of keeping emerging symptoms such as shortness of breath (dyspnea) and fatigue from his teammates.

Will Wedge wrote in the *Sun*, probably humorously, that one person who was not happy with the trade was Babe Ruth, since he enjoyed the challenge of facing Shocker.[17] He had hit seven home runs off Shocker, one of his highest pitcher totals.[18] Both men were probably happy to be teammates, and Ruth soon bestowed the affectionate nickname of "rubber belly" onto him, probably a reference to Shocker's ample waistline. The two soon became part of a regular foursome that played Hearts on train trips, along with trainer Doc Woods and recently acquired catcher Steve O'Neill.[19]

In spring training Shocker faced and beat an old teammate from the Yankees' 1916 spring training, Dazzy Vance, now a star with Brooklyn. Whereas Shocker had been considered old when he won his first game at age twenty-six, Vance did not gain his first victory until he was thirty-one.[20] Vance was depending on a blazing fastball, while Shocker's slow ball was his mainstay.[21] When Shocker beat the Braves on March 12, Ford Frick painted a picture of his change-of-pace pitch for his readers, when he wrote that those pitches "looked as big as trucks and were as elusive as greased fleas."[22]

Miller Huggins was uncharacteristically optimistic about the upcoming 1925 season. A *Sporting News* columnist wrote that he felt this was the best club he ever managed, while the opposition was not as strong as in the previous year. He pinned a lot on the acquisition of Shocker, who "will be living for but one purpose, to redeem himself."[23]

William Hennigan pointed out that Shocker was as daring as ever, still "about the only pitcher in the country" who throws a slow ball with a full count.[24] John Foster wrote that he recently asked the league's top hitters who the best pitcher in the American League was. "Without exception," they replied that Shocker was the man.[25]

A pall was cast on the start of the season when Babe Ruth collapsed on the train to Asheville, North Carolina. He had just hit two long home runs in an exhibition game a day earlier, but was now a very sick man. W. O. McGeehan tagged his condition "the bellyache heard 'round the world," which supposedly resulted from his devouring too many hot dogs and too much soda pop. He was operated on for a stomach abscess on April 17 and would not return to the Yankees until June 1.[26] The whispers were that he was suffering from venereal disease. But the Babe did indeed have an abdominal incision from surgery, which was not the treatment for venereal disease.

Miller Huggins released and traded away many players over the years he managed the Yankees. Urban Shocker was said to be the only man he reacquired. While this is technically not correct, Shocker was the only meaningful player he brought back to the Yankees.[27]

Huggins named Shocker his starting pitcher for Opening Day, a selection that reflected his manager's estimation of him as the ace of the pitching staff. The Yankees hosted the world champion Washington Senators, and Shocker was in total control, a 5–1 win. He even hit a triple and scored, and the Babe's replacement, Ben Paschal, hit his first career home run.

Fred Lieb described Shocker at work. "He pitched an easy, natural delivery yesterday. Urban has reached an age where he knows he must conserve his strength. His slow ball is a work of art and most of the time when he wets the ball, he is merely bluffing a spitter."[28] Joe Vila wrote, "Shocker's control was magnificent. He forced the world champions to hit balls that they didn't like, and in that way he had them completely at his mercy."[29]

Beating the world champions before fifty thousand cheering fans in Yankee Stadium meant a lot to Shocker; Yankee Stadium was now his home. One reporter observed that the trade back to the Yankees "brought balm to his injured spirit."[30]

23

The Season That Wasn't

On May 8, 1925, the struggling Yankees brought their 5-12 record into St. Louis. The big December trade was showcased, as Urban Shocker and Joe Bush faced off in the first game of the Yankees-Browns series. New York prevailed in a rout, 12–0. "Shocker was never better in his life," wrote Martin Haley in a St. Louis paper. "Joe Bush hardly ever was worse."[1] Another St. Louis reporter wrote that Shocker had assumed a haughty demeanor and smiled throughout the game, as he five-hit the Browns.[2] He faced only thirty men, as two of St. Louis's base runners were eliminated in double plays. Bush did not survive the second inning, when the Yankees scored six times.

The game was a rare bright spot for both Shocker and his club. Interspersed with some effective outings were others in which he was hit hard. By the end of May, when Ruth was about to return, Shocker's record was 4-5, and the New York club was much worse, with a 15-25 mark, just ahead of the last-place Red Sox. Joe Vila was moved to write of Shocker, in late May, "It begins to look like he has seen his best days."[3]

Just how Shocker's shoulder operation affected him this season is not known. But in early 1926, he told a reporter that the first couple of months of the previous season were trying. Each time he pitched, he felt his arm would fall off, he said.[4] He received another setback when he dislocated his finger in batting practice in early June and missed ten days.

The team that Huggins expected so much from had seemingly grown old overnight. He admitted he had badly misjudged this club's potential. "Colonel Ruppert and I thought sure last winter that the Yankees would not only last one more season, but that they would be strong enough to win the pennant."[5]

An anti-Huggins clique, which had been the bane of the manager's existence from 1920 to 1922, resurfaced in the clubhouse. Joe Vila was harshly critical of those players: "Several veterans, disgruntled and indifferent, are said to have joined in the abuse of the Yankees' manager, perhaps for the purpose of driving him out of his position."[6]

But Huggins had the full backing of Colonel Ruppert. On June 18, with his club mired in seventh place, 15 games out of first, he told the *Sporting News*, "I'm going to stick, and for a long time.... Several radical changes will be made before next year."[7] Huggins had already begun to make changes, benching older veterans. They included shortstop Everett Scott (age 32), whose consecutive-game mark of 1,307 ended when Huggins sat him, center fielder Whitey Witt (almost 30), catcher Wally Schang (almost 36), and second baseman Aaron Ward (only 28, but dropping off significantly in performance).[8]

On June 1, the day that Ruth returned to the lineup, Lou Gehrig pinch-hit and started what would become his streak of playing 2,130 games in a row. The following day, Gehrig started at first base, replacing Wally Pipp (age 32).[9] The club hit rock bottom on June 17, when the Tigers beat them, 19–1, including a 13-run sixth inning.

Many New York newspapers listed the names of disgruntled players, those who were on the trading block. Some names appeared repeatedly, including Scott, Schang, Witt, and pitcher Sam Jones. Other names surfaced occasionally, including pitcher Waite Hoyt and outfielder Bob Meusel, but not Babe Ruth.[10] Hoyt was immensely talented but headstrong. As historian John Mosedale wrote, "Hoyt's competitiveness was of the hair-trigger kind. It might be measured by incidents that more or less bracketed his playing career."[11]

Meusel was a puzzle to Huggins, at least in their early years together. In 1923 the manager said, "All he has ever lacked is an aggressive spirit. He has been content thus far to drift along, playing brilliant ball one day and lapsing into mediocrity the next, simply for lack of sustained effort."[12]

35. When Urban Shocker returned to the Yankees for the 1925 season, he was nine years the senior of Waite Hoyt. Here the two men discuss pitches and grips in spring training in St. Petersburg. © *Bettmann/CORBIS*.

The reticent Meusel was also an enigma to other observers. Fred Lieb called him "the most undemonstrative player I ever saw."[13]

One name never appeared in reports as a malcontent on that club: Urban Shocker. If ever there was an environment in which this man with a reputation for petulance and sulking would follow that form, it was the 1925 Yankees. Yet no complaints or problems were reported. And this colorful character receded into the background on the Yankees, where he gradually became known as colorless, quiet, and even withdrawn, the polar opposite of what he had been.

How can this change be explained? Why did it occur? The change was real and had a few causes. Shocker was not the first—and would not be the last—athlete to go from a team he dominated with his personality to a club where players were more forceful than he was, including one of the biggest in sports history, Babe Ruth. The Babe attracted the media attention, was a lightning rod for controversy, and thus shielded his teammates from the glare of the spotlight. A man who is a negative force in one clubhouse sometimes gets submerged in another.

But Shocker had not joined a team in the midst of a dynastic run. This was not the Yankees of the late 1920s or late 1930s. The 1925 Yankees were a disaster, and they had to have been an immense disappointment to Shocker. Yet despite the negativity around him, including a strong anti-Huggins group that surely would have welcomed him, Shocker was a model citizen.

The answer may be found in some other factors, too. First, Shocker was very content to come home to the Yankees, back from a seven-year exile. It was a dream come true. He was also getting older, entering the latter stages of his career. He was reportedly going on thirty-three years old in 1925, "getting up" in the years. Yet in reality he was even older; approaching thirty-five, an age when a ballplayer—if he is still active—is nearing the end of his career. Add to that his discovery that he had a fatal illness, and his change in outlook and behavior is more easily understood. Shocker did not know how much time he had left in baseball—and in life—and he was going to savor it.

The most effective pitcher on the 1925 Yankees was left-handed veteran Herb Pennock, with Shocker not far behind him. Pennock was the last talented player the Yankees had acquired from Red Sox owner Harry Frazee in January 1923. At the time the deal was hardly mentioned, even in the New York press, because he had posted a losing record his previous two seasons. But Huggins and Barrow saw Pennock's potential, and he posted a 40-15 record his first two seasons in New York. He also won two games in the 1923 World Series, including the clincher that brought the Yankees their first world championship.

Unlike Shocker, Pennock was slender and appeared fragile, with only 160 pounds on his six-foot frame. But their cerebral approach to pitching was remarkably similar. "I always claimed that every batter has a weakness. . . . Knowledge of the batter's weakness, to prove worthwhile, must go hand-in-hand with the ability to control the ball."[14] Those were Pennock's words; they could have been Shocker's. Like Shocker, he had

36. While Bob Shawkey (*left*) had seen his best days by the time Urban Shocker returned to New York and won only 16 games for the 1925–27 Yankees, Herb Pennock was in his prime and won 58 games during those seasons. Pennock's slim frame belied his durability. Shocker won 49 games in those years, the same total as Waite Hoyt. *Private collection of Steve Steinberg.*

impeccable control. "Pennock could hang a curve upon a corner of the plate as if it were a hat-rack," wrote Heywood Broun.[15] And like Shocker, Pennock believed he would continue to be effective as he aged. "A pitcher's head doesn't grow old, like his arm or legs. On the contrary, it should improve with use."[16]

Pennock suffered nine one-run losses in 1925, including three by the score of 1–0.[17] On July 4 he won a 1–0 game, a 15-inning four-hitter over Philadelphia A's rookie Lefty Grove. Both men went the distance. James Harrison was moved to write in the *Times*, "The svelte and satiny southpaw pitched what was undoubtedly the finest game of a long and honorable career."[18] Pennock considered this game, in the lost season of 1925, his greatest baseball thrill.[19]

Just a few weeks before Pennock's gem, Ford Frick wrote a column on Shocker. "Shocker is a living example of that thing known as 'cunning' in pitching form."[20] Like pitchers Eddie Plank, Grover Alexander, and Pennock, Shocker let his head do some of the work of his arm. Jacob Ruppert had a very good understanding of this aspect of the game; a reporter for the *Sun* later wrote, "Shocker's cool, crafty mechanical delivery was one of Col. Ruppert's delights."[21]

In July Shocker had some superb outings—but only until the late innings. He took two shutouts into the seventh inning and one into the eighth, only to be driven from games.[22] Was his stamina beginning to desert him?

Babe Ruth struggled when he returned to the lineup. His wife, Helen, had a nervous breakdown, and he returned to his hectic nightlife pace as if he had never been sick. Waite Hoyt said, "He was wolfing it [life] down in immense, oversized doses. Although we all recognized his undiminished baseball genius, we knew we were witnessing the gradual disintegration of Ruth, the man."[23] Huggins fined him on June 30, but the next day Ruth hit two home runs, and the fine was reversed. He continued to excel at nighttime carousing, with only occasional flashes of that baseball genius on the diamond.

The Yankees came to St. Louis on August 28 with a record of 49-70. Ruth was hitting only .265 with 15 home runs. The Browns' Joe Giard, one of the young pitchers they had received in the Shocker trade, shut out Waite Hoyt and the Yankees, 1–0. Before the next game, with the season already gone, Huggins suspended the Babe and fined him $5,000, the largest fine in baseball history. The penalties were for an accumulation of transgressions over a series of years, including insubordination, not staying in playing shape, and not complying with curfews.

More importantly, they were a dramatic move to salvage the career of a great player. Ed Wray noted that this was much more than a showdown between Huggins and Ruth. "There is another and much more serious battle pending for the Bambino. The fight is with himself. His ultimate career is the prize of victory."[24] Heywood Broun worried whether Ruth would be able to flourish when shackled: "You can't make a Spartan out of an ancient Goth."[25]

Ruth's initial reaction was to tell reporters that Huggins was incompetent and to declare he would never play for him again. Huggins had finally exercised his authority against the biggest celebrity of sport, and he had the full backing of Ruppert and Barrow. The Babe meekly backtracked and accepted that there were limits to his behavior and that Huggins was the team's leader. He would never challenge his manager again. Damon Runyon pointed out, "In the days when Mr. Ruth was busting those home runs all over the landscape, he rarely, if ever, had to apologize to anybody."[26]

Shocker played a couple of roles on the edges of that famous showdown. He introduced a young St. Louis reporter he knew, Ray Gillespie, to Huggins as a "good guy." Gillespie got the scoop on the story, but not before his editor on the telephone challenged him. "If this story is incorrect, you're fired," he told Gillespie.[27] The story ran, and the *St. Louis Star*, not a dominant paper in that market, had the breaking story.

Shocker took to the mound that day, and despite the controversy that was swirling, he went the distance and beat the Browns and Milt Gaston, 4–1. "Shocker pitched a typical Shocker game," wrote another St. Louis reporter. "He was hit frequently, except when there were men on base."[28] He scored the go-ahead run, after walking in the eighth inning. He also made a sparkling fielding play when he dove toward the plate to catch a bunt and then doubled a runner off first base. Nineteen twenty-five was the second year in a row in which he was perfect in the field.

Shocker was the only Yankees starter who did not have a losing record in 1925, with a 12-12 mark.[29] He must have been terribly disappointed; he was further away from the World Series than ever. Even his old team, the Browns, had a better record than the Yankees. They finished the season in third place, 13½ games ahead of the seventh-place New York.

He was part of an emerging nucleus of Yankees who quietly went about their business on the field and did not get involved with clubhouse politics. First baseman Lou Gehrig and outfielder Earle Combs were rare New York bright spots on the diamond that year. Gehrig hit .295 with 20 home runs in his first full season, and Combs hit .342 with 203 hits in his first. When Combs was inducted into the Baseball Hall of Fame forty-five years later, he said, "I thought the Hall of Fame was for superstars, not just average players like me."[30] The modesty was genuine and not the least bit forced. He and Gehrig typified the consummate professionals around whom Huggins was rebuilding his team.

After the season, Huggins let it be known that only two pitchers were sure to return to the club in 1926, Shocker and Pennock.[31]

24

Hope Springs Eternal

Most observers did not expect the Yankees to compete for the pennant in 1926. Their middle infielders, second baseman Tony Lazzeri and shortstop Mark Koenig, seemed too young to excel in their first full season. Many pundits and fans felt the aging Babe Ruth, on the other hand, would not come back. Four of their five starting pitchers were over the age of thirty.[1] Chicago sportswriter Warren Brown wrote that the club's "ancient and honorable corps of flingers are creaking their aged limbs into shape."[2] When the club was swept in its first three preseason games by a mediocre Boston Braves team, Brown resorted to sarcasm when he filed his final report on the Yankees a few days later. "I was afraid if I stayed any longer, I would make the team."[3] Syndicated columnist Westbrook Pegler leveled withering attacks on the club's manager, whom he dismissed as irrelevant because his players considered Huggins a "sap."[4]

Their former hitting star, Babe Ruth, was an "old" thirty-one. He was a veteran of more than eleven seasons and a lifetime of nighttime carousing. Few expected him to post numbers close to those he had generated in the early 1920s. Many fans were rooting for him, a fallen hero who was also a lovable guy. As one of his contemporaries, Jimmy Austin, told Larry Ritter almost forty years later, "The big fellow wasn't perfect. Everybody knows that. But that guy had a heart. He really did. A heart as big as a watermelon and made out of pure gold."[5]

When the Babe showed up for spring training, he looked incredibly fit. In an open letter to the *New York World*, he declared he was in the best shape ever, after working all winter in Artie McGovern's gym. "I left 36 pounds in his gym. My stomach is where it belongs."[6]

Ruth also had a new relationship with his manager. It showed up in a revealing minor occurrence at a spring training game, one that was mentioned in only one paper. On a chilly afternoon in Birmingham, where the Yankees played the Brooklyn team, Ruth got his overcoat and wrapped it around Huggins, with the words, "You'll feel better with that on."[7] Ruth never again challenged him and actually developed a genuine affection for his little manager.

Fred Lieb felt that "the turning point in the fortunes of the Yanks" that spring was when Shocker and two other New York pitchers one-hit the Braves on March 17.[8] The umpire behind the plate that day was former Chicago White Sox manager Pants Rowland. "I always enjoy umpiring behind the plate when Shocker pitches," he said. "It is a treat to watch a cunning pitcher and note the many deliveries he calls into use."[9]

Many of Shocker's deliveries that day were once again variations on his signature pitch. "Using little more than a slow ball, Urban made the Braves look like monkeys," James Harrison wrote in the *New York Times*.[10] "He pitches more with his head than his arm, half the time lobbing the ball up to the plate much slower than the catcher returns it to him," Will Wedge reported a couple months later: "Care and caution and craftsmanship are Shocker's mottos."[11]

Once again, we are left to wonder just how dawdling Shocker's slow ball was.[12] Roger Peckinpaugh, his Yankees teammate in 1916–17 and one who faced him for many years thereafter, recalled Shocker's special pitch in 1938, perhaps with a bit of embellishment.

> Well, there never was a pitcher who could throw a slow one like Shocker. His slow ball never did look like it was going to get to the plate. He'd throw it 20 feet into the air sometimes. And he'd make an awful sucker out of a hitter, especially when he had two strikes on him and two were out. Shocker'd throw his slow one in that high arc and then start walking for the dugout, perfectly confident that the side was retired.

37. Despite having won 94 games through the 1924 season, Waite Hoyt was still a relatively young player at twenty-six. Here he and Urban Shocker are in a serious discussion early in the 1926 spring training before the Yankees started their long winning streak, one they replicated early in the regular season. © *Bettmann/CORBIS*.

> By the time the ball came across the plate, Shocker would be across the foul line and headed for a drink of water.[13]

Shocker was very superstitious, and Huggins was a worrier. How they reacted to a near-tragedy during spring training is not known. Shocker, Lou Gehrig, Yankees scout Paul Krichell, and two other club members were on a fishing boat in the Gulf of Mexico, twenty-three miles from St. Petersburg, where the Yankees were training, when the vessel sprung a leak. Eight inches of water swamped the boat before their distress signal was heard by another ship that rescued them.[14]

Huggins was confident Shocker would have a much better season than he had in 1925, and he was equally bullish on his club as a whole. He already had released or traded away veterans Steve O'Neill, Wally Pipp, Wally Schang, Everett Scott, and Whitey Witt. His two key additions, both from the San Francisco area, had never played a game in the Major Leagues before they came to the Yankees: infielders Tony Lazzeri and Mark Koenig. Huggins decided to entrust his middle infield with these youngsters, ages twenty-two and twenty-one, respectively. Each man was acquired for $50,000, Lazzeri from the Salt Lake City Bees of the Pacific Coast League and Koenig from the St. Paul Saints of the American Association.[15]

Major League teams had shied away from Lazzeri because he had epilepsy. Former Yankees scout Bob Connery, who now owned the Saints club from which Koenig came, had observed Lazzeri in Salt Lake City. His report to Ed Barrow: "I don't care what he's got. Buy him. He's the greatest thing I've ever seen."[16]

Koenig was often his roommate on the road, and late in his life he told Dave Newhouse, "Lazzeri was combing his hair and—zoom—the brush flew out of his hand and hit the wall. He was having an epileptic fit. Then he flopped on the ground and started convulsing. I was stark naked, but I ran out in the hall and banged on Waite Hoyt's door. I knew he was a coroner's helper. He got Lazzeri's head up and his tongue out."[17]

Lazzeri never had a seizure during a game. Like Shocker with his heart condition, Lazzeri's illness remained a secret from fans. Unlike Shocker, Lazzeri's condition was known by his teammates.

38. Tony Lazzeri was the key addition to the 1926 Yankees and played second base (his regular position had been shortstop in the Minors) with the aplomb of a veteran. He also helped settle down the club's other young infielders, Lou Gehrig and Mark Koenig. His on-field performance (117 RBI, 14 triples, and 18 home runs) later earned him the 1926 Retroactive Rookie of the Year Award. *Cleveland Public Library Photograph Collection.*

Colonel Ruppert believed in his manager and his players. After those early spring training losses to the Braves, he told a *New York American* reporter, "The worst trick you can play on anybody is to bury him before he is dead. When you are talking about the Yankees, don't say it with flowers yet."[18]

Huggins used the newspaper attacks on him and his team as a rallying cry. The Yankees started winning and kept winning—their final 16 exhibition games. They beat Wilbert Robinson's Brooklyn Robins 12 games in a row during that stretch, as the teams moved north together. Uncle Robbie, as he was affectionately known, was a member of the powerful Baltimore Orioles of the 1890s. "It's a long time since I saw such a bunch of sluggers," he told reporters. "It's a lineup which doesn't give a pitcher any breathing room. Mark my word, that club will win a lot of games in any league."[19] Fred Lieb, after following the Yankees during spring training, agreed and was a rare sportswriter who picked them to win the 1926 pennant.[20]

Huggins felt good about his club's hitting. If the veteran pitchers came through, he believed his Yankees would contend for the pennant. Shocker planned on improving in 1926; he had worked out strenuously all winter. When he arrived in St. Petersburg, Ford Frick commented, "His expansive waistline is positively sylphlike."[21] On April 1 Shocker told Fred Lieb, "I am going to be mighty tough out there this year."[22] That very day, Ruppert was quoted in the *Sporting News*: "Shocker, at his best, is an inspiration for the other Yankee pitchers."[23]

25

The Comeback

The sweetest songs come after saddest sighs;
The clearest light shines from the darkest room,
The brightest gleams come from the blackest skies,
When once the rift has opened in the gloom.
The greatest rest will follow hardest toil;
The best content comes after fiercest strife,
The deepest peace aye follows wild turmoil
That wrecks the soul upon the Sea of Life.
—from "Compensation" by Grantland Rice

Most people who think of the Yankees of the 1920s think of their decade of dominance. They overlook the disastrous interlude of 1925 and how few people gave New York a chance to come back from that debacle of a season. They also may not realize how different the championship teams of the early 1920s were from those of the late '20s. The distinction is that the latter were the direct result of Huggins's fining and suspending Babe Ruth in 1925. Ed Barrow later put that chastening of Ruth in perspective. "You can call it the turning point in the history of the New York Yankees. Thereafter the so-called bad boys realized that we meant business."[1]

The pennant winners of the early 1920s included Carl Mays and Joe Bush, stars before they came to the Yankees and men from whom Huggins could not command respect. The pennant winners of the late 1920s included Earle Combs, Lou Gehrig, and Tony Lazzeri, who did not see their role as judging their manager. They did their "talking" with their bats and gloves.

It is true that three of those "bad boys" remained on the team: Ruth, Hoyt, and Meusel. But now they understood that there were repercussions for bad behavior. Westbrook Pegler, formerly a harsh critic of Huggins, explained with wry humor how Huggins was handling his troublemakers. "One by one he eased them out of his force, until finally the greatest cut-up of them all [Babe Ruth] found himself considerably outnumbered by nice young men with respect for authority and an understandable desire to stay up where the wages were good."[2]

The 1926 Yankees carried their spring training winning ways into the regular season. When Shocker won his third April game, a 7–2 decision over the Washington Senators, he pushed New York's record to 12-3. James Harrison waxed on about the winner's change of pace. "Shocker can throw fifty-seven varieties of slow ball, and he threw all fifty-seven yesterday. Urban mixed fast with slow until the [1925 American League] champions were dizzy."[3]

The Yankees set the baseball world on its ear when they put together a 16-game winning streak in May, as they pushed their record to 30-9 on May 26. Six of the wins came by only one run. They were winning big, and they were winning close.

Three of those wins were by Shocker. When he beat the White Sox on May 17, he gave up 10 hits but won comfortably, 5–3. Fred Lieb described what he called a typical Shocker game now that he was getting older. "He doesn't bear down until it really is necessary. When things are breaking his way, he is inclined to float along with the tide and play with his opponents. . . . Matty [Christy Mathewson] used to pitch the same way late in his career."[4] As for "playing with" the hitters, umpire and columnist George Moriarty compared Shocker to the spider dealing with the helpless fly caught in its web.[5]

Shocker had two sacrifice hits in the game, 2 of the 20 he would execute this season and again in 1927.[6] That is a very large number of sacrifices for a pitcher, who has a limited number of plate appearances.[7] As with his high walk rate and on-base percentage, Shocker was as meticulous at the plate as he was on the mound. Will Wedge pointed out after the Chicago game, "He learned the value of slow and precise work when he was a toolmaker in a twist drill factory in Cleveland during his days as a sandlotter."[8]

Bob Meusel provided the margin of victory in the game with his fifth home run of the season. He pushed his batting average up to .389. That month Miller Huggins told reporters he would not trade Meusel for any other American League outfielder.[9] Huggins finally was beginning to fully appreciate Meusel, whom Will Wedge once described as "an odd mixture of placidity and fire."[10]

Huggins told reporters that they did not understand Meusel, and perhaps he did not either in their first years together. Meusel was not lazy, he said. "You'll never see him give the old college try in a play he figures is hopeless. But when it counts most—when there is a catch to be made, a hit beaten out, or an extra base to be got in a pinch—there are few ball players I've ever seen whom I'd bank on so heavily."[11] Meusel told *Baseball Magazine* during the 1926 season, "Hustling is overrated in baseball. . . . It's a showy quality about looks and counts for little."[12]

What Lieb and Evans saw as smart pitching, George Daley saw as a weakness. When Shocker beat the Senators, 9–5, on June 2, he had let up with a 9–2 lead. "Urban doesn't thrive on prosperity," Daley wrote under his pseudonym of Monitor. "When his team is ahead, he takes things too easy."[13] The losing pitcher in that game was Joe Bush, whose career was on a steep decline. The Browns had dealt him to Washington earlier in the year. The loss dropped him to 1-6 for the season, and on July 1 the Senators sold him to Pittsburgh.[14]

A big factor in the Yankees' 1926 success was the return of the game's biggest star, Babe Ruth. His off-season training regimen had paid off, as had his determination to return to form. After the first week of the season, his batting average never dipped below .363, and he finished at .372, with 47 home runs and 153 runs batted in.[15] Arthur Robinson wrote of the Babe in the *New Yorker*, a year-old weekly, "He no longer has a genius for getting into trouble, and, repentant and determined, he is currently smacking that ol' apple, or onion, as well as he did in 1921, his greatest year."[16] Ruth's biographer, Robert Creamer, put it more succinctly. "From the ashes of 1925, Babe Ruth rose like a rocket."[17]

39. Urban Shocker fathered no children with either of his two wives, but he adopted his second wife's son, Cletus, late in 1924. In 1926, sixteen-year-old Cletus helped Eddie Bennett with some of the batboy responsibilities. *Private collection of Bill Loughman.*

On June 4, Shocker's son, Cletus, turned sixteen. He joined the Yankees that spring as an assistant to batboy Eddie Bennett. Bennett was then given some responsibilities in the club's business office.[18]

Less than two weeks later, the Yankees went into St. Louis, and Shocker easily beat another pitcher for whom he had been traded, Milt Gaston.[19] Browns fans booed Shocker throughout the contest. Tony Lazzeri's home run gave the Yankees the lead in that game and pushed his RBI total to 52, second best in the league, behind Ruth (who already had 72). They would finish one-two at season's end. Lazzeri played in every game of his rookie season, most of them at second base, even though he had played primarily shortstop in the Minors.[20]

In his Sports of the Times column, Arthur Daley wrote that Lazzeri was "quietly efficient . . . he steadied the jittery Koenig on one side and settled down the yet uncertain Gehrig on the other. Lazzeri was truly the pivot on which the Yankee pennant hopes spun."[21]

Koenig needed steadying. He was a sensitive and brooding young man. He led the league with 52 errors in 1926, and many of them cost the Yankees games. Just five days after that St. Louis win, in which Koenig made two errors, his error and a misplay cost Shocker a game in Chicago.[22]

Koenig's fretting over his fielding only made him more nervous. "It got so bad," he admitted, "every time a ball was hit down to me, it became a mental hazard I had to handle."[23] He never forgot the support he got from Huggins. More than a half century later, Koenig told Dave Newhouse that Huggins understood human nature. "When the New York sportin' writers were saying, 'Koenig's got to go,' he called me in and said, 'Listen, as long as I want you to play, you're going to play.'"[24]

By mid-June New York led the American League by 10 games.[25] The Yankees were back. No one was more instrumental in the team's fast start than Shocker. In the first half of the season, he made six starts against the defending American League champion Senators and won four of them, against a solitary loss. By the time he beat Walter Johnson for the second time for his 11th win on July 1, the Yankees had a 49-23 record and maintained a 10-game lead.

Now that he was in New York, Shocker was often quoted about his pitching philosophy. Billy Evans said that the pitcher's favorite advice was,

"Pitch to the small end of the bat."[26] Another columnist had Shocker's version of Willie Keeler's classic saying. "Make 'em hit it where you want 'em to hit it," he said.[27]

Shocker was also a voracious reader of newspapers for the information the box scores and game accounts revealed. He explained to William Hanna what they told him.

> There are lessons and tips in there if the pitcher can read them. What do they tell you? They tell you at particular times just who is hitting and who isn't; also, what the good hitters, the ones in whom you are most interested, are doing. . . . If a good hitter is having an off spell, you'll pitch to him accordingly. It's useful to know . . . just how far you can take chances with him. The scores also will tell you what style of game the other team is playing, the sacrifices or the hit and runs. . . . The box scores ought to be an open book to a pitcher.[28]

Chief Bender, the pitching great of the Philadelphia Athletics from 1903 to 1914, told reporters that he found the story of Shocker studying box scores quite interesting.[29] He explained that A's pitchers used to study box scores for hours every morning. "They knew what batters were hitting and what batters were in a slump. They didn't have to look over to the bench for instructions. . . . They had all of this stuff memorized."[30]

Shocker's pitching style must have been maddening to opposing hitters. Ford Frick called it "tantalizing" and explained, "At times, he appears to be 'loafing' on the job, kidding and clowning in an absurd manner. He scores few strikeouts, and base hits resound with increasing frequency. But he keeps the runs down. And does it with cunning rather than force, with good judgment rather than blinding curves. Shocker's last six starts have been jewels."[31]

On July 19 Shocker completed a trade trifecta of sorts when he beat the third pitcher for whom he was traded, Joe Giard. It was an 11–2 massacre, and Giard did not survive the first inning, as his record for the season fell to 1-7. Fred Lieb was again enamored with Shocker's slow ball, the likes of which had not been seen, he said, since Brooklyn's Nap Rucker.[32] "It frequently is amusing to watch famous sluggers almost tear themselves apart trying to connect with this [Shocker's] slow ball."[33]

When Shocker led the American League in strikeouts in 1922, he was fanning almost four men per nine innings. In 1926 he struck out just over two men per nine innings. He completed just over 56 percent of his starts in 1926, lower than the almost 66 percent he had finished in his career up until then.

To what extent Shocker's style and performance were influenced by his illness and not simply from getting older is not known, but it must have had an impact. He certainly did not discuss the loss of stamina he was experiencing because of his heart disease, and there were virtually no clues in the press. A rare one was Lieb's mentioning that Shocker had "a dizzy spell" during his June 2 start.[34]

Shocker beat the Browns on July 28, 3–2, and ended the game with what Ford Frick called his "caginess," when the pitcher picked pinch-hitter Herschel Bennett off second base to end the game. Two days later Shocker topped St. Louis for the fourth time—as a reliever in this game—to push his record to 15-5.

That week's *Sporting News* carried Joe Vila's column, in which he wrote about the spitballer's season. "Shocker is worth his weight in diamonds. He is the Yankees' 'mainstay,' and his winning delivery has had more to do with keeping the Hugmen on top than any other factor."[35]

On September 7 Shocker won his 19th game of the season when he beat the Red Sox, 4–2. Frick again commented on his seeming to be "loafing," yet the many hits he allowed (11) came when they meant nothing, and the result again was that he allowed few runs.[36]

A week later the Yankees arrived in Cleveland for a six-game series against the second-place Indians. Shocker started and lost the fifth game of the series, 3–1, to his friend George Uhle. Three New York errors, including Koenig's 50th of the season, cost New York dearly. Cleveland's player-manager, Tris Speaker, taunted Shocker when he intentionally walked him, and Miller Huggins was so upset that he had to be restrained from going after Speaker. It was the Indians' fourth win in a row and shaved New York's lead to only 2½ games. The Yankees were "out in the open country, fleeing madly, a disorganized mob staging a disorderly retreat," in the words of James Harrison. They were "nervous, apprehensive, over-eager and tightened up into a knot," which had undermined Shocker's "excellent pitching."[37]

Barrow and Huggins had strengthened the Yankees' roster that summer. First they added veteran catcher Hank Severeid, who had been Shocker's regular catcher in St. Louis.[38] They also picked up veteran pitcher Dutch Ruether, who had a reputation as a "money pitcher," one who was not bothered by pressure and did well in big games.[39] Ruether also had a reputation as an unruly man who liked to drink, which made his acquisition a carefully calculated risk.[40]

Ruether had pitched well earlier in the Cleveland series, when he lost, 2–1. Now, on September 19, with the Yankees reeling, Huggins started him in the final game of the series. The veteran responded, James Harrison wrote, in his "characteristically cool and unperturbed style" with an 8–3 win, and the onrushing Indians had been stopped.[41] As Frank Graham later wrote, the Yankees clinched the pennant a few days later, but "anybody who was there will tell you they clinched it when Dutch foiled the Indians" with his "magnificent" performance.[42]

Lou Gehrig had three doubles and a home run in the game; he knocked in four runs. The series drew large crowds, and 8,000 fans were allowed on the outfield grass for this game. Harrison criticized Cleveland's management for their greed in going after "the golden shekels," which resulted in "an absurd condition of play." Gehrig took advantage of the shrunken field and stroked three ground-rule doubles down the right-field line into the crowd.[43] Each knocked in a run, and his home run his fourth time up was the exclamation point.

This was the season in which he began to solidify his emergence as a star, with a .313 batting average, 20 home runs, and 47 doubles. Arthur Mann wrote at the start of the 1927 season, "Gehrig is almost a finished player. He is a tower of strength with no apparent weakness. It looks as though the Yankees' first base troubles have been settled for at least ten years. In that time there is no telling what unscaled heights Gehrig may attain."[44]

Shocker dropped his last three decisions of the season, including that loss to the Indians.[45] On September 22 he thought he had his 20th victory, a 1–0 gem against the White Sox. But a ninth-inning, two-out, full-count pitch was called "ball four" by George Moriarty, the umpire-columnist. The White Sox then struck for two runs, and the Indians drew to within two games of first place.

40. Team shots are usually uninteresting, with players appearing wooden and solemn. This image is a rare exception and has an air of informality. Lou Gehrig is smiling (*back row, fourth from right*) and manager Miller Huggins seems unusually relaxed (*middle row, middle*), as does the usually high-strung Mark Koenig (*second from left, middle row*). Urban Shocker strikes a serious pose (*second from left, bottom row*). © *Bettmann/CORBIS*.

The Yankees held on to win the pennant by three games, and reporters wrote of their hanging on and staggering in. After streaking out to a 40–15 record on June 13, they won only 51 of their last 99 games. Still they had accomplished something that had not been done since 1901: rise from seventh place to first in just one season. This was a club Huggins had shaped himself, with four of his eight starting position players coming directly from the Minor Leagues to the Yankees.

While Shocker was a veteran and a star when the Yankees got him back, his 19 wins confirmed the wisdom of that trade. Fred Lieb noted on the eve of the World Series, "The burly Shocker is going into this series with the enthusiasm of a boy. The thrill of a world's series has been denied him for many years."[46]

26

Moment in the Sun

The Yankees prepared to meet the St. Louis Cardinals in the World Series. The Cardinals had edged the Cincinnati Reds for the National League pennant by only two games. Former Yankees Wally Pipp and Carl Mays were key members of the Reds, and had Mays not had arm trouble late in the season, the Yankees might have faced them.[1] Instead, Shocker would face a team from the city he still called home, where he had pitched for seven seasons. He had many friends in St. Louis and was not bothered by the fact that his popularity had plummeted among fans there since the Browns traded him away. Just a few months earlier, a New York reporter wrote, "Shocker is about as popular in St. Louis as a colored person at a Ku Klux Klan wedding."[2]

St. Louis was the only Major League city yet to win a pennant since the turn of the twentieth century. How ironic that Phil Ball, the irascible owner of the Browns, had just remodeled and expanded Sportsman's Park. There was a tradition that after a city builds a new park or improves an old one, a pennant follows.[3] Indeed it did—not for Ball's team, the Browns, but rather for the team he leased the park to, the Cardinals. In George Sisler's third season as manager, the Browns finished in seventh place, with their worst winning percentage in a decade.

As the Yankees had done, the Cardinals picked up veterans for the stretch run. Like Dutch Ruether, Grover Cleveland Alexander found "training rules" too confining. He made no secret of his drinking; he told *Baseball Magazine*, "I have never professed to being an angel, but I do claim I know how to pitch."[4] Unlike Ruether, Alexander had been one of the greatest pitchers in baseball history. Between 1911 and 1920, he led the National League in wins and strikeouts six times and earned run average four times.[5] He had already won 327 games in his storied career.

Now at the age of thirty-nine, on June 22 he was picked up off waivers by the Cardinals from the Chicago Cubs. The Cards' player-manager, Rogers Hornsby, was blunt with reporters when he said of his acquisition, "I don't care what his habits are if he can win ball games."[6] Alexander responded with nine wins for St. Louis. Damon Runyon probably spoke for many observers when he wrote, "Like Pennock, old Alex needs much rest. He is getting along in baseball years."[7] The Yankees did not expect to see him more than once, or possibly twice, in the Series.

Unlike Shocker, Alexander had participated in a World Series, back in 1915 with the Philadelphia Phillies. He won the opening game, but then Boston won the next four. Like Shocker, Alexander understood what an older pitcher had to do to win. "A real pitcher, to my way of thinking, is a fellow who has speed and curves and control and knowledge of the batter, and guts," he told *Baseball Magazine*. "Sooner or later stuff will leave a man. . . . I had stuff once myself, and I know."[8]

The week before they picked up Alexander, the Cardinals had acquired veteran outfielder Billy Southworth in a trade with the New York Giants. After he helped beat his old team in August, Fred Lieb wrote, "Billy Southworth has been a veritable terror in his new St. Louis toggery."[9] Countless columns were written on the upcoming postseason championship. Runyon, a New Yorker, admitted to treasonous thoughts: he was attracted to the St. Louis club. "Rogers Hornsby's team appeals to me, personally, as one of the most dashing crews I have ever slapped eyes on. It has youth, and what goes with youth, which is zip and zest and zing, and all that sort of thing."[10]

Dan Daniel wrote that Shocker would give the Cardinals trouble because of his assortment of pitches and added, "He is especially formidable if you are facing him for the first time."[11] George Moriarty wrote that Shocker was a blend of star and artist. "No other pitcher has ever been more adroit in foretelling the intention of the batsman," he wrote. He added

41. Late in the 1926 season, Miller Huggins checks out the right arm of Urban Shocker. While he did not win a game after September 7, Shocker was both thrilled and confident to finally appear in a World Series. © *Bettmann/CORBIS*.

that if Shocker thinks the batter will not swing at a pitch, "he has a habit of tossing up a strike that could be hit by a school boy."[12]

Shocker himself exuded confidence. He reminded reporters that, as a member of the Browns, he had beaten the Cardinals with regularity in the annual St. Louis city series.[13] Bozeman Bulger of the *New York Evening World* wrote that Shocker was the Yankees pitcher the Cards feared the most. He had beaten them "more consistently than any man in America."[14] But Sid Keener looked over the layout of Yankee Stadium with its short right-field porch and saw a real opportunity for the Cards. "I will be bitterly disappointed if [Cardinals Jim] Bottomley or [Billy] Southworth or both do not shove drives into the seats during the games here. . . . If the Cardinals, with their right-field offensive punch, do not batter the Yankees here, they will have no one to blame but themselves."[15]

The first two games of the World Series, along with the last two, if needed, were scheduled for Yankee Stadium. The Yankees won the first game, 2–1, behind the masterful three-hit pitching of Herb Pennock. They now had the advantage, with Shocker slated to start Game Two. After the possibility of rain had loomed over Game One on Saturday, Sunday's forecast called for clear skies, with temperatures in the upper 70s. The old World Series attendance record of 62,817, set in Game Five of the 1923 Series, would be threatened.

On Sunday morning, from afar, Yankee Stadium seemed like the crater of an enormous volcano, with the rising smoke of thousands of cigars and cigarettes. The crowd was orderly, but many women tried to plead and even weep their way in. One gatekeeper said he could have made a year's salary by admitting "crashers," and perhaps other gatekeepers did so.[16] Almost 64,000 fans managed to get inside.

Shocker drew Grover Cleveland Alexander as the Cardinals' starter. He felt a little odd; the Yankee veteran whose time had finally come was facing an even more veteran pitcher. He knew he could best this man from the past, though this opponent had a great past indeed.

At 2:00 p.m. Graham McNamee began his radio broadcast: "What a corking day it is, the sky is blue, just a few fleecy clouds. You can see all the apartments a couple of blocks from here are crowded with thousands of people who could not get into the stands."[17]

42. Before taking the mound for Game Two of the 1926 World Series, Urban Shocker poses with his wife, Rene, at Yankee Stadium. *Private collection of the family of Roger Shockcor.*

Alexander struggled early. With one run in, two Yankees on base, and only one man out in the second inning, he seemed rattled. He gave up another run because of his own error and seemed to be a hit away from being pulled from the game. But he got out of the jam when he struck out Shocker to retire the side. The Cardinals got him even with two runs in the third inning. Then the two pitchers took over. Shocker was perfect in the middle three innings. Alexander matched him and then continued with his mastery. After he gave up a lead-off single in the third, he retired the final twenty-one men he faced.

In the seventh, the first two St. Louis batters got on base, but as he had done so many times in the past, Shocker reached back and retired the next two men. He was back in control and expected he would soon be out of the inning unscathed, with little Billy Southworth, who hit lefty (he threw with his right arm) coming up to bat. McNamee described the action to his radio listeners: "If he pitches himself out of this hole, this man Shocker, he is just as smart as they say he is."[18]

Then came the pitch and one of those baseball moments suspended in time, as Southworth hit a fly ball to right field. It seemed to take forever to come down, and the drama centered on Babe Ruth, racing after it. Grantland Rice captured the scene. "He took both a single and a double grab of the wire mesh and must have lifted his huge form two or three feet above ground when the ball sailed over his head into the crowd. For a moment, he looked like a scaling party from the First Punic War attempting to surmount the barricades of Carthage."[19] Yankee Stadium's famous short porch in right field had claimed another ball, another game, and another pitcher.

Shocker was crestfallen. As he headed back to the dugout at the end of the inning, he walked slowly and never looked up. Alexander now had a 5–2 lead.[20] He got stronger as the game went on and did not allow another Yankees baserunner. The Cardinals added another run in the ninth, for a final score of 6–2.

Alexander's performance, and not Shocker's, was the subject of the newspaper columns written after the game. Rice described it as "One of the pitching masterpieces of all time. It was sheer art raised to the zenith, for it came from an arm grown old in many wars. . . . He turned back the hands of the clock from middle age to morning, from the dusk of twilight to the dew of a long ago dawn."[21]

The Yankees' clubhouse was subdued after the game. Shocker's head was bowed in his hands, "his huge frame quivering with the sudden disappointment of a dream gone awry," in the words of Ford Frick.[22] "Eleven years he waited, and yesterday opportunity finally came. But it was too late," Frick continued. Miller Huggins was talking to reporters about the key play, Southworth's home run: "That one was safe by mere inches. A foot shorter, and it would have been a putout. . . . Nothing but a high fly that drifted with the wind."[23]

Not far away, the Babe was grousing to some writers. "That ball of Southworth's, hell, I was all set for it when the wind lifted it over the screen. It was only about a foot out of my way."[24] Frick praised Ruth's efforts for tearing across the outfield after the ball and leaping "like some giant behemoth suddenly turned hawk or buzzard."[25] Frick felt that the ball had eluded him by only two inches.

Just a few days earlier, Southworth's home run had helped beat his former team, the New York Giants, and clinch the National League pennant for St. Louis. He hit it into the right-field stands of the Polo Grounds, just across the Harlem River from Yankee Stadium. Shocker may have beaten the Cardinals with regularity when he was with the Browns. But he had not faced Billy Southworth before.

Surely the pitcher's meticulous preparation included a review of the tendencies and weaknesses of the St. Louis outfielder. Before the Series, Bozeman Bulger had written, "Personally, I think Shocker will prove one of the most effective pitchers in the series. . . . Shocker is one of those cool, deliberate fellows, who studies his batters as a cat would a mouse."[26]

What then went wrong? First of all, it was a short fly ball. Shocker knew the short distance down the right-field line of Yankee Stadium as well as anyone.[27] But he had been vulnerable, even though it had not been mentioned in the press. In 1925 and 1926, he gave up a total of 33 home runs, and 28 of them were hit in the stadium. Of those, 24 were hit by lefties, whose natural swings sent the ball to the right side.

There was a lot of commentary on the pitch Southworth drove out of the park. New York sportswriters had covered him during his more than two seasons with the Giants and knew he had trouble hitting a low ball, around the knees. They also knew Southworth was "poison" on high inside balls. Observers agreed the pitch in question was high. Some thought it was a slow ball; others felt it was a spitter that did not break downward, as was intended.

Brooklyn manager Wilbert Robinson could not believe that Southworth got such a ball, which "the whole National League knows" he clobbers.[28] Southworth said he was expecting a spitball, with which Shocker had fooled him earlier in the game, and Shocker confirmed that was indeed the pitch.[29] James Harrison noted that while Shocker's slow ball and curve were working well in the game, his spitter was not breaking for him.[30] But what if the ball was not intended to break down from Southworth's "sweet spot"? What if Shocker's hubris had caused his downfall? John McGraw wrote that Shocker was always a daring pitcher and may have decided to surprise his opponent by pitching to his strength.[31]

Roy Stockton, who knew Shocker as well as anyone in Yankee Stadium that day, agreed. "Shocker was not worried. Shocker never is worried. He is a great pitcher, a shrewd craftsman. He was turning back the Cards so regularly that the old Shocker smile was beginning to show itself. . . . Shocker is like Bill Tilden that way. He enjoys pitching more when the enemy thinks he has a chance. Shocker likes to pitch to a batter's strength and make it his weakness. . . . Not a fastball inside but a half-speed pitch inside."[32]

Nowadays sports fans can view a key play over and over again. With the aid of instant replay, observers can usually determine what had occurred. Of course, even nowadays, the intent of a player—what he was thinking—remains a mystery if he chooses not to elaborate. And Shocker never did, at least not publicly. Roy Stockton had covered Shocker for years in St. Louis and knew him well as both a pitcher and a person. In the absence of conclusive data, his assessment (similar to the opinions of George Moriarty and John McGraw) is the most plausible. Shocker may have mellowed with his return to the Yankees. But at heart his audacity remained.

However short the drive off the bat and however close it came to being caught, the result was undeniable. As George Daley wrote in the *World*, it was the "life hope of a good pitcher shot to smithereens in a single fleeting second."[33]

Damon Runyon noted that, once again, a relative unknown had risen to postseason stardom. "Billy Southworth is one of those peripatetics of the big leagues who come bobbing up occasionally in a world series."[34]

The Series moved to St. Louis for the next three games. Jesse Haines shut out the Yankees in Game Three, 4–0. Dutch Ruether did not pitch well enough to win. For the second time in the Series, Bob Shawkey was perfect in relief.

The Yankees evened the Series the next day, when Babe Ruth hit a postseason record three home runs in a 10–5 victory. He had hit two home runs in a World Series game before, as had three other players.[35] But three such blows made for a stunning performance that left reporters grasping for superlatives. "It was a superhuman Babe Ruth. . . . Ruth seemed to go berserk," wrote veteran sportswriter Henry Edwards with a representative comment.[36]

Waite Hoyt pitched a complete game for New York, though he gave up 14 hits and was shaky early in the game. The first three Cardinals he faced singled, and Miller Huggins had Shocker warm up in the bullpen.[37] But Hoyt got out of the jam, though he gave up three runs in the fourth inning. With the way Ruth and the rest of the Yankees were hitting (all the starters except Hoyt had at least one hit), just about any New York pitcher would have won on this day.

Herb Pennock started Game Five, and once again he was brilliant, as he went the distance in a 10-inning 3–2 New York win. His seemingly delicate physique continued to hold up, in part because of his fluid and graceful delivery and in part because of his focus on control. "If you do not pitch bad balls, you do not have to pitch so much," he once said.[38] This was the eighth straight year he had tossed 200 or more innings, and his 23 wins in 1926 were a career high. He now had a 4-0 World Series record. Huggins called him the greatest left-hander of all time because he was "so coordinated in thought and action."[39]

The Series moved back to New York, with the Yankees needing just one more win. Shocker looked forward to facing the Cardinals again; after his Game Two loss, he said, "I'll have another crack at them, maybe, and I'll get them."[40] He was surely disappointed when Huggins gave the nod to Shawkey to start Game Six, but few could find fault with the choice. Shawkey was the senior on the staff; the Yankees had acquired him in 1915, and he had won 166 games for them. He had the honor of pitching the first game in Yankee Stadium on Opening Day of 1923 and supported Huggins through the turmoil of the early 1920s. Like Shocker, Shawkey was a serious student of the game, but unlike the spitballer, he was mild-mannered and soft-spoken.

Alexander was the starter for St. Louis, and again he was hard to hit. The Cards scored three times in the first inning, and when Southworth doubled in the seventh to extend the St. Louis lead to 5–1, Shawkey was done. As the game progressed, Shocker realized there would probably be a Game Seven, which he very well might start. His disappointment in not starting today—and in the Yankees losing—was tempered by the approaching opportunity. When the bullpen phone rang in the seventh inning, he figured either Dutch Ruether or Sam Jones would get the call to relieve and finish the game. No, Huggins wanted Shocker. James Harrison had a revealing commentary in the *New York Times*. "Urban was furious at being called as a relief pitcher. He gave vent to his feeling when the telephonic orders came out to the bullpen; his wish was to start today's game, if not yesterday's, and it is more than possible that Shocker's anger got the better of his pitching."[41]

Shocker came in with one out and two men on base; the Yankees were already down, 5–1. Whether Huggins was using him in a mop-up role or to keep New York within striking distance is unclear. But the way Alexander was pitching—he had given up only four hits so far—Huggins probably felt the game was out of reach.

Shocker gave up a single, followed by a home run (this one to deep left field) and a double. He got out of the inning, but the damage had been done. The rout was on, with the Yankees looking up at a 9–1 deficit. Alexander finished with a complete-game 10–2 victory. There would be a Game Seven, and Shocker would have no part in it. Huggins had decided to go with someone else.

Sunday was a cold and wet day, quite a contrast from the Indian summer of a week earlier. Only thirty-eight thousand fans attended; they had reached into their cedar chests for their topcoats, and the odor of camphor hung in the air. It was a tense, low-scoring affair. Waite Hoyt started for the Yankees and looked sharp, as did the Cardinals' starter, Jesse Haines. When Ruth hit his fourth home run of the Series in the third inning, it seemed one run might be enough. And it almost was, as the Cardinals did not score an earned run in the game. But in the fourth inning they scored three times, on two New York errors, by Koenig and Meusel, and one misplay, a ball that dropped between them. Years later, Koenig said of the double-play ball he muffed, "I couldn't get the damned ball out of my mitt." He bemoaned his small hands and added, "I was never the player I should have been. I was too hard on myself."[42]

Surely Hoyt must have thought about the final game of the 1921 World Series, when he was brilliant but beaten, 1–0, by an unearned run. Now in 1926, unearned runs were undermining his efforts again. The Yankees did close the gap to 3–2 in the sixth inning. When they mounted a rally in the seventh and loaded the bases with two outs, and Jesse Haines had developed a blister on his pitching hand, Hornsby went to his bullpen.

Alexander had not expected to be called upon the day after his Game Six win, and there has been much written about his condition for Game Seven. His catcher, Bob O'Farrell, provided the inside story, despite denials from many other players. Alexander's friends had bought him a drink after his 10–2 win, O'Farrell explained, but "you weren't doing Alex any favor by buying him a drink, because he just couldn't stop. . . . So in the seventh inning of the seventh game, Alex is tight asleep in the bullpen, sleeping off the night before when trouble comes."[43] Dan Daniel confirmed that the pitcher was indeed sleeping when the call came.[44] Bozeman Bulger added that Alexander had "a nice drink of stimulant in the bullpen before being called that day."[45]

Richards Vidmer of the *New York Times* vividly set the scene, as "a ghostly figure walked through the dull gray haze that shrouded the Yankee Stadium." Alexander, he said, "lumbered, his shoulders bent, his crooked legs wobbling, his shoulders drooping. Not an imposing figure, nor a fearful one. He looked more like an old man, bent with age."[46] James Harrison wrote of the veteran, "He warmed up in that leisurely, methodical way of his, and as he faced Lazzeri, fresh young slugger from the Coast, he was outwardly as unconcerned as if it were a spring exhibition game."[47] Alexander realized the rookie Lazzeri, who had already struck out twice in the game, was more nervous than he was. "How did I feel?" he was asked after the game. "Go and ask Lazzeri how he felt. I felt fine. I have no nerves; the strain naturally was on Lazzeri."[48]

Radio broadcaster Graham McNamee described what happened when Alexander delivered the third pitch with a one-and-one count: "a foul, a long shot into the left field stand for the second strike."[49] Just how close that foul came to being a home run seems to have grown in legend and shrunk in distance over the years. Not a single newspaper from among the dozen I examined made any point about the foul being even remotely close to a home run. Many of the papers did not even mention the foul and focused only on the final pitch of the at-bat.

When Alexander spoke to Francis J. Powers about this being his greatest day in baseball, he said that "the drive had a tail-end fade and landed foul by eight-ten feet in the left-field bleachers."[50] He may have helped Lazzeri with a self-deprecatory comment he made many times over the years. "A foot or two made the difference between being a hero and a bum."[51] In 1930 Lazzeri matter-of-factly said, "I fouled the third and then made up my mind to crack the next one."[52] Fred Lieb was there and wrote in his book on the history of the World Series (first published in 1949) that Lazzeri's "vicious line drive sailed down the foul line several feet outside of third base."[53] Frank Graham was also there, and he described a more dramatic drive, one that "curled just inside the foul pole."[54]

Perhaps the final word should come from the man who was best situated to judge the flight of the ball, Cardinals third baseman Les Bell. He told baseball historian Donald Honig, "Now, for fifty years, that ball has been traveling. It has been foul anywhere from an inch to twenty feet, depending on who you are listening to or what you're reading. But I was standing on third base, and I'll tell you—it was foul all the way. All the way."[55]

Alexander then struck out Lazzeri on a sweeping curve ball that he swung at and missed badly to end the threat. He retired the next five batters and then pitched carefully to the Babe with two outs in the ninth and walked him. It was the slugger's 4th free pass in the game and 11th in the Series.[56] The game ended when Ruth attempted to steal second base and was thrown out by O'Farrell. One New York writer said, "It was a case of the behemoth thinking itself a gazelle."[57]

Vidmer and Sid Keener wrote that it was a botched hit-and-run when Meusel swung and missed, though most reporters saw it as simply an attempted steal.[58] Ed Barrow said it was the only dumb play he ever saw Ruth make. Yet it may not have been that poor a decision. The Babe had stolen a base off Alexander the previous day, and he felt the pitcher was not paying attention to him. Even though Meusel was at bat and Gehrig was on deck, Ruth also figured the Yankees might get one hit off Alexander, but not two. So he wanted to get into scoring position. Miller Huggins confirmed that the Babe ran on his own; he also defended Ruth's decision. "We needed an unexpected move. Had Ruth made the steal, it would have been declared the smartest piece of baseball in the history of World Series play."[59]

Mercifully for Koenig and Meusel, they did not have to live with the lifetime tag as "goats," the way other New York players, Fred Merkle and Fred Snodgrass, had suffered.[60] Koenig's and Meusel's mistakes were overshadowed by Alexander's heroics. That made far better copy and a more stirring story than the fielding flubs.[61] But Lazzeri had to live down the famous strikeout for the rest of his life. While he went on to a Hall of Fame career with many great seasons and game performances, that one unsuccessful at-bat against Alexander remained supreme.

Sportswriter Red Smith noted that while Lazzeri was one of the game's greats, "the most vivid memory he left in most minds concerned the day he failed."[62] "Funny thing, but nobody seems to remember much about my ball playing, except that strikeout," Lazzeri told Bob Considine in 1945. "There isn't a night goes by but what some guy leans across the bar, or comes up behind me at a table in this joint, and brings up the old question. Never a night."[63]

Joe Vila raised a shocking possibility in a front-page article in the October 21 *Sporting News*. He suggested that gamblers may have influenced the outcome of the World Series and won big on the Cardinals. He focused on the strange fourth inning of Game Seven, Ruth's attempted steal to end the Series, and even Shocker's poor performance in Game Two. He also noted that "a notorious gambler from Boston," who had been charged in the Black Sox scandal, was spotted and asked to leave the stadium during Game Seven. Vila also wrote that "American Leaguers were extremely bitter in their criticism of Shocker's ragged exhibition."[64] He added that Meusel and Shocker would not be with the Yankees in 1927.

How likely is it that the 1926 World Series was fixed? While possible, it is highly doubtful for a number of reasons. The first is that there is no supporting evidence that points in this direction. The second is that big-time gamblers bet on things that were far less uncertain than the 1926 Series. The Yankees came so close to winning, far too close for "fixers." The Babe almost caught Southworth's home run in Game Two. Lazzeri might have homered before he struck out in Game Seven. Even Meusel came close to hitting a home run in Game Five. Moreover, Vila knew that Koenig had attacks of the nerves all season long and that the sensitive young man would never make an intentional error.

And not only did Meusel and Shocker return in 1927, but Huggins had been praising Meusel's play during the season and told sportswriter Bill Slocum that Pennock, Shocker, and Hoyt would definitely be hurling for New York the next season.[65] Finally, my friend Gene Karst (1906–2004) provided a 1926 perspective in 2002. The only man alive in the early twenty-first century who had been a reporter in 1926, Karst wrote: "Remember, [Commissioner] Landis was the big boss, and he was fighting gamblers at every turn. . . . Landis had put the fear of god in all players of that era."[66] Simply put, players were frightened of raising any suspicion on Landis's part.

St. Louis sportswriter Bob Broeg (1918–2005) told me he had never heard anything about a 1926 fix. While Broeg was too young to remember much about that Series, he was mentored by Roy Stockton and therefore had inside information on many little-known baseball events.[67] When I queried other baseball historians on the subject, they all said they had never heard even "talk" about gamblers influencing the outcome of the 1926 Series.[68]

Vila was a very opinionated man and was also a close friend of American League president Ban Johnson, who had been fighting a losing battle with Landis. Aspersions cast on the integrity of the Series would have reflected poorly on Landis. Vila also had a long history of confrontation with and criticism of Babe Ruth. During the 1921 World Series, Vila incorrectly accused Ruth of fabricating his elbow injury, which hampered his play

43. After his heroics in the 1926 World Series, Grover Cleveland Alexander returned to his hometown of St. Paul, Nebraska, for a joyous welcome. He appears content and relaxed here with his wife, Aimee, a stark contrast to the many photos of Alexander that seem to show a troubled soul, a man plagued by both alcoholism and epilepsy. When he joined the Cardinals, Aimee traveled with the team to help control his drinking. *Private collection of Steve Steinberg.*

and kept him out of a few games. The reality was that Ruth's elbow was severely infected.[69] After the 1925 World Series, Vila sharply and unfairly criticized the Washington Senators for "maudlin sentiment" in leaving Walter Johnson in the end of the final game and costing the American League the Series.[70]

Alexander's heroics brought the Cardinals a world championship. Cleveland sportswriter Ed Bang wrote after the Series, "Let the name of Grover Cleveland Alexander ring down through the ages and echo back year after year, for that name will be remembered and revered just as long as there is such a thing as a baseball classic."[71] Shocker's misfortune was a mere footnote and a lesser one than Lazzeri's strikeout.

Heywood Broun had not forgotten the drama of Shocker's heartache, even as Alexander was basking in the spotlight. "Something ought to be said about the tragedy of Urban Shocker," he wrote after the Series. "Here is one of the truly great pitchers in the game, and for years and years, he had no chance to show his prowess in a series. And then the chance comes too late. Opportunity dawdled. Shocker had gone over the crest of his best before Fate gave him a tumble."[72]

"We got beat with the pop-up to right field. It was a Yankee Stadium home run. We got beat with a 315-foot home run. The ball went 315 feet, and it was a home run. That's the way it is here."[73] These comments came not from Miller Huggins in 1926 but from Atlanta Braves manager Bobby Cox, after Chuck Knoblauch's eighth inning home run for the Yankees had tied his Braves in Game Three of the 1999 World Series.[74] The Yankees eventually won in 10 innings.

27

The Master at Work

Swiftly winter moves again to another spring;
Day by day through frozen glen where the ice is king;
But the old boy in his den rubs an ancient wing.
"You have one more year to ride up among the great,
One more year to nail the slide coming to the plate;
Then I'll leave you, worn and dried, to the busher's fate.
You have one more year to shoot on the same old line;
One more year—and some recruit sends you to the brine,
Where you'll be like Dead Sea fruit on a withered vine."
—"The Veteran" by Grantland Rice

The winter of 1926–27 was a time of recovery and healing for Urban Shocker. There was the sheer strain of pitching 266 innings in 43 games. There was the bitter disappointment of the World Series. And there was the progression of his illness, as his heart disease surely was advancing. He was becoming more reserved and subdued than in his St. Louis days, as he was facing an opponent he knew he could not overcome.

Miller Huggins once said there was a "fatality" about Shocker. While he never elaborated, it suggests he sensed a predetermined course the pitcher could not change, as if he were in the hands of fate. Such a perception on the part of Huggins, a sensitive and insightful man, may have drawn him closer to Shocker.[1] Huggins also had a sense of his own frailty and probably could relate to and identify with Shocker, once he began to see his pitcher's physical deterioration. As Shocker became more reticent and reclusive, he in turn may have been drawn closer to his manager, who Ford Frick described as "a man with the cool aloofness of a banker; the keen analytical sense of a trained engineer . . . as methodical as a milkman; and about as given to enthusiasm as a hitching post."[2]

Once he came to the Yankees, there was never an incident in which Shocker disappeared for a period of time because of a drinking problem, as had happened in St. Louis. Whether he was better able to handle liquor or whether he cut back on it to keep his body as strong and healthy as possible is not known.

Before Shocker hung up his glove for the year, he joined Babe Ruth and Lou Gehrig on their barnstorming tour to the Midwest and then Canada right after the 1926 World Series. The pitcher still had a following in the greater Montreal area because of his Ottawa days more than a decade earlier, as well as because of his pitching for the Yankees. Such exhibition games in the hinterlands gave fans in areas with no Major League team nearby an opportunity to see the stars up close.[3]

Shocker joined Gehrig's Larrupin' Lou's, as they faced Ruth's Bustin' Babes, on teams populated with local players. A highlight for the fans was Ruth's playing different positions, including pitcher. In one game near Montreal, the Ruth-Shocker team won, 4–3, in a contest that had to be stopped short of nine innings because the clubs ran out of baseballs. The Babe had hit thirty-six of them into a nearby river in pregame batting practice.[4]

As spring training approached, Huggins continued to shape his ball club. Both Sam Jones and Aaron Ward were traded away, and Joe Giard, one of the pitchers who went to the Browns in the Shocker deal, rejoined the Yankees.[5] Huggins and Ed Barrow added depth to the team by acquiring some talented utility players.[6]

Despite the fact that the Yankees were the league's defending champions, most observers picked Connie Mack's Athletics to win the 1927 American League pennant. Huggins's pitching staff was now a year older, and even he did not know how they would perform. "If they stand up," he noted, "my team has a wonderful chance to repeat."[7]

44. Urban Shocker worked as a jewelry salesman in the off-season. He is seen here in the store of Gerhart-Bauman Jewelry Company of St. Louis. © *Bettmann/CORBIS*.

Shocker had a brief salary holdout in March. He suggested he would go into the jewelry business full time if he did not get a sufficient raise. "I don't think my salary demands are unreasonable. I pitched good ball last year," he told a reporter for the *Sun*.[8] He had made the same $12,500 in 1926 that he earned in 1925. He soon signed for $13,500 for the upcoming season. As a comparison with teammates' 1927 salaries, Herb Pennock made $17,500; Waite Hoyt and Dutch Ruether each earned $11,000. Babe Ruth was by far the highest-paid player in the game at $70,000. His emerging slugging partner, Lou Gehrig, was paid just $8,000.[9]

Huggins put Shocker in charge of the young pitchers during spring training. "Yesterday he had the rookies standing open-mouthed while he told them some of the intimate details of working in the box," Ford Frick wrote. And when Shocker started describing the hitting styles and weaknesses of American League players, the youngsters took notes and looked like "school kids listening to the master." Shocker's most important message? "You cannot strike out every batter. The business of good pitching is to make the hitter hit the ball—and hit it where you want him to hit it. Save the strike-out stuff for the pinches." Frick went on to describe Shocker's daily habit of buying eight to ten newspapers to follow opposing hitters. Frick wrote a little Shocker poem in that column:

> I've watched Shocker pitching his slow one,
> I've studied his style like a book;
> And he taught me the way to hold bunters at bay,
> And the use of a "fast one" and "hook."
> Oh, he's wily, cagey and clever—
> Oh, he's studious, careful and grim,
> When his arm won't come through,
> Then he makes his brain do—
> And I've learned about pitching from him."[10]

The Yankees put the favored Athletics in their place by beating them three straight times at the start of the season. Hoyt was given the honor of starting on Opening Day and won easily. For years Huggins had told him to focus more and take the game more seriously. Late in the 1926 season, when Hoyt threw a tantrum after being removed from a game, an

45. By spring 1927, Urban Shocker had recovered from the rigors of the 1926 campaign and the disappointment of the 1926 World Series. Seen here in St. Petersburg in March 1927, he seems fit and ready to help the Yankees repeat in 1927. *Private collection of Steve Steinberg.*

exasperated Huggins said, "The thing must end. After ten years in the big leagues, Hoyt or any other player should know how to curb his temper."[11]

Before the 1927 season, Fred Lieb wrote that with "his natural stuff," Hoyt should have been a better pitcher than he was. "He is quick to lose his temper, and is inclined to be flighty when things do not break well."[12] John Sheridan had written a year earlier that a pitcher's "disposition to get angry when hit hurts his effectiveness more than loss of confidence in his fastball."[13] However, Sheridan was writing about Shocker, who seemed to have curbed that temper since he returned to New York.

It is hard to know if Hoyt took any cues from Shocker's evolution. Years later Hoyt told the story of a spiritual awakening he had before the 1927 season.[14] In his unpublished autobiography, he wrote that after a spring training lecture from Huggins, the message finally got through. "That night, in answer to some mysterious urge I walked far out on the pier at St. Petersburg. . . . I was conscious suddenly that there was some Power somewhere that had lit the lights of these countless stars and kept them spinning through their appointed orbits, that this same Power had ordered my life too, and that it was meant to be more than baseball, more than today—that I could become something more important than just a ballplayer bent on having fun."[15] Nineteen twenty-seven would be his finest year, with personal bests in wins (22) and earned run average (2.63). The pitcher known as the "schoolboy wonder" since his days at Brooklyn's Erasmus Hall High School was finally becoming a man at the age of twenty-seven.

Philadelphia did beat New York and Shocker on April 20. The winning pitcher was fellow spitballer Jack Quinn, who was just a few weeks short of his forty-fourth birthday and would pitch into 1933. Another aging spitball pitcher, Red Faber of the White Sox, was thirty-eight years old and coming off a 15-win season in 1926. In the National League, spitballer Burleigh Grimes, approaching thirty-four, would win forty-four games the next two seasons. Fred Lieb noted, "It is amazing how long these spitballers stick around."[16] Their "wet" pitch seemed to be prolonging their careers.[17] As Faber observed at the age of forty-one, "It's because I'm a spitball pitcher that I am able to keep on going. The spitter is the easiest delivery there is upon the arm."[18]

Ironically, when the debate was raging in the 1910s whether the spitter should be banned, many voices were heard that the pitch was dangerous. Even Billy Evans had spoken out against it. "I have seen a score of pitchers drop out of the majors," he wrote in *Harper's Weekly* in 1914, "because of the strain placed upon their arm through using the spitball. . . . The history of the spitball is that it has ruined many an arm of steel."[19]

Since the pitch was banned for new pitchers in 1920, Shocker and six others were part of a small—and dwindling—fraternity. As Clifford Bloodgood wrote in *Baseball Magazine* during the 1927 season, "Each reunion the ranks are thinned, but the survivors totter along proudly, stubbornly refusing to bow to the inevitable. The sand is seeping rapidly through the hour glass now, the breath of Old Pop Time as he whets his scythe falls hot upon their necks."[20] They may have avoided Organized Baseball's Rules Committee, but they would not outrun Father Time.

Shocker had an injury-plagued season in 1927. What is perhaps more notable was how fast he mended and got back into action. On May 31 he was hit in the head and knocked unconscious by a pitch from Eddie Rommel of the A's. He completed the game despite suffering a serious concussion and missed a couple of starts; he returned on June 10. Exactly four weeks after Rommel hit him in the head, he did so again.[21] On July 3 Shocker twisted his ankle rounding third base (he managed to limp home and score), but had to leave the game after pitching to two batters in the next inning. Initial reports said he had broken a bone in his foot and would be out a month.[22]

He returned just a few days later, but the ankle was still sore and he had to retire in the third inning. He was back in form on July 12, when he shut out Cleveland. But the ankle gave out on the game's final play, and he had to be carried off the field. On August 22 a line drive hit by Cleveland's Joe Sewell broke a finger on Shocker's left hand, and the next day one New York reporter wrote of Shocker's "bothersome" year, one in which he had used "a great supply of liniment, splints, and bandages."[23] Once again Shocker bounced back, each time sooner than trainer Doc Woods had expected. Just six days later, he was back in action. Whether or not his reaction time was slowing and made him more prone to injury is hard to say, but his recuperative powers and desire to get back into the action had not diminished.

Neither had his wiliness on the mound. He beat the Browns in St. Louis on May 11, one of twenty-one straight New York victories over the Browns that year.[24] Shocker had his former teammates "hacking and swinging wildly" that day, in the words of James Harrison.[25] The way New York was slugging the ball moved former Yankee Milt Gaston to say, "I would rather pitch a doubleheader against another club than one game against the Yankees. There isn't a moment's mental rest for a pitcher in that batting order."[26]

New York's young players were a year older and emerging as explosive offensive weapons. Tony Lazzeri increased both his batting and slugging averages significantly, but the biggest improvement came from Lou Gehrig, who was hitting right behind Ruth in the batting order. He hit .373 with a record 173 runs batted in in 1927.[27]

The Athletics still had thoughts of catching the Yankees in late May. They were just four games back on the morning of May 31. In that doubleheader the day after Decoration Day, Hoyt and Shocker pitched complete-game wins over the A's by the scores of 10–3 and 18–5.[28] New York had 37 hits, including six home runs—two by Ruth, who drove in seven runs. Tommy Holmes, who covered the Yankees for the *Brooklyn Eagle* in 1927, said late in his life, "Some 20 years ago, I stopped talking about the Babe for the simple reason that I realized that those who had never seen him didn't believe me."[29]

Shocker won his seventh game of the season on June 17, a four-hitter against the Browns. James Kahn of the short-lived *New York Graphic* was moved to write, "How the professor continues to do it remains a mystery. Shocker hasn't the varied assortment of deliveries that he once had, but it has leaked out that his arm has passed by a studious and diligent process into his head. Professor Shocker is nobody's straight man, though he makes the batters look like a very droll lot of comedians."[30]

Frick wrote an amusing column that season in which he commented on Shocker's superstitious nature. "No greater believer in the occult ever lived." Frick went on to describe his rituals. "He tried hanging his shoes from the chandelier; he sprinkled salt in a magic circle around the Yankee bats; he even slept with his hat on."[31] One historian wrote that Shocker practiced voodoo, but this Frick column probably should not be taken literally.[32]

Perhaps the Washington Senators entertained the idea of competing for the pennant when they came into Yankee Stadium for a July 4 doubleheader. They were in second place, 9½ games behind New York. A sweep would bring them within striking distance. Instead, the Yankees swept them in decisive fashion before more than seventy-two thousand fans, by the scores of 12–1 and 21–1. Once again they pounded out 37 hits on a single day. Perhaps more importantly, they got complete game wins from two pitchers who had won a combined two games in their Major League careers before 1927, George Pipgras and Wilcy Moore.

The Yankees had acquired Pipgras in January 1923 in a trade with the Red Sox. He won one game that season but had control problems. Huggins saw his potential and kept a string on him for four years. Sportswriter Bozeman Bulger later wrote that Huggins had "the patience of a Chinese philosopher" with a player he believed in, and Bulger used Pipgras as an example.[33] Just five days earlier, Pipgras had tossed a three-hit shutout for his first Yankees win. Huggins started him 21 times this year, and he won 10 of them with only three losses. In 1928 he would lead the league in wins with 24.

Moore had posted a 30-4 mark with the Greenville Spinners of the Class B South Atlantic League in 1926, and on that basis Ed Barrow signed him. After breaking his arm in 1925, he had developed a terrific sinker, which one writer described as "almost impossible to hit. It sinks so rapidly the Yankee catchers have to get closer to the plate to keep from picking the ball from the dirt and to prevent the umpires from misjudging the pitches."[34] Huggins used him as a spot starter but more often as a relief pitcher when one of the starters ran into trouble.[35] "He is as cool as a cake of ice, has splendid control, and a deceptive delivery," said Huggins. "He is always ready . . . as nonchalantly as if he were going up to pitch to the batters in practice."[36]

As the season progressed, writers sometimes mentioned that Moore was important for Shocker's success in 1927, since he often came in to save games for the aging spitballer. Shocker completed just under half of the games he started in 1927. Up to that point in his career, he had completed almost two-thirds of his starts. Typical was Frank Graham's comment: "But for the great relief work of Wilcy Moore, [Shocker] would have had many other defeats chalked up against him."[37] Yet such commentary was not correct. Moore saved thirteen games that year, and only three were for Shocker.[38] In three other games, he relieved Shocker with men on base and was not effective.[39] On April 20, for example, Shocker left in the seventh inning of a tie game with the bases loaded. Moore let all the base runners score, and Shocker took the loss.

The July 4 doubleheader sweep may have effectively ended the 1927 pennant race, as New York extended its lead to 11½ games. There were no cliques on the team, and the players were having fun. A story from Billy Werber revealed just how loose they were. Werber was a college player from Duke who spent a couple weeks with the Yankees in the summer of 1927, when he was just a teenager.[40] During a game at Yankee Stadium, Werber related, Shocker walked to the end of the dugout to get a drink of water. As he walked back to his seat, backup catcher Pat Collins, unloaded a big spit of tobacco juice and water onto Shocker and "painted an additional (brown) pinstripe from Shocker's shoulder all the way down his arm."[41] Werber feared a fight was about to break out, but it was just a practical joke. Shocker returned the favor a few innings later, when he spat tobacco juice and water into the face of Collins, who had been his teammate on the Browns for six years.

The modest Pipgras said, "When we got to the ball park, we knew we were going to win. That's all there was to it. We weren't cocky. I wouldn't call it confidence either. We just knew. Like when you go to sleep, you know the sun is going to come up in the morning."[42]

Mark Koenig again led all American League shortstops in errors in 1927 with 47. "I was ordinary, a small cog in a big machine," he told Dave Newhouse more than fifty years later. "The Yankees could have had a midget at shortstop."[43] Huggins would not have agreed with that statement and continued to start Koenig. He hit a solid .285 with 11 triples and 99 runs scored.

Despite the nonexistent pennant race, the Yankees drew large crowds wherever they played, because of a race of a different kind. Gehrig was matching Ruth, home run for home run, an individual competition unlike any the fans had ever seen. Ruth's 1921 record of 59 home runs was being threatened; the question was which man would top it. They each had 25 home runs at the end of June, and a month later Gehrig had the edge, 35 to 34. After the Labor Day games, they were again tied at 44. The Yankees were playing .700 ball, with a record of 91–39 and a lead of 16 games over second-place Philadelphia. Sports cartoonist and columnist Robert Edgren pointed out that this home run race was a significant development, one that is inherent in spectator sports nowadays. "Until the last two or three years, baseball fans used to watch their favorite teams. Now they watch their favorite individual players. A Ruth or a Gehrig is like a boxing champion, monopolizing all the ballyhoo."[44]

The contrast between the two men was striking, both in their personalities and their hitting styles. Paul Gallico wrote that "Ruth is either planning to cut loose, is cutting loose, or is repenting the last time he cut loose."[45] Gehrig said simply, "I'm not a headline guy, and we might as well face it."[46]

Edgren provided a vivid picture of their different batting styles. "When Babe Ruth knocks out a home run, he puts everything, from his ankles to his ears, into the clout. Babe follows through like a golfer. . . . Lou Gehrig is a shoulder hitter. He takes a short chop at the ball. He is not a long swinger like Ruth. He is a tremendously powerful man, built like a wrestler."[47] Gehrig was becoming as frightening for pitchers as the Babe. Sportswriter Ed Sullivan, who would go on to a successful career as a television personality, wrote a little ditty in the summer of 1927, the chant of opposing pitchers to Huggins. "You can bring Babe and Tony too, but for gawd sake, Don't bring Lou, Lou!"[48]

And then there was Shocker. When he came back from the ankle injury and shut out the Indians on July 12, W. B. Hanna wrote of Shocker's control. "He could have driven tacks at 30 paces. The ball broke exactly as he asked it to, and he used a fast ball only occasionally."[49] He also continued to show his skill at the plate, with three of his season's twenty sacrifice hits in the game.

Shocker beat his old team, the Browns, five times. The Yankees also won a sixth start he made against St. Louis; Moore was credited with the victory in relief. On August 28 the Yankees were in St. Louis almost two years to the day after Huggins had his showdown with the Babe at Sportsman's Park. That year the Yankees came to town in seventh place. This year they arrived in first place, where they had been all season. They were threatening to set an all-time American League record for wins.

Shocker was anxious to pitch again after suffering his broken finger. He won that day, with more than five innings of three-hit pitching in relief of Ruether. Frank Graham wrote afterward what was becoming increasingly obvious, yet remarkable nonetheless.

> Any successful bit of pitching by Shocker, whether for one inning or nine, is purely a triumph of mind over matter, for Urban has little left but his famous dry spitter. He has, however, a brain as keen as that possessed by any pitcher in either league, and with that brain and good control, he is a match for the hitters as they step to the plate. It isn't lack of stuff, but lack of control that brings on his losing games. When he has his control, he doesn't need any stuff.[50]

"Pitching," he said not long ago, "is just this and that." "This" was a gesture to the right of an imaginary plate, and "that" was a gesture to the left, by which he meant that pitching was purely a matter of working the corners. Shocker's "this and that" was good enough for an 18-6 record, the league's second-best winning percentage, and a 2.84 earned run average, the league's third best.

In the twilight of his career, this had to be a bittersweet season for him. With the inexorable progression of his heart disease, he could no longer take his part in the game for granted. He probably had an appreciation of the opportunities he had to pitch. Whether he savored them or was too preoccupied with his illness is unknown.

Babe Ruth beat Lou Gehrig for the home run title with an explosive September. Ruth slugged 17 that month, bringing his total to a record 60. Gehrig, perhaps subconsciously conceding to his more famous teammate, hit only 6 that month and just 2 after September 6, to finish with 47. Ruth hit 2 in Shocker's last start of the season, September 29 against the Senators.

The Babe's second home run that day, his 59th of the year, came against a twenty-two-year-old pitcher making his Major League debut, Paul

46. The seven mainstays of the pitching staff of the 1927 Yankees: L-R: George Pipgras, Wilcy Moore, Dutch Ruether, Waite Hoyt, Herb Pennock, Urban Shocker, and Bob Shawkey. While the '27 Yankees are remembered for their slugging, led by Babe Ruth's 60 home runs, they had outstanding pitching as well. This photo, probably taken in September 1927, shows a Shocker whose uniform seemed to be hanging on the formerly stocky pitcher. *National Baseball Hall of Fame Library, Cooperstown, New York.*

Hopkins. One sportswriter wrote of Hopkins's good fortune. "Hopkins should be grateful. Less than 24 hours ago, he was unknown. Now he is celebrated."[51] Hopkins's fame grew as he outlived all the other pitchers who had given up Ruth home runs that historic season.[52]

The Yankees won 110 games and finished 19 games ahead of the second-place Athletics. As good as was the hitting of the 1927 Yankees, their pitching was outstanding, though often overlooked. Their earned run average of 3.20 was far lower than that of any other team. They had the league's three best earned run averages (Moore, Hoyt, and Shocker), as well as the top four winning percentages. Even Dutch Ruether was terrific. His win over Cleveland on July 30 pushed his record to 12-2, though he tired as the season went on and finished at 13-6.

The Yankees met the Pittsburgh Pirates in the World Series. The possibility of a rematch with the Cardinals or an all–New York World Series with the Giants were real possibilities, but the Pirates edged them both in a heated race. Based on the season's performances, observers expected Shocker to start one of the games. Joe Vila wrote in the *Sporting News* that Shocker would probably pitch the second game. "He is better right now than in mid-summer. His spitter is more puzzling than ever before, and he has great control of it."[53] Arthur Mann added, "Shocker has been better against strong clubs this year than against the weaker ones. Give him a flock of heavy hitters, and he is in his glory."[54]

But Vila and Mann were not observing Shocker as closely as was Miller Huggins. Shocker won four games in September, but made only four starts that month. He had pitched only six innings in the two and a half weeks leading up to the Series. His illness was progressing and apparent to those close to him, including his manager.

In the latter stages of his heart disease, not only was his stamina deserting him but so was his weight.[55] A photograph of the Yankees pitching staff on the eve of the Series shows the once-burly pitcher as thin and gaunt, with his uniform hanging on his shriveled frame. "Rubber Belly" was the nickname the Babe had bestowed upon Shocker, and it was not a random name for the pitcher who had packed some heft in his midsection. Before the start of the series, Huggins talked to reporters about the three starters he was considering to pitch the opening game: Hoyt, Pennock, and Moore.[56] Shocker was not in the mix.

Hoyt started the first game of the World Series in Pittsburgh, and he was not sharp. He gave up two runs in the first three innings. Shocker was up in the bullpen, but Hoyt worked through the threats. When he ran into trouble in the eighth inning, Huggins called on Moore, who nailed down the win, 5–4. Pipgras was the surprise starter in Game Two, also at Forbes Field, or at least a surprise to the public. Huggins had already made that decision early on and informed the rookie a day in advance. Shocker would be the first man out of the bullpen, should Pipgras run into trouble. Expecting to see action, Shocker told him, "When you leave the game, leave the ball rough."[57]

When Lloyd Waner led off the game with a triple, Shocker probably figured he would make an early appearance. But while Waner did score, Pipgras settled down. He then held Pittsburgh scoreless until the eighth inning, and by then the Yankees were up, 6–1. They won, 6–2.

Herb Pennock won the third game, at Yankee Stadium, 8–1, to push his World Series record to 5-0. He took a perfect game into the eighth inning. The Yankees had just broken open a tight 2–0 game by scoring six times. "Sometimes I wonder," Pennock later said, "if maybe I wouldn't have had a no-hitter all the way if we hadn't scored six runs in the seventh. That sewed up the game, and a pitcher is bound to let down with such a lead."[58] In 1948 Dan Daniel wrote, "I have seen a lot of glorious World Series pitching. But none more glorious, from all angles, than the job Pennock achieved in the third game of the 1927 classic."[59]

Moore started Game Four and went the distance in another one-run New York win, and the Yankees were world champions for the second time.[60] They also became the first American League team to sweep a Series.[61] Mark Koenig was the improbable star of the Series, with nine hits. He batted .500 and played errorless ball.

No member of the Yankees was happier for their World Series win than Shocker, Joe Vila wrote. He brought a reputation back to New York that he was hard to handle. "But when Huggins took him back," Vila added, "Shocker became a conscientious and willing worker, obedient and loyal."[62]

Shocker helped the Yankees return to the mountaintop in 1927, yet he did not appear in that World Series. Or did he? Late in 2001, Major League Baseball, in conjunction with a computer simulation company, conducted what it called the SimSeries, a tournament of 64 of the best baseball teams of all time.[63] There was the usual controversy of determining which 64 teams belonged, but of course the 1927 Yankees were there. And they were standing at the end, when Babe Ruth's 14th-inning home run in the seventh game of the finals beat the 1975 Cincinnati Reds, with Pete Rose, Johnny Bench, and Joe Morgan.

The pitching star of the SimSeries? None other than Urban Shocker, who had a perfect 6-0 record, including a one-hitter against the 1954

Cleveland Indians. He really did get another chance, a chance to compete against the best of all time. And he did just fine.

In Mike Schacht's collection of letters of baseball memories, Reba Shimansky wrote, "Last year when I went to Yankee Stadium, the little boy sitting behind me had apparently seen *Field of Dreams*, and it must have made a strong impression on him. He asked his father whether he would see Babe Ruth play today. 'That would be impossible,' his father answered, 'because Babe Ruth is dead.' Disappointed, the boy replied, 'Why should that make a difference?'"[64]

28

Promises and Secrets

Here's to the goal I may never hope to gain;
Here's to the dream that I hope will never die.
The dream of marching onward through the sunlight and the rain,
And never turning backward as the last night rides the sky;
A dream of slogging upward through the barricades that wait,
And of groping nearer, nearer to the finish of the race.
Where the soul may find its answer in the grim set war with Fate,
And shall pass along, unbeaten, through the endless sweep of space.
—from "To the Goal" by Grantland Rice

For Urban Shocker, the end of the 1927 season was the start of a battle that was getting tougher and tougher. Tougher to keep his promise to stay in the game and tougher to keep the secret of his illness from others. Barnstorming with the Babe was out of the question. He was now losing weight at an alarming rate.

Shocker had a reputation for pitching with his head, but he understood that his physical condition was vital to his success. John Sheridan had written in the *Sporting News* earlier in the year, "Stuff does cut a big figure even with the smartest of pitchers. If stuff did not mean anything, a smart pitcher could pitch forever."[1] One Yankee who had lost his stuff was veteran Bob Shawkey, and the Yankees released him after the 1927 season. No other team claimed him, and he was waived out of the league.

Like Shocker, he had turned thirty-seven in the fall of 1927. But he won only two games that year and was used almost exclusively in relief. Since Shocker returned to New York, he had won 49 games; Shawkey, only 16.

In his original *Historical Baseball Abstract*, Bill James discussed these two pitchers with similar-sounding last names.[2] Through 1927, Shocker had won 187 games with an earned run average of 3.17; Shawkey had won 195 (he had 33 more losses than Shocker) with an ERA of 3.09. James suggested they are more deserving of being in the Hall of Fame than their Yankees teammates Waite Hoyt and Herb Pennock, who were inducted.[3] He discussed "the vagaries of history" and noted that "the best pitcher on the 1927 Yankees, in terms of either peak value or career value, was Urban Shocker."[4]

As they said their good-byes after the World Series, these two veterans, both keen students of the game, Shocker and Shawkey, likely did not recall a line from the *New York Evening Post* of a year earlier: "Veterans never hold on. They are brought down by the fatal waiver poison, just as old men die of heart disease."[5]

Just two weeks after the World Series, New York Giants outfielder Ross Youngs died at the age of thirty. "He was the greatest outfielder I ever saw on a ball field," said his manager, John McGraw. "A gamer player than Youngs never played ball."[6] He had experienced severe weight loss as he lost his battle to Bright's disease, a kidney ailment. The initial stages of heart disease involve weight gain, as fluids are retained. But weight loss is a complication of the final stages of that illness, too.[7]

The inability of doctors to save Youngs and the final phase of his illness must have struck a chord with Shocker. "Last December I was in bad shape," Shocker told sportswriter Bill Corum in July 1928. "When I gave out my first interview on salary—fellow telephoned me from downtown—I weighed a hundred and fifteen pounds. We kept it quiet and worked on gaining."[8] Shocker may not have accepted the likely prognosis of his doctor: time was running out. He would not recover. But he refused to give up and walk away from the game. He would regain as much weight as possible and return to the Yankees in 1928, as they went after their third straight pennant.

When Shocker was battling heart disease in the mid-1920s, the subject of what was then inaccurately called an "athletic heart" appeared on the nation's sports pages. The phrase referred not to the efficient heart of a well-conditioned athlete, who has a slow heart rate, but rather to heart diseases that could not be better diagnosed at the time. It was an open question whether healthy athletes who exercised too much could develop stressed and enlarged hearts, resulting in deadly heart disease.

In one chapter of Ty Cobb's syndicated life story, sportswriter H. G. Salsinger wrote that athletes like Cobb had enlarged hearts because of the action demanded of the heart. He added that when athletes retired, "the heart, veins, and lungs collapse because only the normal parts of each organ are used. The result of this collapse is often fatal."[9]

An early 1926 *New York Evening Post* article reflected the lack of medical consensus on the relationship of athletics and heart disease. The piece was headlined "Effects of Sports on Hearts Still Thing of Conjecture" and talked about the "mystic athletic heart."[10] It focused on the recent deaths of college football player and coach Percy Haughton (1876–1924) and German wrestler and bodybuilder Strong Man Sandow (1867–1925). The reporter wrote that Haughton "without doubt was the victim of an overworked heart."

In January 1928 New York sports editor Max Kase examined both sides of the issue, after the premature deaths of football player and coach Bob Folwell (1885–1928) and track star Alvin Kraenzlein (1876–1928).[11] Kase went on to name a half dozen track stars, including Martin Sheridan (1881–1918) and Ralph Rose (1885–1913), who died young, and quoted a well-known physician: "Strenuous exercise and athletic competition brings about a wear and tear on the heart which weakens the muscles of that organ and brings about harmful results." While many of these athletes died of other causes, including typhoid fever and influenza, it was commonly thought that their hearts and resistance to disease were weakened by strenuous athletics.

World heavyweight champion Gene Tunney weighed in on the subject a couple months later. He noted that the early deaths of young sportsmen generated publicity but represented a tiny fraction of athletes. "I have always contended that athletics lengthen rather than shorten the average life," says Tunney. He added that many athletes "rest upon their laurels" and do not exercise enough after they retire from sports. "Inactivity is one of the most devastating forms of dissipation," he concluded.[12]

If indeed Shocker's heart disease was mitral valve failure, the malfunctioning valve was putting added strain on his heart's main pumping chamber. The heart compensated with extra pumping, which resulted in an enlarged heart and, ultimately, heart failure.[13]

With spring training starting only a few weeks after Christmas, Shocker realized he would need more time to gain back that weight. He developed a plan. He would create a cover story to explain his absence from the Yankees' upcoming training camp. Thus began a subterfuge that was to confuse the baseball world in early 1928.

Starting in December, Shocker dropped hints—via telephone and telegraph—that he might retire, that twelve years in the Majors were enough. He also spoke of devoting time to his radio business, with the growing popularity of the medium. He had invested a lot of money in an electronics business that sold radios and related products back home in St. Louis, he explained. By February, he was ready to announce his formal retirement. His telegram to the Yankees was brief and to the point: "Received letter. Due consideration of present state of affairs urges me to voluntarily retire from major league baseball for the furtherance of my business interests at home."[14]

Reporters assumed the Yankees wanted to cut Shocker's salary for 1928, but business manager Ed Barrow said that the club had not cut his proposed salary "by as much as a thin dime." He said the Yankees were happy to develop their younger pitchers and pointed out that Wilcy Moore had "rescued him many times." Barrow added nonchalantly, "Of course, we could probably use Shocker next season. He is one of the smartest pitchers in the game, and he has done good work for us."[15] Shocker reaffirmed it was purely a business decision. "I am not a hold-out. The end of my career will come eventually, so why not resign while I can leave a good record behind me?"[16]

Reporters still believed he was bluffing. In his Sports of the Times column, John Kieran wrote that things just didn't add up. "Few ballplayers quit the game while they are still hale and hearty enough to hobble out on the diamond or at least stagger up to the pay window twice a month. A few have done it, but only a few. And most of them repented. . . . It's even money that Shocker will be among those present on opening day in the stadium."[17] Had Shocker reported to St. Petersburg in early March, his physical activity would probably have been limited to hobbling and staggering.

Meanwhile, the lack of physical and competitive sport was making Shocker restless. He decided to take up flying and entered an aviation school in Okmulgee, Oklahoma.[18] The adventure of the new frontier intrigued him, and now he would have the time to focus on it. Flying did not demand too much physical exertion, and it was both energizing and liberating. Flying would keep his mind sharp.

Fellow spitballer and St. Louis pitcher Marvin Goodwin used to describe the thrills he got as a pilot. The fact that he was killed while flying in October 1925 did not lessen the attraction for Shocker.[19] If anything, the danger may have heightened it. Shocker flew to Okmulgee in mid-February. He was welcomed as a celebrity and spoke to the Okmulgee Aviation Club and at the New Melton Hotel. The *Okmulgee Democrat* reported that Shocker was "an aviation enthusiast . . . gaining a reputation in aviation circles as a student of aviation."[20] The March 15 *New York American* had a photo of Shocker in Okmulgee in a two-seater airplane, about to take off.

Will Wedge injected a sense of humor into the discussion. He wondered if the "fiddling tediousness" of Shocker's slow ball pitching and bunting had begun to "irk" his soul. "From slow balling he wants to fly to the other extreme of zipping around in an airplane. It's a daring thing. Especially for a novice. But, as Ed Barrow says, there may be benevolence in Shocker's purpose. He may want to help out Waite Hoyt's undertaking business." Wedge also wondered why the spitball pitcher went to Oklahoma, a dry state, where the moisture was underground in the form of petroleum. "Petroleum is of no good to a pitcher—at least not on the mound. The oil-ball has been blacklisted, along with the emery ball." Wedge noted the variety of vocations the pitcher had been dabbling in. "The way Shocker shifts jobs or interest in jobs is startling. Pitching, jewelry store clerking, radio, electronic supplies, and then aviation. Back in the old Cleveland days of his youth, he worked in a machine tool factory and played with a brewery ball club, and then was a catcher in Canada."[21]

There was little contact between Shocker and the Yankees during March, the month of spring training. He rejected the club's final contract offer on March 8, and Huggins said he would move Wilcy Moore into the starting rotation.[22] Meanwhile, Shocker focused on flying and on gaining weight. Just what foods his diet consisted of—whether he consumed

47. When Urban Shocker realized his baseball career might be coming to an end, he looked for another challenge and took up flying in the spring of 1928. He planned to continue doing so in Denver that summer, after the Yankees released him in early July. *Associated Press.*

fatty foods and milkshakes—is not known, but slowly he put on some weight. His smokescreen was working well enough. It was buying him precious time to recover.

By mid-April, Shocker was ready to make his move back to baseball. He took the formal step of asking Commissioner Landis to reinstate him from the voluntary retired list. But he was not above creating leverage before he signed. Some newspapers carried Shocker's comments on the burgeoning business he had entered. "There is more money in the radio line. People are more and more coming to depend on A and B batteries, AC sets, and the proper kinds of serials." He then added, "Besides, I am not satisfied with the contract offered me."[23] James Harrison wrote, "It is all a very delightful mystery. Could it be possible that Urban really has an overweening love for the good old radio business and cares so little for baseball that he won't even be bothered by having to state why and where his contract is defective? Could it really be possible?"[24]

While sportswriters were puzzled, the Yankees' management appeared to be getting irritated. Huggins said, "We don't care whether Shocker reports or not. As a matter of fact, I had not counted much on him this year."[25] But with the club's struggles in spring training, he surely could use the veteran. This was different from 1926, when Huggins was using the exhibition season to experiment and rebuild. These were mostly members of the mighty 1927 Yankees. After the Yankees lost five games to Minor League teams, a creative Nashville reporter wrote that "the thundering herd of 1927 has become the blundering herd of 1928."[26] Fred Lieb noted, "Today we have the entire baseball world standing aghast at these Yankees.... No other great baseball club has ever put in a training season as the Yanks."[27]

Huggins met with Shocker to finalize his contract in late April. Reporters assumed the pitcher had reported late to avoid training camp, while he told a parallel story of his business partners "doing him" and his working with an auditor to straighten out the mess.[28] Shocker missed his original meeting with Huggins; he was reportedly suffering from a "severe cold." Huggins included a clause Barrow had insisted on, that the pitcher's salary would not begin until he had worked back into shape. Huggins would make the final determination of when Shocker was ready. Shocker said he had been working out with the Cardinals in St. Louis and would need no more than a week to be fit to pitch.[29]

If Barrow had gotten his way with one clause in the contract, Shocker got the edge with another—with the full knowledge of Huggins. The contract called for a $15,000 salary, a $1,500 increase over what Shocker was paid in 1927. When Huggins traded for Shocker after the 1924 season, he had promised him $1,500 for moving expenses. Shocker explained to Bill Corum, "Barrow hadn't authorized the payment.... Hug wanted to pay me out of his pocket, but I wouldn't take it. I wanted it from the club. Well, it took nearly four years, but I got it."[30]

Shocker also told Corum and Arthur Mann, a young reporter, "Miller Huggins knew I couldn't pitch.... Holdout! I couldn't throw my voice across the room. They gave me up as dying that day [Christmas]. I fought back." Shocker explained, "The boys were swell, printing those holdout stories. When I weighed enough, I came east and saw Huggins."[31]

Corum asked him directly if Huggins knew Shocker had been in bad shape. "Oh, sure," replied the pitcher.[32] It is likely that the perceptive Huggins knew Shocker was a sick man as the 1927 season ended. Whether Shocker confided in him at that time is not known. If he did, then Huggins's remarks to the press—wondering what Shocker was up to early in 1928—were part of the ruse.

The next three weeks, Shocker pitched batting practice, yet it was apparent he was not his former self. A bruised wrist from a batting practice line drive, at first feared to be a fracture, didn't help matters.[33] Neither did a jawbone infection. He finally made his first appearance of the year on Decoration Day, against the Washington Senators. The Yankees had started strongly in the regular season. That morning of May 30, they had a 33-7 record, good for an 8½-game lead over the second-place Athletics.

In two innings of relief, Shocker held the Senators scoreless, though they did beat the Yankees, 5–0. Reporters didn't note anything unusual or different from the Shocker of 1927. Even if they did, they weren't going to write about it. Did any of them consider that this, his 412th Major League game, would be the final appearance of Shocker's pitching career?

His symptoms persisted. Shortness of breath and dizziness were becoming more commonplace now. Rumors begin to circulate about a bad heart.

Less than two weeks later, the Yankees went to Chicago for a series with the White Sox. On a warm morning in Comiskey Park, Shocker didn't feel right as he started pitching batting practice. Suddenly his legs went out from under him; he gasped for breath and collapsed. As Doc Woods and the players rushed to his side, they yelled for the White Sox doctor. The few fans who had arrived early for the game leaned from their seats for a better view. Shocker lay near death, ashen gray with barely a pulse. "I collapsed that day in Chicago and almost died in the clubhouse," Shocker told Mann. "It's my heart."[34]

He was carried into the clubhouse, where he was revived, though still dizzy. Reporters were everywhere, trying to get the story. Shocker tried to brush it off as a fainting spell resulting from dehydration and the heat. He asked them not to write about the incident; he did not want to upset his wife, who read the sports pages. The reporters agreed. "One of the best-kept secrets on the Yankees that spring," Corum wrote, "was Shocker's collapse while pitching batting practice in Comiskey Park."[35]

It wasn't the first time, nor would it be the last, that sportswriters did a favor for a player or a team by not reporting a story. They were in the business of making players look good, not tearing them down.

On the morning of July 4, the Yankees had extended their lead to thirteen games, but it was a difficult day for Huggins. He called Shocker into his office to give him his unconditional release. Frank Graham conveyed the manager's sadness. "Although in releasing Shocker, Huggins took the only course that was left open to him as manager of the Yankees, he was affected to a greater extent by his enforced action than this writer has ever seen him affected by anything."[36]

Shocker was offered the position of Yankees pitching coach but turned it down. He was not ready to give up pitching and wanted to do so when he got better. Fred Lieb noted of Shocker, "His plans are to go somewhere out into the wilds to regain his health."[37] Bob Shawkey had served in that coaching role in 1927, when he pitched only occasionally. Ironically, he left the club this season because, like Shocker, he was not willing to retire as a player. He went to the Montreal Royals of the International League, where he appeared in twenty-three games that season.

Ford Frick wrote that, in Shocker's case, "illness had stepped in where age had failed."[38] He also quoted Babe Ruth commenting on the empty seat at the bridge table. "It seems funny without old Rubber-belly in here," said the Babe. "I sure hope he gets straightened out soon."[39]

Shocker did not question the release. Based on his condition, he could not do so. Instead, as he told Corum, "I'm going to Denver to fight this thing."[40] Eleven years to the day before Lou Gehrig made his emotional "luckiest man" remarks to a packed Yankee Stadium crowd, Urban Shocker left quietly. He was not ready to accept his fate. There was no speech to remember because Shocker expected—or at least hoped—to return. He would make the speech when he came back.

His traveling roommate, batboy Eddie Bennett, also took the news very hard.[41] Shocker spoke to only a handful of reporters before he left for Denver, where the mountain air was thought to help people suffering from various ailments. James Harrison's comment suggested reporters had been aware of Shocker's health issue, at least in a general sense. "It was apparent that he was a sick man and not himself. His stomach gave him trouble, and it was also whispered that his heart was ailing."[42]

For some reason, Bill Corum sat on the story for almost thirty years and revealed it only two years before his death. Arthur Mann related the story a decade after it took place, in a *Sporting News* piece on ballplayers who had lived "Hell on earth," yet continued to play the game. "Most memorable is Urban Shocker, one of the greatest right-handers of the game, and a giant of gigantic courage—bravery of a kind that never creeps into the box scores or the weekly averages. . . . So when you start listing the game ball players, please begin with Urban Shocker."[43]

The Yankees were on the road in Washington DC at the time, and Shocker spoke to Corum and Mann at the Wardman Park Hotel. It is not known if he met with them separately; they both described a shaken and shaking Shocker, who needed a bottle of what Mann called "synthetic courage" and what Corum simply called "contraband Scotch." Between a few forced smiles and some tears, he told them he had been sleeping the past two or three years sitting up. "Lying down even a little smothers me, chokes me," he told Mann. "I . . . don't know what the end will be . . . where I'll go . . ."[44]

As the word of Shocker's release came out, the acclaim came rolling in. Syndicated columnist Joe Williams called him one of the greatest spitball pitchers of all time and noted, "He pitched with his arm, his heart, and his head."[45] Fred Lieb said that, next to Walter Johnson, he was the greatest pitcher of the last decade.[46] Shocker surely did not invent the slow ball, but he "grafted dilatory new tricks onto the horsehide," wrote Will Wedge.[47] Frank Graham detailed Shocker's three main assets: his spitball, his intelligence, and his courage. "If Shocker did not achieve greatness as a pitcher, there were times when he appeared to miss it by the narrowest of margins," he wrote.[48]

Perhaps the most ominous headline came from the July 7 *New York World*, which shouted, "Champions Mourn Passing of Shocker." He was not dead yet, but he knew he would feel alive only if he kept his promise to stay in the game. Somehow, somewhere.

29

A Star Surfaces and Crashes

Denver was a hotbed of baseball in the 1920s. The nearest Major League teams were in St. Louis, more than 850 miles away. Both of that city's teams, the Browns and the Cardinals, had many fans in the West. People in Denver could not help but follow Shocker's success when he pitched for the Browns. And for the past few years he had been a member of the most renowned team in baseball.

The *Denver Post* tournament, which began in 1915, was one of baseball's biggest events west of the Mississippi. Semipro teams from hundreds of miles away were invited to play for the glory and money that went to the winners. Teams often brought "ringers" on board, stars from other teams, even from the Majors, who were not under contract at the time.

As the train pulled into Denver on July 27, 1928, eleven-year-old Frank Haraway could hardly contain his excitement. Urban Shocker, star pitcher of the New York Yankees, was coming to town to pitch in the tournament for his father's grocery team, Piggly Wiggly. Bill Haraway owned the supermarket chain and sponsored the team.[1]

Frank loved baseball. The fact that he was confined to a wheelchair, because of tuberculosis of the bone he had developed at the age of seven, did not lessen that ardor or his willingness to play the game.[2] He was in awe of the Yankees, the team of Ruth and Gehrig. Just last fall, the Babe and Lou had brought their barnstorming tour out to Denver. The Bustin' Babes had played for Bill Haraway's Piggly Wiggly team, while the Larrupin' Lou's played for the Denver Buicks. The two sluggers had come to Frank's house that afternoon (he had been too sick to attend the game) to autograph a baseball for him in his presence. He would never forget the thrill of that moment.

Now Piggly Wiggly, a semipro team in Denver's City League, had the most famous ringer ever to play in the tourney, which would be held the first thirteen days in August. Frank had asked his father why Shocker was available when the Yankees were in the heat of a pennant race with the surging Philadelphia Athletics. Bill had explained that Shocker's health hadn't been great and that he was coming to Denver to rest and recuperate in the mountains where the air was so crisp and therapeutic. More importantly, Shocker told him he was coming to Denver to help the supermarket team win the tournament. Bill had paid the ex-Yankee a lot of money to join the team, and the grocery man had to admit he really didn't know what was wrong with the pitcher or why he had been released.

As the train came to a stop, Frank waited eagerly. As the passengers disembarked, Frank looked ahead with astonishment. There was Urban Shocker . . . or was it someone else? The man had Shocker's face, but he looked pale and drawn. His suit hung loosely on his body, and he had a faraway look. "Shocker looked bad, a sick man, not flamboyant," Frank recalled.[3] Maybe the long trip had tired him out, he thought. Still, something didn't seem quite right.

With his train approaching Denver, Shocker thought about the Yankees' shrinking lead over the Athletics. What had seemed unthinkable at the start of July, a real pennant race between the two teams, now appeared possible as August had arrived. The Yankees' 13½-game lead after the games of July 1 was only 5½ games on the first of August.[4]

A heart disease story of a different kind was making headlines in late July 1928. Percy Williams (1908–82) was a Canadian athlete who had suffered from rheumatic fever at the age of fifteen, and doctors advised him to avoid strenuous physical exercise. That childhood illness often caused mitral valve failure, which was inoperable at the time. Williams trained anyway and was a surprise Olympic qualifier at the Canadian nationals.[5] The twenty-year-old went on to win gold medals in track in the 1928 Olympics in Amsterdam, in both the 100 and 200 meters. His

48. Urban Shocker's heart failure began progressing late in 1927, and he had lost so much weight by the end of the year that he could not appear for spring training 1928 until he presented the semblance of an athlete ready to compete. Yet even when he did report, he was tiring often and easily. It was obvious that something was seriously wrong. *Private collection of Steve Steinberg.*

first victory, in the 100m, was such a surprise, says the Olympics website, that "Olympic officials were forced to delay the medal ceremony as they hunted for the Canadian flag and national anthem."[6]

Shocker most likely was aware of this story, especially with his Canadian connections from his early baseball career. Perhaps he wondered what glory awaited him at the end of his long journey. He had traveled alone to Denver. The plan was to get settled and then perhaps have Rene and Cletus join him. He really did not know what to expect out west. He knew the baseball scene here would be very different from the Majors. Would it be like his summer in Toronto?

He did know that his arrival was being touted in the local press, which referred to him as "the famous Yankee pitcher." The *Denver Post* credited Bill Haraway for "a daring stroke" that "cost a lot of money" in signing Shocker.[7] "What a treat for baseball lovers, this appearance of one of the greatest pitchers the game has ever known," a *Post* reporter wrote a few days later.[8]

Shocker also planned to resume flying lessons, which provided him with that sense of adventure and excitement he craved. The irony must have occurred to him that he and his old antagonist, Browns owner Phil Ball, both had this passion for taking to the skies.

The *Denver Post* tournament was a double-elimination event that involved sixteen teams. Shocker had planned to pitch in the opener for the Piggly Wiggly team on August 1, but he didn't feel well enough to take the mound. There was an awkward moment when he told manager Tommy Collins that he would eagerly coach first base, but he would like to wait until the next game to play. He would have to settle up with Bill Haraway, who certainly had expected him to pitch this game. As he walked out to the coach's box, Shocker put his Yankees jacket over his grocery team uniform. It turned out that he wasn't needed on the mound, at least on this day. His team won easily by the score of 17–3, and he got quite a workout waving runners around the bases.

Frank Haraway watched the tournament games from a special box seat at Merchants Park, one that could accommodate his wheelchair, which he needed to get around with his leg in a cast. On August 3 the *Denver Post* ran a photo of Haraway in that location behind home plate.

Sunday, August 5, Shocker's day to pitch, was at hand. Merchants Park was filled with eight thousand fans. Automobiles lined the outfield edges of the park. Piggly Wiggly was going to face the Cheyenne [WY] Indians, perhaps the best team competing here. The Indians had not lost a game all year. Hundreds of their fans had made the 100-mile trip to Denver.

Opposing Shocker on the mound was a pitcher he had faced back in 1917. One of the first Major Leaguers from Russia, Dmitri Ivanovich Dimitrihoff had changed his name. Now he was known as Rube Schauer. Nineteen-seventeen was his last year in the Major Leagues, after which he spent a few years in the Minors and then a few more playing semipro ball in the Midwest.

As the game began, Shocker did not have his best stuff. His spitter was not an option; it was not allowed in the tournament. He would have to be very smart, mixing up his slow pitches, and a little lucky to win today. When one of his outfielders made a sensational catch in the first inning, it looked like maybe this would be his day. But his luck quickly deserted him when an outfielder misplayed a ball in the fifth inning. It bounced over the fence for a home run under the rules of play.

Schauer was sharp and seemed to be growing stronger as the game went on. Shocker, on the other hand, was getting weaker. In the eighth inning, with his team down 3–1, he was dizzy as he walked to the mound. Three batters later, after giving up two triples and a single, he could pitch no more.[9] He stumbled to the dugout, as the field seemed to be spinning around him. The last thing he remembered was his teammates rushing over to prevent him from toppling over.

Shocker was taken to St. Luke's Hospital, and a call went out to his wife. He protested to his doctors, as he had to the reporters in Chicago, not to bother her. But the doctors would not listen. Rene would be bothered. She would be told to come to Denver immediately. In the ensuing days, the hospital reported that he was suffering from pneumonia and heart trouble, and his condition was described as "critical."[10]

I started conversing on the phone with Frank Haraway (1916–2005) in 1999, and we met for lunch in the Denver airport in 2000. Haraway was getting around on crutches, but his illness never stopped him from leading an active life. A longtime sportswriter for the *Denver Post*, he still remembered overhearing the family doctor telling his mother more than seventy years earlier that "the boy will be lucky to make it to his twelfth birthday."[11]

30

A Day of Death and Rebirth

If I may call you friend, I wish you more—
A rare philosophy no man may fake,
To put the game itself beyond the score
And take the tide of life as it may break.
To know the battle that a man should know
Before he comes through with the winning hit.
And though you fall before the charging foe,
To love the game too well to ever quit.
—from "The Gift of the Gods" by Grantland Rice

THURSDAY, SEPTEMBER 6, NEW YORK CITY
The showdown was approaching. Baseball had rarely looked forward to a day so big. The mighty New York Yankees were fighting for their baseball lives. New York's 13½-game lead of early July was being washed away by the steady waves of Connie Mack's Athletics, who had not won a pennant, or even been close to winning one, for fourteen years and had now won more than 70 percent of their games these past nine weeks. Fans were talking of a comeback similar to that of the 1914 "Miracle" Boston Braves, who climbed from last place to first in a similar time frame, and then won the National League pennant. Ironically, those Braves had stunned Mack's last great team in the 1914 World Series in four straight games.

The Yankees had basically the same squad they had the past couple of years, when they won a combined 201 games. The team just wasn't hitting. It was as if their bats had gone dead the past few weeks. Mercifully for them, heavy rains cancelled their game against Washington on Thursday. For at least one more day, New York would remain two games ahead of the Athletics, who were rained out, too, in Boston. But the storm did nothing to dampen the baseball fever of thousands of fans who showed up at the Yankees' offices. They wanted tickets for the four-game showdown between New York and Philadelphia that would start on Sunday in Yankee Stadium.

THURSDAY, SEPTEMBER 6, DENVER

Urban Shocker devoured newspapers in his playing days, and now in St. Luke's Hospital, he was doing the same. Since his collapse at the *Denver Post* tournament, he had been laid up here. He was more concerned about dying from boredom than any heart condition, he was telling visitors. He had been joined by Rene and Cletus in mid-August.

Shocker was no longer in the game; he was a mere spectator. He was following his Yankees like a fan in the grandstand, able to cheer but helpless to contribute. And these past few weeks, it was the Yankees who had appeared helpless, unable to stop the tide of the surging Athletics.

FRIDAY, SEPTEMBER 7, NEW YORK CITY

The weather was wreaking havoc on the baseball schedules and pitching rotations. The Athletics would play doubleheaders in Boston both on this day and the next, while the Yankees would play two against the Washington Senators at home on Friday and a single game against them on Saturday. On Sunday, the A's and Yankees would have their doubleheader showdown at Yankee Stadium. Six games in three days for Philadelphia and five in three for New York.

The Athletics' climb back toward the top had been steady these past few years. By 1927, when they were ready to compete for the pennant, an exceptional Yankees team had simply overwhelmed them. In 1928 the Athletics had a wellspring of support and goodwill throughout the country, which was also tiring of yet another New York team winning a pennant.[1] Sentiment aside, the A's were a very good team, potentially as good as the Yankees of the past couple of years. The oldest manager in baseball, Mack, had a young team, with a few aging stars playing part-time and one playing a key role.

They had young Mickey Cochrane behind the plate (age 25), Al Simmons in the outfield (age 26), and 20-year-old Jimmie Foxx splitting time between catcher, first base, and third base. Veterans Ty Cobb (age 41), Eddie Collins (also 41), and 40-year-old Tris Speaker played occasionally. On the mound Lefty Grove, at 28, led the team in wins with 24, while veteran Jack Quinn, who had turned 45 in July, was second with 18 wins. Three years after he was picked up off waivers from the Red Sox, the spitballer was one of baseball's best pitchers.

The rains stopped on Friday, but the Athletics did not. They swept the Red Sox, 1–0 and 7–3. Lefty Grove was brilliant in the opener, giving up only four hits and striking out eleven men. The Yankees did not stop either—losing, that is. They dropped two games to Washington, 11–0 and 6–1. They were staggering, not helped by the loss of Herb Pennock and Tony Lazzeri, out with shoulder injuries. The Athletics had pulled even, at 87 wins and 47 losses.

Miller Huggins confided to Dan Daniel that he was having a recurring nightmare. "You know, whenever I get a bad dream, it takes the form of a doubleheader with pitchers running out of the bullpen faster than I can call them in. I've stopped eating bedtime snacks. Only last night, I dreamed that I had to drag in poor Shocker from the pen. Man, that was a real nightmare."[2]

Preparation for the big series proceeded on many fronts. The president of the American League assigned four umpires to the games, as in the World Series. New York City police began to brace themselves for a Sunday crowd of more than 80,000. Deputy Chief Inspector John O'Brien said he would have 120 patrolmen, including 20 on horseback. The IRT announced additional subway service.[3]

Ed Barrow said that all the reserved and box seats for Sunday's doubleheader had been sold.[4] He had to deal with crowds that had been converging on the Yankees' offices. A police lieutenant told him they had been turning away imposters all day long. There had been, in the words of one reporter, "a half a dozen Miller Hugginses, three Colonel Rupperts, and a Herb Pennock or two."[5]

Harry Stevens, stadium concessionaire extraordinaire, wondered how he would feed the 60,000 fans in the general admission sections who would show up for tickets in the morning. He had to be thinking of breakfast, lunch, and dinner. It would be a long day.

SATURDAY, SEPTEMBER 8, BOSTON AND NEW YORK CITY

Saturday was warm and sunny in the east, with a game-time temperature of 75° at Yankee Stadium. Perfect weather for a baseball game, and finally the Bronx Bombers awoke. Led by Babe Ruth's home run that broke a 3–3 tie in the seventh inning, New York won, 6–3. The Babe's 48th homer of the season brought hundreds of straw hats onto the field in celebration.

Still, the Athletics simply would not be denied. They swept another doubleheader from Boston. In both games, Philadelphia came from behind to win. At the end, the Boston fans did something totally unexpected, something that Red Sox infielder Billy Rogell remembered seventy-five years later. They cheered and applauded the visiting team.[6]

Even Yankee Stadium was filled with cheers when the Athletics' victories were announced. A Chicago reporter wrote, "Treason stalks the alleys of the Bronx."[7] Perhaps the explanation was far less sinister, though no less complex. Connie Mack's fourteen-year climb into sole possession of first place, by a half-game, was now complete. After a wilderness that included five seasons with 100 or more losses, Mack and the A's were back. The stage was set for the showdown in New York.

SATURDAY, SEPTEMBER 8, DENVER

Back in St. Luke's, Shocker was lying in bed, absorbing Friday's double defeats from the newspapers, playing the games over and over in his head. The Yankees were not hitting. Richards Vidmer wrote in the *Times*, "Those ball-busters from the Bronx who spread terror wherever they roamed only a few short weeks ago. . . . Alas, and also alack! These are tense times."[8]

Ford Frick captured the approaching drama of Sunday's games. "Never before has staid old New York so given itself to baseball frenzy. There's drama, folks—crude, bloody cold drama of the sort that New York loves. . . .

The hysteria that comes when the commonplace suddenly becomes dramatic, and Mr. Average Man awakens to find the world turned upside down at his doorstep."[9]

Friday's *Evening World* had an article that juxtaposed with the reports of the tailspin of the Yankees, an aging club. Robert Edgren looked at older stars from various sports, men like Cobb, Dempsey, and Tilden, and noted that they were "'through' when the old legs weaken or the heart doesn't pump record-breaking strength through the old veins the way it used to."[10]

SUNDAY, SEPTEMBER 9, NEW YORK CITY

Sunday morning in New York was warm. A game-time temperature of 80° was expected. Many fans armed with food and soda spent the night outside the stadium, to be assured of good seats when they went on sale the next morning. Throughout the night, youngsters did a brisk business selling sandwiches and wooden soapboxes for chairs. By midnight, there were hundreds of fans in line.

The automobiles began arriving during the night. They came from hundreds of miles away, with license plates that gave a geography lesson of the surrounding states. By 9 a.m., the air was filled with fumes and honking horns, as hundreds of vehicles were backed up for miles. In the meantime, a dozen special trains began arriving at Penn Station in Manhattan from the Philadelphia area, bringing 10,000 fans into the city.

The day had a World Series feel to it. Deputy Inspector O'Brien arrived at 6:00 a.m. He was pleased to learn that the crowd had been well behaved during the night, and he was amazed that there were already 20,000 people awaiting the sale of tickets. In the meantime, ticket scalpers were doing a brisk business. They had been getting up to ten dollars in the last few days for a two-dollar reserved seat. Now they were getting twenty dollars for that same ticket.[11]

Just before noon, the police had to deliver the bad news to the horde: There were no more tickets available. Almost 60,000 people had bought one-dollar grandstand seats and 50-cent bleacher seats. Estimates ranging from 40,000 to 200,000 people were turned away. Tens of thousands of them did not leave; they would linger outside the stadium all afternoon.

49. On September 9, 1928, Connie Mack's Athletics came to Yankee Stadium for a doubleheader before an enormous crowd. They had rallied from 13½ games back to take a half-game lead over the Yankees. Here the managers of the two teams, Miller Huggins and Mack, shake hands before the games. On this very day, Urban Shocker died in Denver, and New York swept and went on to win the pennant. *Rucker Archive.*

They were orderly and wanted to remain close to the action. They would have to listen to the *Evening World*'s radio broadcast on WMCA.

SUNDAY, SEPTEMBER 9, DENVER

Shocker had floated in and out of consciousness during the night. Rene stayed at his bedside. When he awoke early Sunday morning, he asked the nurse on duty for the morning papers. He wanted to see the details of Saturday's games and the pitching match-ups for today's showdowns. The nurse replied that his condition did not permit this.

"Oh yes, I can read it. I must see who pitched yesterday and who will do the hurling today."[12] Shocker got the papers and saw that, despite Saturday's victory, the Yankees had fallen out of first place. He had grieved over the slump of "his champions" in recent days. "I'll be better today," he said. "I'll be able to enjoy the two victories of the Yankees today." Less than an hour later, conscious until the end, he died.

SUNDAY, SEPTEMBER 9, NEW YORK CITY

Miller Huggins did not make clubhouse speeches very often. That just wasn't his style. He had tried so many things to shake up his team this summer, from lineup changes to pitching rotation adjustments, and nothing had worked. Today he would speak to his troops, a group he believed in, a group that had played so much great baseball for him for the past three seasons, at least up until the last sixty days.

"You fellows are standing with your backs against the wall," Huggins began. "Have you got the heart to keep fighting? Have you got the 'guts' to come back for more when you're being licked? That's what I want to know. You've got to show me this afternoon."[13]

No one spoke for what seemed like a long time. Finally, Babe Ruth said, "We can beat the Athletics any old time, and they know it, and act as if they know it. If this pennant depends on licking those birds, we're in already."[14] The Babe's comments were more than wishful thinking. The Athletics were much better than six teams in the league, but not nearly as good as the seventh. The Yankees had already beaten them thirteen times in eighteen meetings this year.[15]

A little bravado would not hurt. As the Philadelphians were taking batting practice that day, the Babe drifted over to the Athletics and bellowed, "Well, how does it feel to be in first place, fellows? Take a good look at it, you bums, because you'll be in second place when the day is over!"[16]

Shocker was gone, but the doubleheader went on. There were contradictory reports as to when his teammates learned of his passing. The account that said they got the news before the games described "a grim intensity" to the Yankees as they took the field.[17]

Both games were tense affairs until the late innings. In the first game, Jack Quinn, who had won eighty-one games for the Yankees in years past, was brilliant early for the Athletics, with five scoreless innings of three-hit ball. Then New York broke through for three runs in the sixth inning. In the eighth, young Jimmie Foxx came to the plate for the A's with the bases loaded and the Yankees up only 3–0. But heroics were not meant to be, not on this day. Foxx struck out to end the threat.[18]

Led by Lou Gehrig's double and triple and George Pipgras's 23rd win of the year, the Yankees prevailed, 5–0. Pipgras later called the game the biggest thrill of his career because "if I had not won it, there might not have been a World's Series for the Yankees that year."[19]

The second game was also tight and low-scoring much of the way. The Athletics led after six innings, 2–1, as the Yankees could manage only one hit. But in the eighth inning, with the game tied at 3–3, Bob Meusel's bases-loaded home run broke a tie, and the Yankees completed the sweep by the score of 7–3. They were back in first place by 1½ games, just as the Babe had predicted. Connie Mack left the dugout very slowly, not because of his age but rather due to his disappointment at having finally reached the top, only to be pushed back.

Joe Williams, perhaps with a bit of hindsight, wrote that the outcome was never in doubt. "At no time did the A's play as if they were confident of winning either game. By contrast, the Yankees, manifesting neither anxiety nor arrogance, just rolled along."[20]

The official attendance was 85,265, the largest crowd ever to witness a Major League game. It broke the old Yankee Stadium mark, set on July 4, 1927, by more than 13,000. Those 13,000 fans did not have seats in the typical sense of the word. They perched on awnings, dangled from steel rafters, and crammed the concrete runways. Ushers relayed offers of five dollars for a seat from standees. Another 5,000 people saw the games from the balconies of nearby apartments.

After the games, the Yankees' clubhouse was filled with singing and cheering. Lou Gehrig told the *New York American*, "If I live to be a hundred, I can never forget this day. . . . Nothing that I can recall brought such thrills."[21] "We broke their hearts today!" shouted Babe Ruth.[22] Then, according to the accounts that the players were not informed of Shocker's death until after the games, they learned the news.[23] Another heart had broken earlier that day: Urban Shocker was dead.

The Yankees beat Lefty Grove in the next game. While the A's salvaged the final game of the series and got within a half-game of first place later that week, they never again caught the Yankees. New York went on to capture their third straight pennant, this one by 2½ games.

They went into the World Series as underdogs to the St. Louis Cardinals, mainly because of shoulder injuries to Earle Combs, Tony Lazzeri, and Herb Pennock.[24] The Yankees swept the Cardinals and extended their postseason streak to eight games. The win was all the sweeter because they shelled Grover Alexander in Game Two.[25] Before the game, Yankees pitcher George Pipgras met with Alexander to pose for pictures. "I put out my hand for him to shake," said Pipgras, "and he reached for it and I swear missed it by a foot, he was so drunk; either that or he had a wicked hangover. He just waved his hand around in the air until we made contact."[26]

Ruth and Gehrig hit a combined seven home runs in the Series and batted .625 and .545, respectively. When they distributed their World Series money, the Yankees gave Rene Shocker five hundred dollars.

Doctors said Shocker had died of an athletic heart. While the primary cause of death was pneumonia, the secondary cause was listed as "calcaneous degeneration of the mitral valve." An autopsy revealed that the valve failure had led to an overworked and enlarged heart, half again as large as a healthy heart. This explained all the symptoms Shocker had fought the last two or three years of his life: shortness of breath, dizziness, fainting spells, even his inability to sleep while lying down. He simply could not pump enough blood through his body.

Rene had feared for the worst the last few days, but still she was not prepared for it. She told reporters it was a broken heart, not an athletic or diseased heart, which took the life of her husband. "He played the game to the last. If the Yankees had not lost the lead of the American League," she said, "he would still be alive. He began to sink Friday when his beloved Yankees, as he called them, dropped two games, and the Philadelphia Athletics won two games. If you put a baseball in his hand, he would believe anything. His love for the game was more powerful than the word of a score of physicians."[27]

50. Urban Shocker began and ended his career as a New York Yankee, the team he called "my Yankees." He was distraught when they traded him away and overjoyed when they reacquired him seven years later. *Private collection of Dennis Goldstein.*

Epilogue

Urban Shocker died on September 9, 1928, one of the most dramatic days in New York Yankees history. That day saw the convergence of two of the greatest baseball dynasties: the 1926–28 New York Yankees and the 1929–31 Philadelphia Athletics. This was an exquisite moment of transition. A great team was holding on for one more championship. Another great team was attempting its first since 1914. The 1927 Yankees won the pennant by nineteen games over the A's. The A's would win the 1929 pennant by eighteen games over the Yankees. In September 1928 the teams were almost even; the pendulum was almost perfectly balanced. The Yankees managed to nudge that pendulum in their favor once again the day that Shocker died.

At his peak in the early 1920s, this complex man was mercurial and moody. He played the game with a swagger, an arrogance born of excellence. He did not have humility in his makeup, and his temper was often roiling just beneath the surface. His indomitable spirit was matched by his physical strength. He was a workhorse. Later in the 1920s, when his physical strength was ebbing, Shocker's spirit became the driving force of his personality.

He came back to his Yankees in 1925. One St. Louis reporter was struck by how "very happy" he was at that time.[1] Shocker told Fred Lieb he was jubilant to be coming "back home."[2] Even as he pitched his first game that season, a brilliant opening day win over the world champion Senators, he was seriously ill. It was reported as a bad cold. George Daley wrote that Shocker had trouble breathing while he was laid up.[3] Was it an early sign of something far more serious?

Upon his return to New York, Shocker was undergoing a transformation. There was a mellowing and sense of contentment. He became a model citizen, and his almost signature temper and flamboyance vanished. He was now a veteran player with a new maturity. It was, after all, his second Yankees stint. He was returning to the team he never wanted to leave. Perhaps there was also his realization that he would not stay in the game forever, and he had a newfound appreciation for this opportunity. There was the poignancy of facing his own mortality. The combination of all these aspects was reflected in his markedly different disposition.

Ironically, without his volatility and irrepressible personality, the New York Shocker became more easily overlooked. When the Yankees released him in the summer of 1928, sportswriter Joe Williams discussed the key elements that create lasting fame for a sports star. While he called Shocker "one of the greatest spitball pitchers of all time," he wrote that Shocker did not have a large amount of "that thing called color." Williams went on, "The colorful ball player—the one with the flair for the spectacular or the unusual—will frequently be rated much higher than his intrinsic values warrant." Williams went on to compare Ruth and Gehrig, and noted that Gehrig, like Shocker, lacked that color. "The Babe was fortunate in that he had color to team with genius. This made the outlines of the picture all the more heroic and majestic."[4]

Williams explained that color made a player more "heroic." Yet was he confusing and mystifying the nature of fame and heroism? Does color denote or earn heroism for a man? Should it? Sportswriter William McGeehan realized this distinction: "In this sporting game more than in any other walk of life, they raise false idols. They make heroes of brutes, they make demigods of inconsequential young men without character or true courage; they make saintly characters out of the vicious."[5]

Courage has to be taken into account: exemplary achievements in adverse situations, done with great risk and at great personal cost. In Shocker's case, as the color receded from view, courage moved to the forefront. Perhaps this is why he can be called a hero.

One of the most intriguing comments about Shocker came in a 1931 article in *Baseball Magazine* on spitball pitchers. The writer referred in passing to "the much misunderstood but inherently gentle Urban Shocker"—just eight words whose meaning is open to conjecture.[6]

During the 1926 season, St. Louis sports editor Sid Keener observed, "I doubt there is another pitcher in the game who studies his batters as carefully as Shocker and gives them just what they don't want. Shocker is my selection for the smartest pitcher I have ever seen."[7] John Sheridan of the *Sporting News* declared during Shocker's magical season of 1927, "I believe Shocker to have had more variety of stuff than any other pitcher I have ever seen."[8]

One New York reporter wrote that Shocker had indeed taken up magic at the end of his career, when he had little of his physical prowess remaining. He made the "baseball stand still, or nearly still, in the air," wrote Will Wedge, "and then wobble to the plate in an eye-popping debutante slouch."[9]

Sabermetrician Mark Wernick has noted that Shocker's sabermetric numbers compare extremely well with those of pitchers in the Baseball Hall of Fame. And Bill James has noted Shocker's remarkable consistency over his career.[10] In a 2007 study, using an advanced analysis, James determined that Shocker was the most consistent pitcher in the history of the game.[11]

Miller Huggins explained that Shocker's acumen did not come easily or naturally.

> One of the greatest students I ever have known is Urban Shocker. He generally was credited by other ball players with being as smart as any man that ever stood in the box, and he was, but I don't think that great knowledge of his came to him overnight. He watched the hitters like a hawk at batting practice and in games, talked over his findings with pitchers on other clubs, and I guess thought about little else from one end of the season to the other. He was the greatest fellow I ever saw for getting the dope on hitters he'd never seen.[12]

Despite his virtuosity as a pitcher, playing and excelling while coping with a deadly illness, and his untimely death, Shocker has been virtually forgotten. He also starred on one of the greatest teams in baseball history. Memory is a funny thing, Damon Runyon wrote: "You never can tell about history, baseball or otherwise. An exploit that seems prodigious at the moment dwindles down to nothing with the passing years; a feat that doesn't seem such-a-much at first hand enlarges to gigantic proportions as time goes on."[13]

Memory of events and people does indeed slip away. In his book *History as an Art of Memory*, Patrick Hutton wrote that "the lived experience of the past can never be directly retrieved. What had been lost was the presence of the past." He went on to observe that history begins where memory ends, the horizon between the known and unknown, or the known and the forgotten. Countless stories have been lost and are awaiting recollection, just beyond that horizon.[14] Shocker's story has been waiting decades for rediscovery.

George Underwood, a New York sportswriter, was uniquely qualified to comment on the effervescence of fame. He was a gold medal winner in track in the third Olympic Games of 1904, held in St. Louis. He wrote a couple of decades later, "Memory is kaleidoscope, fitful, capricious. It leaps from event to event, from year to year, with no order or sequence, showing no partiality to either the insignificant or the important, passing over one thing, snatching at another, storing this and that away for you to sort out as you may, or to have recalled a thing foreign to that which it suggests."[15]

Urban Shocker's fierce love for and mastery of the game of baseball stayed alive through illness and live on well past his death.

Notes

1. PASSING BY AND DRAWN IN

1. Calvary Cemetery is one of the nation's largest burial grounds, with 470 acres and more than 300,000 graves. Shocker's burial followed a funeral ceremony at All Saints Catholic Church in the University City neighborhood of St. Louis, where the Shockers lived.
2. The six pallbearers were Yankees Waite Hoyt, Lou Gehrig, Earle Combs, Gene Robertson, Mike Gazella, and Myles Thomas. Shocker's wife and son are also buried in this family plot.
3. Shocker's funeral took place on Saturday, September 15, 1928. The Yankees were scheduled to play in St. Louis that weekend. Later that day, they lost to the Browns, despite Babe Ruth's 50th home run of the season. Former Yankees pitcher Jack Quinn tossed a shutout against the Cleveland Indians on that day, which drew his Philadelphia Athletics to within a half-game of the first-place Yankees.
4. The graveside prayers were translated from Latin by historian and genealogist Tom Bourke.
5. James Gould, Gould's Gossip, *St. Louis Star*, September 11, 1928.
6. Heydt and I saw Mark McGwire and the Cardinals host Sammy Sosa and the Cubs. Rennie Heydt's obituary appeared in the *St. Louis Post-Dispatch* on March 20, 2000.

2. MIDWEST CONNECTIONS

1. Before I located Urban's Cuyahoga County birth record, I made fruitless searches in the St. Louis Catholic Archdiocese records, assuming Shocker was born into that religion because he is buried in a Catholic cemetery. But my

mistake was assuming Urban was of the same religion as his second wife (who survived him), with whom he is buried in Calvary Cemetery. His parents are buried in the nondenominational Brooklyn Heights Cemetery in Cleveland.

2. In the 1910 census, the spelling is slightly different, "Schockor." In the 1920 census, William's family name returns to "Shockcor." And on his 1920 marriage license, Urban listed his father's last name as "Schockcor."
3. Alsace-Lorraine was part of France until 1871. From the end of the Franco-Prussian War (1871) to the end of World War I (1918), it was part of Germany. After 1918, it was returned to France.
4. The Shocker genealogical research was done by historian and genealogist Tom Bourke.
5. John B. Sheridan, "Players Never Old," *Sporting News*, November 11, 1915.
6. I furnished the documentation to SABR's Biographical Research Committee, which formally made the correction to Shocker's baseball entry and announced the change in its July-August 2005 newsletter. There has also been some confusion about Shocker's actual birthday (month and day). This is probably a result of confusion he created in his own mind by using different years. November 22 occasionally shows up, as does September 20.
7. The 1900 federal census is the only one that, in addition to age, lists month and year of birth.
8. Brookside Park drew enormous crowds for semipro games. A Google search for "baseball at Brookside Park, Cleveland" brings up numerous articles, including photos of a 1915 semipro championship game that drew an estimated 115,000 spectators.
9. Will Wedge, Games, Gossip, and Guff, *New York Sun*, February 23, 1928.
10. Cora, born in 1882, and her husband, Fred Nieman, are already listed in the 1910 Detroit census. They later moved to Sylvan Lake, a Detroit suburb.
11. Shocker shows up in the Detroit directory from 1909 to 1917, except in 1914. His name is listed as "Urban" or "Urban J.," except in 1911, when he appears as "Herb," and 1917 is the first year his profession is listed as "ballplayer."
12. "Yankees Pound Gaston in Eighth," *St. Louis Post-Dispatch*, August 30, 1925.
13. See, for example, Will Wedge, "Shocker a Big Yank Asset," *New York Sun*, May 18, 1926. "Care and caution and craftsmanship are Shocker's mottoes. He learned the value of slow and precise work when he was a toolmaker in a twist drill factory in Cleveland during his days as a sandlotter."

3. SANDLOTS AND LOVE OF THE GAME

1. McKenna, "Logan Squares," SABR BioProject, sabr.org/bioproject.

2. The Tigers lost all three World Series, two to the Chicago Cubs (1907, 1908) and one to the Pittsburgh Pirates (1909).
3. Among these ballplayers were Shocker's future teammates on the Yankees, Wally Pipp and Frank Gilhooley, as well as Johnny Lavan, Johnny Mitchell, Elmer Smith, and Frank Snyder.
4. There are brief references to Shocker's 1911 and 1912 playing in the *Reach Guides* of 1912 and 1913, as well as on his Hall of Fame contract card. The Detroit newspapers had good coverage of these games. One account says he started out with Ypsilanti of the Trolley League. *Philadelphia Bulletin*, September 10, 1928.
5. *Windsor Evening Record*, June 14, 1911. This issue of the paper may have had the first published photo of Shocker. Windsor was not a professional team until 1912, when the Border League was formed.
6. *Windsor Evening Record*, July 11, 1911. Bay City released Shocker when their catcher had recovered from injuries, and Shocker returned to Windsor.
7. "Shocker Is Fined $100," *Windsor Evening Record*, July 3, 1912. His Hall of Fame contract card confirms the suspension. He was rumored to be pitching for Marquette of the Upper Peninsula at the time.
8. *Windsor Evening Record*, August 8, 1913.
9. Schmitz & Schroder was a Detroit department store that fielded a top semipro team. For accounts of the games, see the *Detroit Free Press*, September 29, October 6, and October 13, 1913. See also "Pitching Ace of Browns Started In as Catcher, *Boston Daily Globe*, May 11, 1924, and "Shocker Started Baseball Career behind the Plate," *St. Louis Star*, April 4, 1923.
10. Frank G. Menke, "Busted Finger Back in 1913 Made Shocker Decide to Be Pitcher," *Birmingham News*, February 7, 1924.
11. Lane, "Urban Shocker, One of the Great Pitchers of 1920," 381.

4. AN EMERGING STAR IN THE MINORS

1. *Ottawa Citizen*, April 28, 1914. Ypsilanti tried to claim Shocker, and John Farrell, the secretary of Minor League baseball's governing body, the National Association, ruled against them. *Ottawa Citizen*, May 8, 1914.
2. Indoor baseball was popular in the winter in the early twentieth century. Under George Hancock's 1887 rules, bases were 27 feet apart, though that could vary, based on the size of the facility. The pitcher threw only underhand, 23 feet from the plate. The bat was no more than 30 inches long. Patrick Mallory, "The Game They All Played," 109.
3. *Sporting Life*, May 2, 1914, listed Minor League rosters. Shocker's contract

card at the Baseball Hall of Fame Library and Archives shows his May 9 release by Fort Wayne.

4. The Canadian League had been a Class C league the prior year. Windsor's 1913 Border League, by comparison, had been a Class D league, the lowest level of professional league. Shaughnessy later was the president of the International League, from 1936 to 1960. See Bevis, "Frank 'Shag' Shaughnessy," SABR BioProject, sabr.org/bioproject.
5. "Senators to Have Pick of the Detroit Spare Recruits," *Ottawa Journal*, February 23, 1914. Claude Varnell owned the Fort Wayne club.
6. *Ottawa Journal*, April 23 and May 5, 1914.
7. *Ottawa Citizen*, May 17 and May 20, 1914.
8. *Ottawa Citizen*, May 13, 1914.
9. *Ottawa Citizen*, April 24, 1914.
10. Frank Graham, *New York Sun*, July 6, 1928.
11. Some spitball pitchers chewed on the bark of the slippery elm tree to generate more saliva.
12. Joe King and Cy Kritzer, "The Frank Shaughnessy Story," *Sporting News*, December 14, 1960.
13. *Ottawa Citizen*, September 10, 1914.
14. *Ottawa Citizen*, August 21, 1914.
15. *Ottawa Journal*, October 6, 1914.
16. The game was reported in the *Ann Arbor Times* and the *Detroit Free Press*, September 17, 1914.
17. Ty Cobb, On and Off the Field with Ty Cobb, *Detroit Free Press*, September 27, 1914. He wrote that Shocker had struck out twenty-two men. Other accounts said twenty-three.
18. In the 1910s, many stars had columns ghost-written by reporters under their names. But Cobb had the personality that wanted control of content that appeared under his name. If he did not write the column himself, he was involved to some extent. Both of Cobb's biographers, Charles Leerhsen and Tim Hornbaker, expressed this opinion in e-mails dated February 9 and February 15, 2016, respectively.
19. *Detroit Free Press*, October 6, 1914. Siever, who led the American League in earned run average in 1902, had won eighteen games for the 1907 Tigers. He died at the age of forty-four in 1920.
20. An account of the game is available at http://articles.petoskeynews.com/2013-08-23/detroit-tigers_41442215. The Tigers' George Moriarty, who later became an American League umpire, wrote about this game years later.

He noted that Shocker had thrown the spitter repeatedly, but later "wisely learned to cut the damp fling to a minimum." With George Moriarty, *Uniontown* [PA] *Morning Herald*, October 6. 1926.

21. "Manager Shaughnessy Claims Fort Wayne Has No Claim," *Ottawa Journal*, April 15, 1915.
22. *Detroit Free Press*, August 15, 1915.
23. David McDonald, "The First Diamond Dynasty," *Ottawa Citizen*, May 4, 2013.
24. Latest News, Telegraph, *Sporting Life*, September 11, 1915.
25. *Detroit Free* Press, September 30, 1915, and *Sporting Life*, October 29, 1915. The weekly incorrectly stated that the game took place in Medford.
26. Pertinent Comment on Sportdom Happenings, *Ottawa Journal*, September 2, 1915. Gilks also would sign Muddy Ruel and Aaron Ward for the Yankees. Ford C. Frick, Frick's Comments, *New York Evening Journal*, March 11, 1925.
27. *Ottawa Citizen*, September 20, 1915. The contract was approved by American League president Ban Johnson on October 18. This document was sold in the Robert Edwards Auction of May 3, 2008.
28. *Ottawa Citizen*, May 13, 1914.
29. After finishing far out of first place from 1910 to 1914 (they came closest in 1911, when they were 13½ games out), the Tigers fell just 2½ short of the Boston Red Sox and the 1915 pennant. They are one of the few teams in baseball history that won 100 games and did not make the postseason.
30. "If Mr. Jennings Could Develop One More Pitcher, He'd Be Happy," *Detroit Journal*, April 7, 1915.
31. E-mail from Peter Morris, August 1, 2002.
32. *Ottawa Journal*, April 28, 1914. Historians David McDonald and Peter Morris provided specifics on the confusing path of Shocker to and from Ottawa, in e-mails dated September 9, 2002 and August 1, 2002, respectively. They too did not uncover an article on a Shocker tryout with the Tigers.
33. *Detroit Free Press*, August 15, 1915.
34. "I Would Have Pitched My Arm Off to Defeat Tigers," *Detroit Journal*, September 15, 1916. It is unknown when the unnamed Tiger said this.
35. American League News in Nut-Shells, *Sporting Life*, April 4, 1914.
36. "History of League Shows Not More than 6 Capable Spitters, Says Jennings," *Detroit Journal*, March 22, 1915. Jennings actually had two spitball pitchers on his team in this period, Ralph Comstock and Ross Reynolds. They were not very successful.
37. Ray Gillespie, "Star Slabman Wishes Browns Best of Future," *St. Louis Star*, December 18, 1924. Also see David Pietrusza, *Minor Miracles*, 121.

38. *Detroit Journal*, March 22, 1915.
39. E-mail from historian Peter Morris, May 17, 2002. Jennings's first team pitchers: Mathewson, Johnson, Rusie, and Waddell; second team: Alexander, Walsh, Brown, and McGinnity; third team: Young, Donovan, Shocker, and Plank.
40. Jennings, *Rounding Third*. These articles were never published in book form and appeared in newspapers as a syndicated series in 1925. E-mail from historian Peter Morris, March 26, 2003.
41. www.retrosheet.org. The Retrosheet database has selected Pitcher-Batter matchups in its Player database. These are not complete lifetime statistics, as Retrosheet continues to add to its database. There were a number of players who hit Shocker very well, including Al Simmons (.395 batting average), Ray Schalk (.359), Frank Baker (.356), Earl Sheely (.354), Bobby Veach (.341), Lu Blue (341), and Tris Speaker (.337). All had at least 38 at-bats against Shocker.

5. FALSE START

1. Baker and Magee cost the Yankees a total of $60,000; Shawkey was a bargain at $3,000. Baker and Shawkey came from Connie Mack's Philadelphia Athletics, as he continued to dismantle his championship club. Baker had sat out the 1915 season in a dispute with Mack. Magee had been the player-manager of the Brooklyn Federal League club, which folded after the 1915 season.
2. Joe Vila, "Yank Owners to Burn More Money," *Sporting News*, January 6, 1916.
3. "These Rays Give Silver Lining to New York's Cloud," *Sporting News*, June 3, 1915.
4. Harry Schumacher, "Charley Mullen Quits," *New York Globe and Commercial Advertiser*, March 14, 1916.
5. Arthur Mann, *New York Evening World*, July 6, 1928.
6. *New York Evening Journal*, October 21, 1915.
7. "Twenty-Five Yanks to Make Journey," *New York Herald*, March 13, 1916.
8. "Shocker Hurt in Yankee Game," *New York Sun*, March 17, 1916.
9. *Janesville [WI] Daily Gazette*, April 14, 1916. The Yankees had an informal relationship with the Richmond club. Hendryx, Keating, and Angel Aragon all played for both the Yankees and the Climbers that year.
10. *Sporting Life*, April 1, 1916, and *New York Globe and Commercial Advertiser*, April 14, 1916.
11. Bozeman Bulger, "Donovan's $750 Pitcher Brings Better Offers than Tipple," *New York Evening World*, March 30, 1916.

12. Ray Gillespie, *St. Louis Star*, December 18, 1924. The *New York Evening Telegram*, March 29, 1916, had a similar account.
13. "Wily Mack and Lajoie's Bat Beat Donovan's Yanks," *New York Sun*, May 14, 1916. Lajoie's teammate, Harry Davis, was forty-two that year. But he had only one at-bat that season. Lajoie would hit only one more home run in his illustrious career.
14. "All Over but the Shouting, Connie Mack Insists," *New York Evening Mail*, May 31, 1916.
15. Toronto agreed to pay $1,125 of Shocker's $1,350 salary, prorated for the remainder of the season. Jacob Ruppert signed the document on behalf of the Yankees.
16. "Uniform Agreement for Transfer of a Player by or to a Major League Club," May 15, 1916.
17. Cliff Blau, http://cliffblau.ucoz.com/options.htm and http://cliffblau.ucoz.com/waivers.htm.
18. "Shocker Shows Real Championship Calibre," Right Cross, *New York Evening Journal*, August 14, 1916.

6. A MAGICAL SUMMER ON THE ISLAND

1. The island was named after world champion sculler (rower) Ned Hanlan (1855–1908), who settled here in the 1860s. His sister married Toronto businessman Lol Solman.
2. A Canadian author, Jerry Amernic, has written a book around this very story line, *Gift of the Bambino: A Novel.*
3. Murray came out of retirement to play for his childhood friend, Toronto manager and former Major League outfielder Joe Birmingham. Gagnon, "Red Murray," SABR BioProject, sabr.org/bioproject.
4. Levitt, "Paul Krichell," SABR BioProject, sabr.org/bioproject.
5. Tom Flanagan, Flanagan on Current Sport, *Toronto Evening Telegram*, June 8, 1916.
6. Gordon Belyea, "Birmingham at Outs with Toronto Public," *Sporting News*, June 22, 1916.
7. "Leafs Beaten 7–6 in Eleven Innings," *Toronto Globe*, June 23, 1916.
8. "Leafs Advance by Getting Even Break," *Toronto Globe*, July 10, 1916.
9. Don Drysdale of the Los Angeles Dodgers broke Johnson's mark in 1968 with 58 innings in a row, and another Dodger, Orel Hershiser, owns the current record of 59, which he set in 1988. Irvin "Kaiser" Wilhelm tossed 56

straight scoreless innings for Birmingham in 1907, when he won 23 games, a mark that was not commonly known in 1916. Brad Thompson broke that Minor League mark when he tossed 57 consecutive shutout innings for the Tennessee Smokies in 2004.

10. Cullop, who won 22 games the prior year in the Federal League, went down with a 9–1 record and a 1.62 earned run average. He is not to be confused with another Nick Cullop, who played for the Yankees in the 1920s. Gilhooley was lost for the year, Maisel for 10 weeks, and Baker for 6.
11. Harry Schumacher, *New York Globe and Commercial Advertiser*, July 31, 1916.
12. John J. McGraw, "Yankees Not Out of American League Race Yet," *New York Evening World*, August 8, 1916.
13. "If Results Count, Here's the Answer," *Toronto Globe*, July 22, 1916.
14. "Shocker Here until Week from Tuesday," *Toronto Globe*, August 3, 1916.
15. Harry Schumacher, *New York Globe and Commercial Advertiser,* August 4, 1916; "Uniform Agreement for Transfer of a Player by or to a Major League Club," May 15, 1916.
16. Editorial, "An Unwarranted Minor Howl," *Sporting News*, August 3, 1916.
17. "Ruppert Defends Recall of Loans," *Sporting News*, August 10, 1916. On the same day, the Yankees also recalled Angel Aragon from Richmond, where he was hitting .317, and Elmer Miller from Baltimore, where he was hitting .338.
18. "International Has Borrowed Heavily," *Sporting News*, August 17, 1916.
19. Pennock won seven games with a 1.67 earned run average for Buffalo. The Red Sox had the luxury of sending him down and leaving him down. Loaded with pitching talent, they repeated as world champions in 1916.
20. Shocker pitched 185 innings in his twelve weeks with Toronto. There were reports in the New York press during the summer, some as early as mid-June, that Donovan was concerned the Leafs were overworking Shocker. See, e.g., *Toronto Mail and Empire*, June 14, 1916, and "May Recall Shocker," *New York Evening Journal*, July 24, 1916.

7. MOTOR CITY MISCHIEF

1. Frederick G. Lieb, "Shocker Always Had the 'Old Confidence,'" *New York Evening Telegram*, December 19, 1924, and Cutting the Plate, *New York Evening Post*, July 7, 1928.
2. Steinberg, "Ray Caldwell," SABR BioProject, sabr.org/bioproject.
3. Schumacher, "Caldwell Must Fight for His Job This Year," *New York Globe and Commercial Advertiser*, January 25, 1917.

4. Joe Vila, "Gotham Prepares to Claim Dodgers," *Sporting News*, August 10, 1916.
5. *Sporting Life*, September 12, 1914. Caldwell then jumped to the Federal League but returned to the Yankees in early 1915, after Ruppert and Huston bought the club. One joke was that Caldwell returned because the team was now owned by a beer magnate who would supply Caldwell with an unlimited supply of beer.
6. The Yankees had shared the Polo Grounds with the New York Giants, who were their landlords, since 1913.
7. Shocker was pulled for a pinch hitter, with the Yankees down, 1–0. He took the loss; the final score was 2–0. He held Nap Lajoie hitless.
8. Right Cross, "Shocker Shows Real Championship Calibre," *New York Evening Journal*, August 14, 1916.
9. "Mullen Hit Ends Long, Bitter Fray," *New York Times*, August 19, 1916.
10. *New York Globe and Commercial Advertiser*, August 19, 1916.
11. "Shocker Foils Foul Plot," *New York Times*, September 15, 1916. Frank Merriwell was the lead character in Gilbert Patten's adventure and sports novels. He was a heroic figure who overcame adversity and solved mysteries.
12. "Shocker Baffles Tigers, Who Lose Chance to Climb," *New York Tribune*," September 15, 1916. Donovan's Yankees executed the play successfully a number of times in 1916 and 1917.
13. Wilcox, "Looking 'em Over," *Detroit Times*, September 15, 1916.
14. "Shocker Trips Up Speeding Tigers," *New York Evening Journal*, September 15, 1916.
15. "'I Would Have Pitched My Arm Off to Defeat the Tigers,' Says Shocker," *Detroit Journal*, October 15, 1916.
16. *Ottawa Citizen*, May 13, 1914.
17. H. G. Salsinger, "Burns' Case: It Proves Where Hugh Jennings Is Lacking as Manager," *Sporting News*, July 4, 1918.
18. H. G. Salsinger, "Salsinger Has Idea That Is All His Own," *Sporting News*, October 5, 1916.

8. THE RETURNED PRODIGAL AND THE COMING PHENOM

1. Tom Thorp, "Yankees Finish Season in Fourth Place," *New York Evening Journal*, October 5, 1916.
2. Obituary, "Ray Caldwell," *Sporting News*, September 2, 1967. Reports surfaced about a sensational American pitcher in Panama named Collins. Visitors to Panama confirmed it was Caldwell.

3. Frank L. Chance, "Caldwell Erased $100 Fine Quickly," *New York Times*, July 27, 1915. Chance did have a specific Caldwell story in this article.
4. "Caldwell Already in Mid-Season Form," *New York Evening Journal*, March 6, 1917.
5. "Frosty Welcome Ready for Caldwell at Macon," *New York Sun*, March 2, 1917.
6. William Hennigan, "Pitcher Unafraid Comes Back to the Yankees," *New York World*, December 21, 1924.
7. Obituary, "Ray Caldwell," *Sporting News*, September 2, 1967.
8. Harry Schumacher, "Bill Donovan Has More High-Grade Pitchers Than He Knows What to Do With," *New York Globe and Commercial Advertiser*, March 23, 1917.
9. Shocker's salary data comes from his transaction card at the Baseball Hall of Fame in Cooperstown.
10. Harry Schumacher, *New York Globe and Commercial Advertiser*, April 14, 1917.
11. Damon Runyon, *New York American*, March 9, 1917.
12. "Hit Famine Proves Fatal to Yankees," *New York Times*, May 4, 1917.
13. *New York Evening Telegram*, July 1, 1917.
14. Harry Schumacher, "Bill Donovan Has More High-Grade Pitchers Than He Knows What to Do With," *New York Globe and Commercial Advertiser*, March 23, 1917.
15. Walter Trumbull, *New York World*, April 19, 1917. The final score was 7–5, but three New York errors led to four unearned runs. Shocker gave up only four hits in the complete-game win.
16. "Sensational Rally by Indians Beats Yanks," *New York World*, May 31, 1917.
17. Bohn, "Rube Schauer," SABR BioProject, sabr.org/bioproject. In 1913 Schauer had been a Minor League sensation, as Shocker had been in 1916. But the former had not yet been drafted, and an intense bidding war ensued and was won by John McGraw and the Giants.
18. "Love and Cullop in Poor Form," *New York American*, July 1, 1917.
19. Joe Vila, "Issue Narrows to Scribe and McGraw," *Sporting News*, July 5, 1917.
20. *New York World*, July 11, 1917.
21. The Yankees sent struggling outfielder Lee Magee to the Browns for Marsans, who became the second Cuban on the team, joining Angel Aragon.
22. Harry Schumacher, "Marsans a Welcome Addition to Yankees," *New York Globe and Commercial Advertiser*, July 16, 1917.
23. *Sporting News*, July 12, 1917, and *New York Globe and Commercial Advertiser*, July 6, 1917. The latter said Shocker had a similar injury in the Minors. It

was later determined that the arm was not broken. In 1933, Red Sox pitcher George Pipgras, a Yankee star in the late 1920s, broke his arm when throwing a curve ball. Liepa, "George Pipgras," SABR BioProject, sabr.org/bioproject.

24. The shine ball was smoother on one side than the other, usually accomplished by the pitcher's rubbing one side of the ball repeatedly against his trousers. This contrast between the finishes on the two sides of the ball has a real—and unpredictable—effect on the flight of the ball.
25. "'Shine Ball a Myth,' White Sox Claim," *New York Times*, September 26, 1917. Even the New York Giants, who would face Cicotte in the 1917 World Series, said it was nothing but a fastball. *New York Globe and Commercial Advertiser*, September 14, 1917.
26. *New York Globe and Commercial Advertiser*, May 16, 1917.
27. Walter Trumbull, *New York World*, August 4, 1917.
28. "Donovan Will Make Many Changes in Yankees Next Season," *New York Evening Journal*, September 17, 1917.
29. *Morning Oregonian*, January 29, 1918.
30. Husman, "Toledo's Flash," 4. Gilhooley's Major League career ended in 1919, and he then went on to a decade-long career as a star in the International League for five different teams.
31. On September 24, for example, Dan Daniel reported in the *New York Sun* that Donovan was done and that Huggins admitted he had been offered the job. The Yankees finished in sixth place, 11 games under .500 and 28½ games out of first place, similar to where they stood in 1914, when Ruppert and Huston bought the club.
32. George Daley, Comment on Sports, *New York World*, October 29, 1917.
33. *Lethbridge [Alberta] Daily Herald*, February 9, 1916.

9. THE DREAM TEAM

1. The All-Stars were heavily weighted to the American League because the National League teams were playing out west at the time. Edd Roush and Benny Kauff were going to play, but the former rushed to the bedside of his dying father and the latter had been injured that week. Rabbit Maranville was the only National Leaguer in the game.
2. Bevis, "Tim Murnane," SABR BioProject, sabr.org/bioproject. The game was organized by the American League and the Baseball Writers Association of America, in conjunction with the Red Sox.
3. Bob Shawkey was also reported to attend as an All-Star, but he did not appear in either the photo or the game.

4. Some reports said Alexander was injured. Actually, he was again closing in on a third straight season of 30 wins and did not want to miss a start. He won his 27th game on the day of this benefit game and won 3 more, to reach the milestone.
5. Caldwell missed the last three weeks of the season. In his last game, on September 12, he gave up seven earned runs. Despite all his problems in 1917, he finished with 13 wins and an earned run average of 2.86, only slightly higher than the league average.
6. "17,000 Out to Honor Murnane," *Boston Daily Globe*, September 28, 1917.
7. For more on the game, see Zerby, "September 27, 1917," SABR Baseball Games Project, sabr.org/gamesproj.

10. THE FIRST TRADE

1. Cullop won only 5 of 14 decisions in 1917. Maisel, who had led the American League in stolen bases in 1914 with 74, barely hit above .200 in 1916 and 1917 combined. The Yankees also sent the Browns $15,000 cash.
2. Pratt had averaged 29 stolen bases and almost 30 doubles in his six seasons. In 1916, he led the American League in runs batted in.
3. Frank Graham, *The New York Yankees*, 103–4.
4. Frank O'Neill, "Yankees Score over Shocker," *New York Sun*, August 7, 1923. It is not known if Donovan and Huggins conferred during the transition.
5. Harry Schumacher, "Huggins Got None the Worst of Trade," *New York Globe and Commercial Advertiser*, January 23, 1918.
6. Joe Vila, "Vila Calls Yankee Discards Useless," *Sporting News*, January 31, 1918.
7. Sid Mercer, All in a Day's Work, *New York Globe and Commercial Advertiser*, January 24, 1918.
8. Dan Daniel, High Lights and Shadows in All Spheres of Sport, *New York Sun*, January 23, 1918.
9. L. L. Arms, *New York Tribune*, January 24, 1918. The Great White Way referred to the theater district on Broadway, with all the theater lights.
10. Til Huston was in France with the Allied war effort, and Ruppert took an active role in the team's operation before Huggins arrived. See Steinberg and Spatz, *The Colonel and Hug*, 78, 87–88.
11. Jacob Ruppert, "Building a Winning Club in New York," 204.
12. "Ruppert Defends Huggins's Trade," *New York Sun*, January 24, 1918.
13. "If He Can't Fix 'em, He Trades 'em Off," *Sporting News*, February 21, 1918. After Ball accused Pratt and teammate Johnny Lavan of "laying down,"

not giving their best, they responded with a $50,000 slander lawsuit. Ball felt he was giving up little in Pratt, whom he could no longer tolerate. See Steinberg, "Del Pratt," SABR BioProject, sabr.org/bioproject.

14. Joe Vila, Setting the Pace, *New York Evening Sun*, October 27 and December 22, 1918.
15. Frederick G. Lieb, "Huggins Will Stay with Yanks Indefinitely," *New York Evening Telegram*, December 26, 1924. Pratt was exempt from the draft because of his family.
16. Frederick G. Lieb, "Pratt and Plank Traded to Yanks," *New York Sun*, January 23, 1918. In his final two seasons with the Browns, Plank had earned run averages of 2.33 and 1.79.
17. Frederick G. Lieb, "Plank Declines to Sign with Yankees," *New York Sun*, February 12, 1919. Huggins would try to lure Plank back with an attractive contract again a year later, unsuccessfully. His auto and garage business was doing well.
18. *St. Louis Globe-Democrat*, February 16, 1918.
19. Sid C. Keener, "Browns Trade Pratt and Plank to Yankees," *St. Louis Times*, January 22, 1918.
20. Frederick G. Lieb, "Half Century of High and Low Points in the Game Recalled by Bob Quinn," *Sporting News*, December 6, 1945. This does not explain what Quinn would have done had Ray Fisher not entered the army. And there is an intriguing February 16, 1918, *St. Louis Globe-Democrat* report that said Quinn was going to send Shocker to George Stallings's Boston Braves, but four AL teams refused to let Shocker pass out of the league on waivers.
21. Monitor, "Shocker Yanks Yanks Out of First Place," *New York World*, June 16, 1919.
22. "Tad Wises Up Fans on How Giants Put Crusher on Huggins' Crew," *New York Evening Journal*, October 10, 1921.
23. Frederick G. Lieb, "Browns Have All the Fun at Yankees' Flag-Raising Party," *New York Evening Telegram*, May 15, 1924.
24. Damon Runyon, "Shocker Tightens in Pinches," *New York American*, May 23, 1920.

11. LOVE AND WAR AND A LITTLE BASEBALL

1. Though Minerva was only twenty-six years old, one report on the marriage stated that she had retired from the stage "several years ago." "Urban Shocker Is Married on Eve of Training Trip," *Detroit Free Press*, March 2, 1918.
2. The Michigan Marriage Index states that Minerva C. Davenport (formerly

Thomas) was born in 1892. Shocker listed his age accurately as twenty-seven on the document.

3. The first draft of June 5, 1917, did not take substantial numbers of men, but the second draft, June 5, 1918, did. By June 1918, two hundred thousand American soldiers were alighting in France each day, numbers that would ultimately help the Allies prevail.
4. *Wilkes-Barre* [PA] *Times-Leader*, January 8, 1918. Whether his subsequent marriage added to his exemption is not clear. At some point during 1918, a young adult male could not avoid the draft by marrying.
5. "Browns May Lose Shocker, Called by Draft Board," *St. Louis Post-Dispatch*, March 20, 1918.
6. "Four Browns Are in Class 1-A of Selective Draft," *St. Louis Post-Dispatch*, March 14, 1918.
7. The Yankees, by comparison, had finished second in 1910 and fourth in 1916.
8. In the late nineteenth and early twentieth centuries, before the introduction of household refrigerators and freezers, ice was manufactured in plants.
9. Dick Farrington, "Phil Ball, Whose Ambition Was Pennant, Dies," *Sporting News*, October 26, 1933.
10. Steinberg, *Baseball in St. Louis*, 79.
11. Ball moved Rickey into a front-office position, and Rickey departed a year later when he became the president of the National League's St. Louis Cardinals.
12. Larson, "Fielder Jones," SABR BioProject, sabr.org/bioproject.
13. His 1915 Terriers finished with an 87-67 record, just .001 behind the pennant-winning Pittsburgh Rebels, who had an 86-66 record. This remains the closest pennant race ever, driven by the fact that the teams did not play the same number of games.
14. Monitor (pen name of George Daley), "Ball Orders Jones to Use 'Iron Fist,'" *New York World*, January 31, 1918.
15. "Four Browns Are in Class 1-A of Selective Draft," *St. Louis Post-Dispatch*, March 14, 1918.
16. "'Shocker's Up-Curve Is a Rarity,' Says Fielder Jones," *New York Sun*, April 4, 1918. Orth won 204 games for three teams from 1895 to 1909 and won a league-high 27 games for the 1906 Yankees.
17. In a January 9, 2006, e-mail, former Major League pitcher Dave Baldwin wrote that the only way a pitcher can make a ball break upward is with a submarine delivery. If Shocker used such a delivery at times, it was not mentioned in the countless accounts I have seen.

18. Sam Crane, "Yankees' Poor Work on Bases Costs Victory," *New York Evening Journal*, May 17, 1918.
19. W. S. Farnsworth, "Caldwell's Ambition to Win 30 Games in 1918," New *York American*, March 20, 1918.
20. Damon Runyon, The Mornin's Mornin', *New York American*, May 6, 1918.
21. George Daley, Comment on Sports, *New York World*, July 15, 1918.
22. Jim Corbett, In Corbett's Corner, *New York American*, July 24, 1918. Dunn not only managed but also owned the Baltimore Orioles of the International League.
23. Shocker struck out Ruth his other time at bat. The run Shocker gave up was unearned. Austin ran the club for 16 games. Then coach Jimmy Burke took over for the balance of the 1918 season.
24. Larson, "Fielder Jones," SABR BioProject, sabr.org/bioproject. McGraw had died less than a month earlier.
25. *Infantry Journal*, 85th Division, U.S. Infantry Association, Washington DC, July 1926. The 85th sailed to Liverpool and then on to France.
26. J. G. Taylor Spink, Three and One, *Sporting News*, April 30, 1942.
27. Live Tips and Topics, *Boston Daily Globe*, October 23, 1926.
28. "Shocker's Narrow Escape," *Louisville Courier-Journal*, May 26, 1919.
29. The fire, at the National Personnel Record Center, destroyed most army records of 1912–60.
30. Spatz, "Dan Parker," *Dictionary of Literary Biography*, 241.
31. Major League Notes, *Sporting News*, April 3, 1919. The *Leviathan* was a German boat (*Vaterland*) that was in an American port when the United States declared war on Germany and then seized the ship for transport during the war.
32. Barry, *The Great Influenza*, 304, 306.
33. Some of Shocker's military information contained herein was gleaned from his wife's 1931 application for benefits, which paperwork was not destroyed in the 1973 fire.
34. Ancestry.com has a file of Michigan divorces.
35. "Ball Player Must Pay Back Alimony," *Detroit Free Press*, July 22, 1919. Shocker owed back alimony, which he agreed to pay at this hearing. In return and on condition he would pay it in a timely manner, it was reduced from $50 a month to only $25 a month.

12. A SUMMER TO REMEMBER

1. In that period, Shocker pitched 62 innings and posted a 6-2 record. He had already beaten New York earlier in the season. The Browns agreed to pay

him $525 a month, which was close to his 1918 contract of $2,400. Of course when he joined the army, he was not paid that full 1918 salary.

2. George B. Underwood, "Shocker Baffles Old Teammates," *New York Sun*, June 16, 1919.
3. Monitor, "Shocker Yanks Yanks Out of First Place," *New York World*, June 16, 1919.
4. "Shocker Avenges Exile by Yankees," *St. Louis Times*, June 16, 1919.
5. Monitor, "Shocker Yanks Yanks Out of First Place." Baker was a very hard man to strike out. He whiffed only 18 times in 623 plate appearances in 1919.
6. George B. Underwood, "Shocker Baffles Old Teammates," *New York Sun*, June 16, 1919.
7. Lane, "Urban Shocker, One of the Great Pitchers of 1920," 381.
8. Harry Schumacher, *New York Globe and Commercial Advertiser*, April 14, 1917.
9. George Moriarty, "Shocker Is Rated with Ed Walsh," *American Newspaper Alliance*, undated column in the Bill Loughman Shocker clippings. Moriarty's last season as a regular player was 1914. He was an American League umpire for more than twenty years.
10. Damon Runyon, "Shocker Kalsomines Yanks," *New York American*, June 16, 1919. Whether Shocker moderated his use of saliva in later years is not known. There really were few in-depth descriptions of the spitballs that were thrown. But in 1927, one of his catchers, Johnny Grabowski, said that Shocker's spitter was easy to catch because it was dry. *New York Sun*, June 2, 1927. Is it possible his catcher was also confusing his spitter with his slow ball? Or might Shocker have changed the preparation of his spitter?
11. Harry Schumacher, *New York Globe and Commercial Advertiser*, April 14, 1917.
12. Burke is the answer to the trivia question Who, besides Branch Rickey and Rogers Hornsby, has managed both of St. Louis's teams, the Cards and the Browns?
13. Fred Lieb, Cutting the Plate, *New York Evening Post*, undated article in the Sporting News archives.
14. Sam Crane, unsourced 1913 article in the Jacobson file, National Baseball Hall of Fame Library and Archives.
15. John B. Sheridan, "Four Reassuring Words," *Sporting News*, October 16, 1919.
16. Ruth was still pitching in 1919. He started 15 games and completed 12 of them, on his way to a 9-5 record. It was the last season he pitched more than a couple of games.
17. Mercer, "The Supreme Value of 'Color' in Baseball," and Lieb, "What 'Color' Means to a Ball Player."

18. Huhn, *The Sizzler*, 135.
19. Mays led the American League in hit batsmen in 1917 and was among the leaders in 1918 and 1919. Ironically, in this game, it was Shocker and not Mays who hit a batter.
20. Spatz and Steinberg, *1921*, 87–88.
21. The sixth-place Red Sox would soon give up on Caldwell, too. They released him on August 4.
22. At this point in the season, Ruth already had hit 16 home runs. He would hit 3 more in the next week. Shocker's third-inning showdown with Ruth came with the Browns ahead, 6–1.
23. *St. Louis Post-Dispatch*, August 13, 1919.
24. Lane, "Urban Shocker, One of the Great Pitchers of 1920," 381.
25. Sid C. Keener, "Urb Shocker Blanks the Yankees," *St. Louis Times*, July 17, 1919.
26. "Burke Explains Why He Expects Team to Crowd Leaders," *St. Louis Post-Dispatch*, March 30, 1920.
27. Only two games separated the second-place Tigers and the fifth-place Browns, and the latter were only 7½ games out of first. The Cleveland Indians were also in that mix. The Yankees would finish in third place, just 7½ games back, while the Browns faded badly, finishing 20 games out.
28. Mays had walked out on his team, and league president Ban Johnson did not want players to force trades by such action. The Yankees sent two pitchers to Boston in the trade, but it seemed fairly one-sided, since Mays was one of the game's best pitchers.
29. Steinberg and Spatz, *The Colonel and Hug*, 110–14.
30. John E. Wray, Wray's Column, *St. Louis Post-Dispatch*, August 8, 1919.
31. "Sisler Wins Three-Round Argument but Mays Wins Game," *St. Louis Post-Dispatch*," August 23, 1919.
32. Mays had a reputation for throwing the bean ball, but not for defacing the ball.
33. Mays was an excellent hitter, with a career batting average of .268 and 111 runs batted in.
34. H. R. Hoefer, "Durable Dave Davenport," 36.
35. W. A. Phelon, "When the Big Clubs Strike Their Stride," 206.
36. One report said Shocker wrenched a ligament under his right shoulder. "Crippled Browns Open Series with Griffith Gang Today," *St. Louis Star*, September 16, 1919.
37. Caldwell's career was resuscitated by the nurturing of the Indians' player-manager, Tris Speaker, who signed him late in the 1919 season. He won

twenty games in 1920, as the Indians won the world championship. See Steinberg. "Ray Caldwell," SABR BioProject, sabr.org/bioproject.

38. "Davenport Suspended for Season after Club-House Row with Burke and Quinn," *St. Louis Times*, September 4, 1919.
39. Scribbled by Scribes, *Sporting News*, February 5, 1920. Fulton, "the Minnesota plasterer," was a fearsome puncher who knocked down world champion Jess Willard in an exhibition match. Jack Dempsey knocked Fulton out in less than 20 seconds of the first round in 1918, a year before he became the heavyweight champion.
40. *St. Louis Star*, "Double-Header in Boston Is Off on Account of Rain," September 10, 1919.
41. *Sporting News*, September 18 and October 9, 1919.
42. The word "tumor" may have had a different medical meaning a hundred years ago. Perhaps it was a cyst. And a ligament injury is not healed by removing anything. Doc Lavan is the same Johnny Lavan who played for the Browns and sued their owner for defamation, along with Del Pratt. He was traded to Washington a month before Shocker came to the Browns. He served as a surgeon in World War I.
43. "Cards Save Effort until It's Too Late," *Sporting News*, September 11, 1919. St. Louis's Grand and Olive district was the city's theater district and also home to many bars.

13. THE END OF AN ERA

1. Irving Sanborn, "Consider the Pitcher," 47.
2. John B. Foster, "Editorial Comment," *Spalding's Official Baseball Guide, 1909*, 35.
3. W. A. Phelon, *Spalding's Official Baseball Guide, 1909*, 47. A decade later, the nation had just suffered from the deadly influenza epidemic, which reminded people of the unsanitary aspect of a ball covered with spit.
4. Shocker, Stan Coveleski, Red Faber, Burleigh Grimes, and Jack Quinn were the best.
5. As Sunday baseball became legalized in more cities (in 1919 in New York City), the working class could attend games on their one day off. They could understand a home run more easily than a walk, stolen base, and sacrifice to score a run.
6. F. C. Lane, "Should the Spitball Be Abolished?" 70.
7. The owners had far more information about the 1919 Series than the fans had. They had looked the other way far too often, whether the issue was

gambling or illegal pitches. It was time for bold and dramatic action. Also, the popularity resulting from an increase in hitting could offset any possible fallout from scandal.

8. Irving Sanborn, "Consider the Pitcher," 475. If a gambler could bribe a starting pitcher, he could likely fix the game. In the 1919 World Series, White Sox pitchers Eddie Cicotte and Lefty Williams confirmed such fears.
9. The debate over the new rules found some surprising positions. Miller Huggins, the Yankees' manager, favored keeping freak pitches, even though his career as a player consisted of trying to gain an edge on the pitcher whenever possible. *Atlanta Constitution*, January 18, 1920. John McGraw of the New York Giants favored the ban, even though he had spitballer Phil Douglas on his team. *New York Herald*, January 15, 1921.
10. Had the spitter not been banned, any time a pitcher threw a freak pitch, he could have claimed the erratic flight of the ball was caused by a legal pitch, the spitter. Roger Peckinpaugh, who spanned both eras, explained this to Donald Honig in an interview. Honig, *The Man in the Dugout*, 216–18.
11. F. C. Lane, "Should the Spitball Be Abolished?" 68.
12. "Umpires Criticize Mays," *New York Times*, August 19, 1920.
13. F. C. Lane, "The Much Discussed Menace of the Lively Ball," 505. For a discussion of how much livelier the ball was in the 1920s, see Spatz and Steinberg, *1921*, 37–38.
14. Ford Frick, "Yankee Ballads," *New York Evening Journal*, March 16, 1927. Frick went on to become the president of the National League (1934–51) and then the commissioner of baseball (1951–65). In the late 1950s and early 1960s, Frick fought a losing battle to legalize the spitter. He wanted to provide pitchers with an additional weapon to reduce the number of home runs. A big fan of Babe Ruth, Frick was not thrilled when Roger Maris broke the Babe's single-season record in 1961. Dan Daniel, "Strong Support behind Clamor for Spitter," *Sporting News*, November 22, 1961.
15. Babe Ruth, "Babe Ruth Tells in His Own Book of Baseball," *New York World*, January 8, 1929.
16. Eller, "Why the New Pitching Rules Are Unjust," 433. Eller won 35 games in 1918–19, with the help of the shine ball. After winning 13 more in 1920, at age twenty-five, his career was finished. He won only two more games.
17. Billy Evans, "Spitter Saves Many," *St. Louis Post-Dispatch*, January 22, 1921.
18. Sid C. Keener, "Browns' Spitball Hurlers Use More Speed and Wider Curve with Ban on Freak Shoots," *St. Louis Times*, March 4, 1920.

14. CHALLENGING THE GREAT ONE

1. Walter Trumbull, "Schang's Homer in Ninth Beats Yanks," *New York World*, April 26, 1917.
2. Hyatt Daab, Timely News and Views in the Field of Sport, *New York Evening Telegram*, June 3, 1920.
3. *New York Globe and Commercial Advertiser*, June 3, 1920.
4. The eastern teams did not meet the western teams until mid-May, their first long road trips.
5. Monitor, "Shocker Gets More Revenge on Yanks," *New York World*, May 25, 1920.
6. Ed Rumill, "Quinn, Nearing 75, Recalls His Thrills in Game," *Sporting News*, February 8, 1945.
7. Sportsman's Park could handle a crowd of 27,526 only by placing several thousand fans on the outfield grass, behind ropes. While that series was going on, the Browns made the decision to rent their ballpark to the St. Louis Cardinals of the National League. The Cards' ballpark was a small, decrepit facility, and the move allowed their president, Branch Rickey, to sell the property for enough money to climb out of debt and start his farm system.
8. Arthur Robinson, "Record Crowds See Yankees Halt Browns," *Sporting News*, June 21, 1920.
9. Babe Ruth, "Off to Real Start Now, Says Ruth," *New York American*, April 21, 1921.
10. "Babe Ruth Drives Ball over Fence—in Practice," *St. Louis Post-Dispatch*, June 21, 1920.
11. Greene, "George Sisler, Picture Player," 50.
12. *New York Sun*, June 24, 1920.
13. Harry F. Pierce, *St. Louis Star*, August 19, 1920.
14. Sam Murphy, Sports Editor's Say So, *New York Evening Mail*, July 14, 1920.
15. *New York Times* and *St. Louis Globe-Democrat*, August 8, 1919.
16. Frederick G. Lieb, "Carl Mays, in Yankee Debut, Beats St. Louis," *New York Sun*, August 8, 1919.
17. Shocker's career fielding percentage of .980 is one of the best of his era.
18. Cataneo, *Baseball Legends and Lore*, 77. Orig. *Saturday Evening Post*, July 19, 1930. Just how often Shocker was "licked" is questionable, though Rommel is making a point about Shocker's superstitious nature.
19. The New York Giants had drawn 38,281 fans to Game One of the 1911 World Series.

20. Frederick G. Lieb, "New York Has Gone Baseball Crazy," *New York Evening Telegram*, July 14, 1920.
21. "38,823 Fans See Yanks Break Even," *New York Times*, July 14, 1920.
22. "How's This for a Star Battery?" *Sporting News*, July 22, 1920. In his book *Babe Ruth: Launching the Legend*, Jim Reisler has a detailed account of this story, but places it during the June 20, 1920, Yankees-Browns game.
23. Lane, "Urban Shocker, One of the Great Pitchers of 1920," 381.
24. James Sinnott, "Ruth Fans 5 Times Trying to Make Homers," *New York Evening Mail*, July 14, 1920. Umpire Billy Evans, who worked that game, noted that only one of Ruth's nine strikes in the three at-bats was a called strike. He swung and missed the other eight times. *St. Louis Post-Dispatch*, January 30, 1921.
25. Frank O'Neill, "Three Seasons' Records Set," *New York Evening Sun*, July 14, 1920.
26. The final score was 6-4. It was 6–0 until the Yankees scored too little, too late. Rube Waddell had 16 strikeouts in a revenge game of his own, also for the Browns, against his former team, the Athletics, on July 29, 1908. Philadelphia had just traded him away that off-season. Bob Shawkey of the Yankees had struck out 15 Athletics in 1919, and Fred Glade of the Browns had fanned 15 Senators in 1904.
27. Joseph H. Holland, *St. Louis Globe-Democrat*, July 14, 1920.
28. Frederick G. Lieb, "'Pay One Dollar to See Ruth Walk,' Is Western Slogan," *New York Evening Telegram*, July 30, 1920.
29. Proposals included giving the man who got the intentional walk more than one base.
30. John B. Sheridan, Back of the Home Plate, *Sporting News*, June 2, 1921.
31. Stoney McLinn, *Philadelphia Evening Public Ledger*, May 26, 1924.
32. Boston pitcher (and future Ruth teammate on the Yankees) Sam Jones beat New York, 9–0. It is somewhat odd that Jones would have walked Ruth after the third inning, when his club was already leading, 8–0.
33. "Shocker's Pitching Puzzles Yankees," *New York Times*, July 29, 1920. This quote may serve as a reminder that sportswriters sometimes clarified and cleaned up the quotes players gave them. It's not likely the Babe used the phrase "means of transportation."
34. Weed Dickinson, *New York Graphic*, July 14, 1920.
35. Sam Crane, *New York Evening Journal*, July 14, 1920.
36. In 1919 Shocker had given up six home runs, and three were hit by Yankees.
37. W. O. McGeehan, *New York Tribune*, August 30, 1920.

38. *St. Louis Globe-Democrat* and *St. Louis Post-Dispatch*, August 30, 1920.
39. Reisler, *Launching the Legend*, 205–6, and "Yankees Nose Out Browns at Finish," *New York Times*, August 30, 1920.
40. Sam Crane, *New York Evening Journal*, July 14, 1920, and Frank O'Neill, *New York Evening Sun*, July 14, 1920.
41. "Ruth Says New Pitching Rules Have Not Helped Him in Breaking Records," *St. Louis Globe-Democrat*, July 25, 1920.
42. "This Kind Must Succeed," *Sporting News*, February 24, 1921.
43. Urban Shocker, "Pitching to Babe Ruth," 540.

15. THE SHOWDOWNS CONTINUE

1. Kamp is listed in the 1920 census as living in St. Louis with his wife, Helen. That same information shows up on his 1918 draft registration card. He would be killed in a streetcar accident in 1923.
2. Shocker's nephew, Roger Shockcor (1920–2003), the son of Urban's oldest sibling, William, provided some of the family information. Roger played Minor League ball for the Cardinals before World War II.
3. Frederick G. Lieb, "Spitballers Want to Stay," *New York Evening Telegram*, May 21, 1920.
4. "Bill Klem Thinks Spitball Will Stay," *Sporting News*, November 18, 1920. See also the November 25 issue of that weekly.
5. Editorial, "Magnates Loath to Bar Spitter Now," *Sporting News*, October 28, 1920.
6. Editorial, "Unmoved by Slippery Sobs," *Sporting News*, November 25, 1920.
7. Ultimately Landis did get involved. The American League owners voted to grant the exemption, but those of the National League were deadlocked, 4–4. Landis broke the tie in favor of "the wet one."
8. Lane, "Urban Shocker, One of the Great Pitchers of 1920," 381.
9. Murdock, *Baseball between the Wars*, 47.
10. Mel Allen, "Pitching Style," 9. Sportswriter Arch Ward originally told the story. *Chicago Daily Tribune*, July 25, 1950. Hildebrand played in the Majors in 1902, was a longtime American League umpire (1913–34), and passed away in 1960. Ironically, he had a role in the development of the spitball. See my website, www.stevesteinberg.net, go to the "Baseball History" tab and then "The Spitball" section.
11. Shocker's recollection was not accurate. He was ejected by umpires Dick Nallin in 1920, Brick Owens in 1922, and Red Ormsby and Pants Rowland in 1923, as well as by Hildebrand in 1925.

12. Francis J. Powers, “Ban on Freak Deliveries Meant Nothing to Erick,” *Sporting News*, December 8, 1921.
13. Ed Rumill, “Shocker Threw Best Spitball,” *Christian Science Monitor*, July 30, 1964.
14. On July 18, 1919, Fohl’s relief pitcher gave up a two-out ninth-inning home run to the Babe (his second of the day) to win the game. Fohl was blamed for bringing that reliever, Fritz Coumbe, into the game in the first place and for not having Ruth walked intentionally. The Indians’ star outfielder, Tris Speaker, had been the fans’ choice to manage the club for some time. After this game, Fohl decided to step aside. See Lewis, *The Cleveland Indians*, 99–102.
15. Lane, “Brooklyn’s New Business Manager,” 302.
16. Godin, *The 1922 St. Louis Browns*, 35.
17. Lammers, “Bob Quinn and the Farm System.” Quinn ran the Columbus club from 1900 to 1916.
18. Ed Rumill, “Quinn, Nearing 75, Recalls His Thrills in Game,” *Sporting News*, February 8, 1945.
19. In 10 of those 21 outfield seasons (three players for seven years), they had batting averages higher than .330.
20. The Federal League operated as a third major league in 1914 and 1915. It was a Midwest minor league in 1913, and Tobin played for the league’s St. Louis Terriers all three seasons.
21. Obituary, “John T. (Johnny) Tobin,” *Sporting News*, December 27, 1969.
22. Ward, “Tobin the Transcendent,” 448.
23. “Forced Out by Illness,” *Sporting News*, February 10, 1921. In 1919 he came back and posted a 10-6 record with a 2.07 earned run average, third best in the league. Weilman died in 1924 at the age of thirty-four.
24. Dave Heller, “The Life and Death of Carl Weilman,” http://seamheads.com/2010/01/10/the-life-and-death-of-carl-weilman/.
25. Okkonen, *The Ty Cobb Scrapbook*, 150.
26. “Ty Cobb’s Own Life Story,” no. 35, *Boston Daily Globe*, January 26, 1926.
27. Jennings, *Rounding Third*. See the Jennings excerpt in chapter 4 here, “An Emerging Star,” from syndicated newspaper series, 1925.
28. Jenkinson, *The Year Babe Ruth Hit 104 Home Runs*, 137–38.
29. Gallico, *Farewell to Sport*, 40.
30. James J. Corbett, “Shocker Suggests Armor Plate for Pitchers with Ruth at Bat,” *New York American*, February 2, 1921.
31. W. O. McGeehan, In All Fairness, *New York Tribune*, January 3, 1921.

32. Davis Walsh, "Yanks Begin Series Here by Beating the Browns," *New York World*, June 3, 1921.
33. Charles Taylor, "Long Drives in Early Innings Rout Shocker," *New York Tribune*, June 3, 1921.
34. "Long Drives by Pipp and Mays Hasten Departure of Shocker," *New York Tribune*, July 14, 1921.
35. Lane, "Urban Shocker, One of the Great Pitchers of 1920," 381.
36. "Shocker Draws Suspension for Failure to Obey Orders to Report," *St. Louis Times*, July 5, 1921.
37. *St. Louis Star*, July 10, 1921, and *St. Louis Times*, July 9, 1921.
38. Martin J. Haley, "Browns Practically Through So Far as 1921 Is Concerned," *St. Louis Globe-Democrat*, July 8, 1921.
39. Stockton, also a Spink Award winner, covered the Browns and the Cardinals first for the *Globe-Democrat* and then for the *Post-Dispatch* and became the sports editor of the latter.
40. Godin, *The 1922 St. Louis Browns*, 83.
41. Damon Runyon, *New York American*, July 28, 1921.
42. William Hennigan, "Shocker and McManus Beat Yanks for Browns," *New York World*, July 28, 1921. Shocker struck out Baker and Meusel in the eighth inning on slow balls. Then, after an error and an infield hit put the go-ahead run on base, Shocker got Schang to strike out on a slow ball.
43. Frank F. O'Neill, *St. Louis Times*, July 28, 1921. The *New York Times* that day called the Browns' manager "Prudence Fohl." By "place," Fohl was probably referring to the fact that the leagues were distributing some World Series money to second- and third-place teams, a policy that started in 1919.
44. See Steinberg and Spatz, *The Colonel and Hug*, chapter 20.
45. *New York Daily News*, August 22, 1921.
46. Sid Keener, "19 Yanks Strike Out when Browns Win Double-Header," *St. Louis Times*, August 22, 1921. Shocker and Bob Shawkey, the Yankees' starter, each struck out 9 men. The Browns' Billy Bayne struck out 10 more in the second game.
47. "Yanks Pennant Chances Weakened," *New York Evening World*, August 22, 1921.
48. *New York Herald*, August 22, 1921.
49. Heywood Broun, *New York World*, September 17, 1921.
50. Johnson would pass Shocker for the strikeout crown by the end of the season.
51. Frederick G. Lieb, *New York Evening Telegram*, September 17, 1921.

52. Sid Mercer, "Shocker Knocks Yanks Out of First Place," *New York Evening Journal*, September 20, 1921.
53. For a detailed account of this series, see Spatz and Steinberg, *1921*, chapter 23.
54. The Yankees sent catcher Muddy Ruel, pitcher Hank Thormahlen, outfielder Sammy Vick, and Pratt to the Red Sox in exchange for catcher Wally Schang, pitcher Harry Harper, infielder Mike McNally, and Hoyt.
55. John Kieran, Sports of the Times, *New York Times*, June 17, 1929. Huggins had planned to get rid of Pratt a year earlier, but his planned replacement, Chick Fewster, was almost killed by a pitched ball during spring training in 1920.
56. *New York Evening Mail*, April 9, 1921.
57. Frank F. O'Neill, "Yanks Nearly Clinch the Pennant," *New York Sun*, September 27, 1921. The Yankees' series with the Indians was played in New York, and Shocker and the Browns were in town to play the Yankees the following day.
58. Sid Mercer, Sid Mercer's Close-Ups, *New York Evening Journal*, August 11, 1920. This was a rare time the New York press pushed back on Ruppert, suggesting he should not focus on such a conspiracy theory.
59. Heywood Broun, "Yanks Win Again, and Odds Favor Big Series Here," *New York World*, September 27, 1921. In the 1945 *Baseball Register*, Fred Lieb picked this game as one of the ten greatest ever.
60. *New York Tribune*, September 28, 1921. The "Kiplingized oath" is based on Rudyard Kipling's "Oath of the Brother-in-Blood" in his poem "The Ballad of East and West."
61. "Yankees Shut Out as Shocker Gains His 27th Victory," *St. Louis Post-Dispatch*, September 28, 1921.
62. Robert Boyd, *New York Evening World*, September 28, 1921.
63. Damon Runyon, "Urban Shocker Calls Old Jinx into Play," *New York American*, September 28, 1921.
64. Frank O'Neill, *St. Louis Times*, September 28, 1921. The *Times* was a smaller St. Louis paper and did not send reporters to away games. Instead, they picked up the column of a New York writer. The article appeared in O'Neill's home paper, the *New York Sun*, that day.
65. Harry Schumacher, *New York Globe and Commercial Advertiser*, September 28, 1921.
66. Editorial, *Sporting News*, September 23, 1920.
67. Sid Mercer, "Big-League Cast-Off Often Comes Back to Take Revenge," *New York Evening Journal*, January 7, 1922.
68. Monitor (George Daley), "Yanks Fall before the Wiles of Shocker," *New York World*, September 28, 1921.

16. THE UNDERDOG ARISES

1. The Browns did finish in third place in 1921, but they were 17½ games back of the Yankees. The batting averages of Sisler, Jacobson, Tobin, and Williams were .371, .352, .352, and .347, respectively.
2. W. S. Farnsworth, "Silent on Ruth Case," *New York American*, December 15, 1921.
3. My story of Dave Danforth, one of the most fascinating and controversial figures in the history of the national pastime, can be found at Steinberg, "Dave Danforth," SABR BioProject, sabr.org/bioproject.
4. Danforth had been on two world championship teams, the 1911 Athletics and the 1917 White Sox. His Columbus manager in 1921 was Pants Rowland, who had led the White Sox in 1917.
5. These pitches, which involved defacing the ball, were not legal even before 1920, though the spitball was. See, for example, the career arc of emery ball pitcher Russ Ford. Morgan and Jones, "Russ Ford," SABR BioProject, sabr.org/bioproject.
6. Harvey A. Miller, The Sport Mirror by H. A. M., *Columbus Dispatch*, January 13, 1922. Miller was the sports editor of the *Dispatch* from 1903 to 1924.
7. The rule banning World Series winners from barnstorming was instituted by the National Commission after members of the 1910 world champion Philadelphia Athletics had toured Cuba and were embarrassed by local teams there. Ironically, a star player could earn more money barnstorming than by winning the World Series. In 1916 Ruth was a member of the world champion Red Sox and disregarded the rule. He was fined a mere $100, and his Series ornament was withheld.
8. "Ruth Is Suspended; Fined World Series Money," *New York Times*, December 6, 1921.
9. The Yankees sent pitchers Jack Quinn, Rip Collins, and Bill Piercy, along with shortstop Roger Peckinpaugh, to Boston for shortstop Everett Scott, as well as Bush and Jones.
10. *Fort Worth Star-Telegram*, January 22, 1921, and *Lexington Herald*, December 29, 1921.
11. Godin, *The 1922 St. Louis Browns*, 26.
12. *St. Louis Times*, February 22, 1922.
13. Martin J. Haley, "Shocker and Sherdel Are Probable Pitchers," *St. Louis Globe-Democrat*, April 18, 1922.
14. Wancho, "Ken Williams," SABR BioProject, sabr.org/bioproject.

15. Hugh Fullerton, On the Screen of Sport, *New York Evening Mail*, August 11, 1922.
16. "Fortune That Attends Browns Proves That Fate Tires of Hammering at Old Target," *St. Louis Star*, September 4, 1922.
17. Heywood Broun, *New York World*, May 20, 1922.
18. "Fortune That Attends Browns Proves That Fate Tires of Hammering at Old Target," *St. Louis Star*, September 4, 1922.
19. Billy Evans, syndicated column. Slightly different versions of this column appeared in a number of papers in 1922. See *Nashville Tennessean*, July 19, 1922, and "Urban Shocker Is at His Best in a Tight Pinch," syndicated column, September 22, 1922.
20. Editorial, "The Season's Best Joke," *Sporting News*, June 8, 1922.
21. While there was never a specific connection made between Baker's hit-by-pitch and his long absence, Baker biographer Barry Sparks believes it did play a role.
22. In Retrosheet's partial data (being added to all the time), Mays hit .389 against Shocker in 18 at-bats.
23. J. Roy Stockton, "Yanks Pound Shocker, and Ruth Gets Homer; Umpires Avert Fight," *St. Louis Post-Dispatch*, June 11, 1922.
24. "Yanks Slaughter Browns, 14–5," *New York American*, June 11, 1922.
25. Shalin and Shalin, *Out by a Step*, 119.
26. Frank O'Neill, "Shocker Shows He's Bad Loser," *New York Sun*, June 12, 1922.
27. "Yankees At Last Subdue Shocker," *New York Evening Telegram*, June 12, 1922.
28. "Call to Conscience and Courage, If Any," *Sporting News*, June 15, 1922.
29. Many newspapers mentioned Shocker's injury. Some said he had ligament damage; others pointed to a ruptured blood vessel. A number of papers said he had an operation, but mentioned no specifics. Shocker did have an extended stay in the hospital.

17. GOOD BUT NOT LUCKY

1. Stewart, "The Man Who Owned Babe Ruth," 55–57.
2. Babe Ruth, *New York American*, September 8, 1922.
3. Shocker had returned to action on July 4, when he relieved in both games of a doubleheader.
4. "Yankees Outluck Browns in Opener," *New York Times*, July 12, 1922.
5. John E. Wray, Wray's Column, *St. Louis Post-Dispatch*. July 30, 1922.
6. Babe Ruth, *New York American*, September 8, 1922.

7. J. Roy Stockton, "The Men Who Lead St. Louis' Pennant Battle," 492.
8. Vangilder also hit .344 in 1922, with 93 at-bats.
9. Arthur Robinson, "Shocker No Longer Shocks," *New York American*, July 12, 1922.
10. "Yankees Outluck Browns in Opener," *New York Times*, July 12, 1922.
11. "Yankees Win Final Game with Browns," *New York Times*, July 15, 1922.
12. New York sent infielders Chick Fewster and Johnny Mitchell, along with outfielder Elmer Miller, to Boston for Dugan and outfielder Elmer Smith.
13. Scribbled by Scribes, *Sporting News*, August 10, 1922.
14. While the trade deadline is nowadays also July 31, it was moved up to June 15 after the Dugan deal. The theory is that teams should have their lineups set earlier in the season.
15. John E. Wray, Wray's Column, *St. Louis Post-Dispatch*, July 30, 1922.
16. Harry Schumacher, "Urban Shocker Showed the Spirit," *New York Globe and Commercial Advertiser*, July 26, 1922.
17. Danforth had started only 10 games.
18. *San Jose Evening* News, July 7, 1922. Evans credited Danforth for having "heart" to continue pitching in the face of all the accusations.
19. Meany, *Baseball's Greatest Teams*, 197. One report said that Danforth slept with his pitching hand soaking in pickle brine to make it more abrasive.
20. Sid C. Keener, "Danforth Used Plank as Mound Model," *St. Louis Times*, March 15, 1922. In 1911 and 1912, Danforth's first two seasons, he was a teammate of Plank's on the Athletics.
21. John E. Wray, Wray's Column, *St. Louis Post-Dispatch*, August 12, 1922.
22. Frank O'Neill, *New York Sun*, August 26, 1922.
23. Martin J. Haley, "Rain Stops Browns and Yankees," *St. Louis Globe-Democrat*, August 28, 1922.
24. Heywood Broun, "Browns Divide with Yanks and Retain League Lead," *New York World*, August 26, 1922.
25. Frederick G. Lieb, "Shawkey Victor in Titanic Debate," *New York Evening Telegram*, August 29, 1922.
26. Meany, *Baseball's Greatest Teams*, 200.
27. The Browns had a successful August, winning 18 of 30 games. But the Yankees caught fire that month and won 20 of 26.
28. "Sisler May Be Out for Rest of Year," *New York Times*, September 13, 1922. Other reports said Hyland called it a bad tear in the fiber around the shoulder joint. *St. Louis Times*, September 13, 1922.
29. Sid Keener, "Sisler, Injured, Unable to Play," *St. Louis Times*, September 13, 1922.

30. *St. Louis Star*, September 14, 1922. Also, the Advertising Club of St. Louis had an event for the Browns at the Missouri Theater in early September. *St. Louis Times*, September 5, 1922.
31. For a detailed account, see Steinberg, "The Little World Series of 1922." The Browns won three of the four games Sisler missed leading up to this series.
32. *New York Globe and Commercial Advertiser*, September 16, 1922.
33. The Yankees (and the New York Giants) did not allow fans on the field in the Polo Grounds because their presence reduced the size of the playing area, and the subsequent ground rules distorted the game.
34. Harry Harlow, "Yankees Fight Good Ball and Poor Sports," *New York Evening Mail*, September 18, 1922. Evans was hit on September 15, 1907.
35. Eventually, a youngster was identified as the bottle thrower. But supposedly he did not hit Witt. He merely threw the bottle onto the field, after which Witt stepped on it and propelled it into his head. Babe Ruth muttered jokingly that maybe they thought Whitey was trying to kill himself.
36. *Sporting News*, February 10, 1944.
37. The Yankees protested vehemently when Wally Pipp drove a ball into the crowd, and the fans had moved and let Jacobson make the catch. The putout was upheld by the umpire.
38. Smith had a career .311 batting average as a pinch hitter, 41-for-132. As a pinch hitter, Smith was 6 for 22 (.273 batting average) in 1922 and would go 10 for 21 (.476 batting average) in 1923.
39. The concept has been borne out by statistics and is now widely accepted: A hitter does better against a pitcher throwing from the other side. A right-handed hitter does better against a left-handed pitcher than against a righty, for example, because he has a better view of the ball and because a breaking ball breaks into and not away from him.
40. Harry Schumacher, *New York Globe and Commercial Advertiser*, September 19, 1922.
41. *New York Evening Telegram*, September 19, 1922.
42. John B. Sheridan, "Change from Joy to Gloom in Final Innings," *St. Louis Globe-Democrat*, September 19, 1922. The *Sporting News* columnist also wrote for the *Globe-Democrat*. Both the weekly and the daily were based in St. Louis.
43. Martin J. Haley, "Game Highlights," *St. Louis Globe-Democrat*, September 19, 1922.
44. Curran, *Big Sticks*, 184.
45. Joe DiMaggio broke the record with hits in 56 consecutive games in 1941. That

is still the record; Pete Rose hit in 44 straight games in 1978. Two nineteenth-century streaks had also exceeded Sisler's mark of 41: Willie Keeler's 45 in 1896–97 and Bill Dahlen's 42 in 1894.

46. Martin J. Haley, "Browns Lose to Nationals, 4–3," *St. Louis Globe-Democrat*, September 20, 1922.
47. Sid C. Keener, "Abusive Fan Ejected from Park," *St. Louis Times*, September 21, 1922.
48. Christy Mathewson (1908), Walter Johnson (1913 and 1915), Grover Cleveland Alexander (1917), and Robin Roberts (1953 and 1954) are the only others to accomplish this unique "power-control" double achievement.
49. Shocker's 24-17 record translates to a winning percentage of .585. The Browns' winning percentage was .604. Extracting his decisions from their record (a truer comparison) raises their percentage to .611. He won only one game after September 4.
50. Meany, *Baseball's Greatest Teams*, 207.

18. A LOST SEASON

1. The Browns drew more than 700,000 fans in 1922, more than double their 1921 figure. Only once before had they drawn more than 420,000 fans. In 1908, when they were in the pennant race until late in the season, they drew in excess of 618,000.
2. Lieb, *The Baltimore Orioles*, 95, and "Browns Receive $20,000," *New York Times*, November 2, 1922.
3. Arthur Daley, Sports of the Times, *New York Times*, April 5, 1954.
4. *St. Louis Star*, August 31, September 14 and 30, 1922. Godin says Shocker got the car before his 24th and final win on September 30. *The 1922 St. Louis Browns*, 187–88.
5. Shocker's nephew, Roger Shockcor, related this story to me. The Marmon was a high-end auto.
6. Roy Stockton, "Urban Shocker, the Lazy Man of Browns' Training Trip, Proves Brain Is Mightier Than the Arm," *St. Louis Post-Dispatch*, May 10, 1923.
7. Huhn, *The Sizzler*, 156–59.
8. Martin J. Haley, "Absence of Sisler Has Changed Outlook," *St. Louis Globe-Democrat*, April 13, 1923.
9. Huhn, *The Sizzler*, 156.
10. *St. Louis Star*, April 28, 1923. Cobb's punch was blocked by a Shocker teammate.
11. Lane, "Urban Shocker, One of the Great Pitchers of 1920," 382.

12. *New York Evening Telegram*, June 14, 1923. Red Ormsby ejected Shocker in the sixth inning of a game he was losing, 1–0, in which he had given up only four hits.
13. Notes of the Nationals, *Washington Post*, August 3, 1923.
14. "Shocker Exponent of Fading Art of Spitball Pitching," *St. Louis Post-Dispatch*, June 29, 1923.
15. John B. Foster, *New York Sun*, September 17, 1921.
16. George Moriarty, *American Newspaper Alliance*, 1928, article in the Bill Loughman Shocker clippings.
17. Gordon Mackay, "Passing of the Spitball Pitcher," *Reach 1924 American League Guide*, 48. Walsh was unhappy in his role as an umpire after years of sharing the camaraderie among players. He served in that capacity only in 1922 before returning to coaching.
18. John McGraw, *Hartford Courant*, July 15, 1923.
19. J. Roy Stockton, "Shocker Scores His 15th Victory and Shows More of the Stuff That Makes Him a Consistent Winner," *St. Louis Post-Dispatch*, July 19, 1923.
20. After posting a 10-5 record with a 2.91 earned run average in 26 games in 1919, Uhle managed only four wins in 1920, when his ERA ballooned to 5.21.
21. Eugene Murdock, *Baseball Players and Their Times: Oral Histories of the Game, 1920–1940*, 130. A pitcher tips his pitches when he does something different in his windup or delivery for different types of pitches.
22. Joe Vila, Setting the Pace, *New York Sun*, August 8, 1923.
23. Sid C. Keener, On the Side Line, *St. Louis Times*, August 3, 1923. It is not known if Keener spoke with Billy Evans about this matter.
24. Sid C. Keener, On the Side Line, *St. Louis Times*, August 3, 1923. I have written a creative account of this 1923 controversy swirling around Fohl, "For the Good of the Game, 1923."
25. "Many Have Failed in Position Sisler Will Be Asked to Occupy," *St. Louis Star*, August 8, 1923.
26. "Yankees Trounce Tigers Again, 6–5," *New York Times*, September 21, 1922.
27. Sid C. Keener, "Balls Pitched by Dave Danforth, Now Held by Fohl, Show Cover Is Rough in Same Spot between Seams," *St. Louis Times*, August 22, 1923.
28. Frank O'Neill, "Fohl to Demand Showdown from Magnate Ball," *St. Louis Times*, August 9, 1923.
29. I. E. Sanborn, "Danforth Has Caused Quite a Bit of Trouble," *Washington Post*, September 19, 1923.

30. Frank O'Neill, "Fohl to Demand Showdown from Magnate Ball," *St. Louis Times*, August 9, 1923.
31. Meany, *Baseball's Greatest Teams*, 197.
32. *St. Louis Post-Dispatch*, August 8, 1923.
33. Sid Keener, On the Side Line, *St. Louis Times*, August 17, 1923.
34. J. Roy Stockton, "Pruett, Sensation of 1922, Waived Out of League," *St. Louis Post-Dispatch*, February 15, 1925. Pruett had a 2.33 earned run average with the 1922 Browns. In his short seven-year career, he never had another season's ERA under 4.00.
35. Pruett said he had worked six or seven games in a row in 1922. Stewart, "The Man Who Owned Babe Ruth," 57. Pruett appeared in five games in a seven-day stretch and five others in an eight-day period that season.
36. *New York American*, July 12, 1922, *New York Times*, August 29, 1922, and New *York Evening Telegram*, August 7, 1923.
37. Arthur Robinson, "Babe Cleans Bases in 8th," *New York American*, August 7, 1923.
38. *New York Times* and *St. Louis Globe-Democrat*, August 7, 1923.
39. Frank F. O'Neill, "Yankees Score over Shocker," *New York Sun*, August 7, 1923.
40. Babe Ruth, *New York American*, September 9, 1923.
41. Hugh S. Fullerton, On the Screen of Sport, *New York Evening Mail*, September 30, 1922. Williams was caught stealing twenty times that year, and Ruth was caught five times.
42. Hugh S. Fullerton, On the Screen of Sport, *New York Evening Mail*, September 30, 1922.
43. Babe Ruth, "Yankees' Slugger Says Rival Has Advantage in Small Park," June 6, 1923.
44. James Murphy, "New Home Run King Hailed," unsourced 1922 article in Ken Williams file, *Sporting News*.
45. Hoefer, "The Reign of the Wallop," 365.
46. Lane, "The Home-Run Epidemic, 372.
47. Frederick G. Lieb, "Big League Pitching Has Deteriorated," *New York Evening Telegram*, August 5, 1923.
48. *New York World*, August 16, 1923.
49. Willie Keeler had hit safely 200 or more times from 1894 to 1901, and Ichiro Suzuki achieved that mark in ten consecutive seasons, from 2001 to 2010.
50. John B. Sheridan, Behind the Home Plate, *Sporting News*, April 9, 1925. Tobin had an interesting anomaly in his game. Though he was quick and hit a lot of

triples, he did not steal many bases. In 1921, for example, he led the league in triples with 18. Yet he stole only seven bases.

51. Frank Graham, "Yankees Release Shocker," *New York Sun*, July 6, 1928.
52. Lane, *Batting*, 47–48.
53. Martin J. Haley, "Urban Allows but Three Hits," *St. Louis Globe-Democrat*, August 27, 1923.

19. FREE AGENCY IN 1924?

1. Friel had played in the Majors briefly in the early 1900s and, from 1909 to 1912, was player-manager for the Columbus Senators, the American Association club that Quinn was running at the time. Friel did not bring the management experience and gravitas to the Browns' position that Quinn had, and on major issues, Ball was making the calls.
2. Ford Frick, "Players' Wives," *New York Evening Journal*, July 16, 1926.
3. The Pirates and Tigers did not allow wives on road trips, while the Giants, Reds, and White Sox did permit them. *St. Louis Globe-Democrat*, December 31, 1923.
4. I. E. Sanborn, "Why Players' Wives Are an Impediment," *Sporting Life*, April 15, 1916.
5. Westbrook Pegler, United News Service, Bill Loughman clippings, February 7, 1924.
6. John E. Wray, Wray's Column, *St. Louis Post-Dispatch*, September 20, 1923.
7. Harry Schumacher, "Mays Should Make Good in National," *New York Evening Mail*, October 23, 1923. The term "red-necked" meant hot-tempered and stubborn in 1923.
8. "American League Magnates Train Their Guns upon Landis, the Friend of the Ball Player," *St. Louis Post-Dispatch*, December 11, 1923. The National Agreement stated, "The Commissioner shall hear and determine finally any dispute to which a player is a party, or any dispute concerning a player, which may be certified to him by either of the disputants." *New York Sun*, December 14, 1923.
9. Seymour and Mills, *Baseball: The Golden Age*, 299–300, 376–77.
10. Ball was a big supporter of American League President Ban Johnson, whose power was dramatically curtailed under the new commissioner system.
11. John B. Sheridan, Behind the Home Plate, *Sporting News*, November 8, 1923, and *New York Sun*, November 27, 1923.
12. Frederick G. Lieb, *New York Evening Telegram*, December 11, 1923.
13. John E. Wray, "American League Reportedly Ready to Withdraw," *St. Louis Post-Dispatch*, December 10, 1923.

14. Murdock, *Ban Johnson*, 207.
15. John E. Wray, Wray's Column, *St. Louis Post-Dispatch*, December 26, 1923.
16. Joe Vila, Setting the Pace, *New York Sun*, December 5, 1923, and Sid C. Keener, On the Side Line, *St. Louis Times*, October 4, 1923.
17. "Landis Considers Shocker Case," *New York Times*, December 4, 1923.
18. Francis C. Richter, Casual Comment, *Sporting News*, November 22, 1923.
19. "Phil Ball," *Reedy's Mirror*, December 18, 1914, 75.
20. Phil Ball to Ban Johnson, January 12, 1923, National Baseball Hall of Fame Library and Archives.
21. Ball to Johnson, January 17, 1924. Joe Gedeon was traded from the Yankees to the Browns with Shocker back in 1918. Judge Landis banned Gedeon for life after the 1920 season because of his prior knowledge of the Black Sox World Series affair. National Baseball Hall of Fame Library and Archives.
22. Bob Quinn to Ball, January 10, 1924, National Baseball Hall of Fame Library and Archives.
23. Johnson to Ball, January 18, 1924, National Baseball Hall of Fame Library and Archives.
24. Ball to Johnson, January 19, 1924, National Baseball Hall of Fame Library and Archives.
25. Johnson to Ball, January 21, 1924, National Baseball Hall of Fame Library and Archives.
26. Ban Johnson had asked the Browns' business manager why the club did not trade Shocker. Billy Friel said, "Sisler insisted on keeping the pitcher." Johnson to Quinn, January 16, 1924, National Baseball Hall of Fame Library and Archives.
27. Daniel M. Daniel, "Phil DeCatesby Ball, Despite Huge Cost of His Hobby, Still Pursues Will o' the Wisp of Pennant for Browns," *Sporting News*, February 11, 1932.
28. Francis C. Richter, Casual Comment, *Sporting News*, January 31 and February 7, 1924.
29. Martin J. Haley, "Ban Johnson Acts for Owner Ball," *St. Louis Globe-Democrat*, January 23, 1924.
30. Shocker had 10 percent more wins than the pitchers with the second-most wins in those years, Urban Faber and Burleigh Grimes, who won 83. Shocker missed five weeks at the end of the 1920 season and four weeks at the end of 1923. He also missed more than two weeks during the 1921 season and three weeks in 1922.

20. THE TEMPERAMENTAL SPITBALLIST

1. Huggins believed in making some personnel moves from year to year. He said, "The secret of it [continuing to win championships] in my mind is to keep on changing about your players." *New York Evening Telegram*, March 27, 1923.
2. Sid Mercer, *New York Evening Journal*, December 11, 1923. Jones had a 21-8 record in 1923, but his 3.63 earned run average was not close to the league's best.
3. Steinberg and Spatz, *The Colonel and Hug*, 215–16. Mays pitched only 81 innings that season.
4. Hoyt posted a 19-9 record with a 3.02 earned run average.
5. Frederick G. Lieb, *New York Evening Telegram*, December 11, 1923.
6. "Sisler Outlines Early Plans for the Browns' 1924 Campaign," *St. Louis Post-Dispatch*, October 23, 1923.
7. *Cleveland Plain Dealer*, April 24, 1924.
8. "Shocker Just Up and Left," *NEA Service*, April 26, 1924.
9. "Shocker Case Lies with Ball or Landis," *Sporting News*, January 10, 1924.
10. Blood transfusions from Urban's sister, Rhea, failed to save their father. The cemetery is nondenominational.
11. "Browns Wreck Yankee Celebration," *St. Louis Globe-Democrat*, May 15, 1924.
12. "Baseball Crown Rests Uneasily on Both New York Champions," *Sporting News*, May 22, 1924.
13. Joe Vila, Setting the Pace, *New York Sun*, May 15, 1924.
14. "Shocker Fined," *St. Louis Post-Dispatch*, May 27, 1924.
15. Joe Vila, Setting the Pace, *New York Sun*, August 8, 1923.
16. Joe Vila, Setting the Pace, *New York Sun*, April 12, 1924.
17. Huhn, *The Sizzler*, 189.
18. Hoefer, "The Return of the Player-Manager," 345.
19. Joe Vila, Setting the Pace, *New York Sun*, February 22, 1924. Sisler was an excellent pitcher at the University of Michigan and when he first joined the Browns in 1915. He won five games as a pitcher in 1915–16. He often said one of his greatest thrills was when he pitched and beat Walter Johnson, 1–0, late in the 1916 season.
20. Huhn, *The Sizzler*, 188.
21. Ford Frick, "Sisler Plays as Well as Ever, but Puzzles Fans," *New York Evening Journal*, June 9, 1924.
22. Sisler, "The Inside Story of Sisler's Great Comeback," 392.
23. Scribbled by Scribes, *Sporting News*, June 5, 1924.
24. Joe Vila, Setting the Pace, *New York Sun*, July 8 and July 12, 1924.

25. "Urb Shocker in Another Row on Club," *St. Louis Times*, and *St. Louis Star*, May 27, 1924.
26. Ban Johnson to George Sisler, June 7, 1924, National Baseball Hall of Fame Library and Archives.
27. Johnson to Sisler, June 3, 1924, National Baseball Hall of Fame Library and Archives.
28. Steinberg, "Dave Danforth."
29. Lane, "Why Dave Danforth Has Been a Storm Center," 353. Carl Mays threw the lethal pitch that fractured the skull of Ray Chapman in 1920. It remains the only on-field fatality in Major League history.
30. Lane, "The Prosaic Career of Elam Van Gilder," 411.
31. "Sisler's Men Spurt with Good Pitching," *Sporting News*, June 12, 1924.
32. "Sislerites Falter as Flinging Fails," *Sporting News*, June 5, 1924.
33. Sid Keener, On the Side Line with the Sports Editor, *St. Louis Times*, June 11, 1924.
34. In 1922 and 1923, Shocker had the lowest walk rate per nine innings in the American League.
35. Billy Evans, "Speaker Owns Critical Eye, Shocker Says," *Alton (IL) Evening Telegraph*, February 20, 1924.
36. Billy Evans, "Winning Pitchers Use Their Knobs," *Bakersfield Californian*, August 18, 1924. The other seven he included were George Dauss, Howard Ehmke, George Mogridge, Herb Pennock, Ed Rommel, Sherry Smith, and Hollis Thurston. Evans added that Walter Johnson had developed into one of the "wisest" pitchers in the game as he lost his speed late in his career.
37. From 1900 to 2013, among pitchers with more than 500 plate appearances, only Clark Griffith had a higher relative walk rate, and most of his pitching was done in the nineteenth century. Griffith's rate was 171 and Shocker's was 154. E-mail from sabermetrician Cyril Morong, October 6, 2015, based on the Lee Sinins's *Complete Baseball Encyclopedia*.
38. E-mail from Joe Haardt, July 4, 2005. For his full career, Griffith drew walks 10.5 percent of his plate appearances and 12.3 percent from 1901 on.
39. Lane, "Severeid, a Catching Hercules," 501.
40. "Tribe Looks Feeble," *Cleveland Plain Dealer*, August 5, 1925.
41. "Yanks Beat Browns Following Dispute," *New York Times*, July 16, 1924. Had the play been ruled a catch, Shocker would have gotten a double play, since he had tagged Ruth on third base; the Babe had run there from first base on the drive. The Democrats nominated John W. Davis for president in 1924 after 103 ballots. He was trounced in the general election by President Calvin Coolidge.

42. "Caught at the Plate," *New York Times*, August 16, 1924.
43. Babe Ruth again led the league with 46 home runs, followed by Joe Hauser of the Athletics with 27. Jacobson finished third, one ahead of Ken Williams. Williams's figure came despite playing in only 114 games. He broke his ankle in late July.
44. John B. Sheridan, Behind the Home Plate, *Sporting News*, April 24, 1924.
45. Lane, "'Baby Doll' Jacobson, a True Clean-Up Hitter," 534. An article in Jacobson's file at the National Baseball Hall of Fame Library and Archives said that when he was with the Giants for spring training (1913 or 1914), John McGraw changed his hitting style to one in which he chopped at the ball, rather than putting all his weight behind the swing.
46. Shocker led the league in strikeouts in 1922, with 149. That number dropped to 109 in 1923 and 88 in 1924.
47. "'Play the Batter,' Advice of Outfielder Who Set Record," unsourced newspaper article in Jacobson's file at the National Baseball Library and Archives.
48. "William C. (Baby Doll) Jacobson," Obituary, *Sporting News*, February 5, 1977.
49. Sid C. Keener, On the Side Line, *St. Louis Times*, July 30, 1926.
50. Sid C. Keener, "Collegiate Pruett Developing Rapidly; Urb Shocker Offers Pitching Advice," *St. Louis Times*, March 15, 1922.
51. The conclusion seems almost counterintuitive, that the longer the top of the first inning takes, the greater the edge in runs for the home team in the bottom of the first. One would think a longer top of the first translates into the visiting team having a great edge in first-inning runs. http://www.retrosheet.org/Research/SmithD/HomeTeamScoringAdvantageRelatedToTime.pdf.
52. Pat Robinson, "Abusive Fans on the Job," *New York American*, August 2, 1924.
53. Urban Shocker, "Pitching to Babe Ruth," 540. In this article, Shocker claimed that Ruth hit a home run off him "two seasons ago," when Shocker was trying to walk him intentionally. I have not come across confirmation of such an occurrence.
54. The feat would be accomplished only once more, in 1926 by Dutch Levsen of the Tigers. Both Dave Davenport (1916) and Carl Mays (1918) had done this. Only Grover Alexander (1916, 1917), Joe McGinnity (three times in August 1903), and Ed Walsh (1905, 1908) accomplished this more than once in the twentieth century.
55. Sisler still had trouble seeing the ball clearly. He would never regain the form of 1920–22, when his batting average was exactly .400.
56. Damon Runyon, Says Damon Runyon, *New York American*, August 30, 1921.

21. BACK WHERE I BELONG

1. Norman Macht interview of Milt Gaston, 1985, Norman L. Macht Baseball Research Collection, DeGolyer Library, Southern Methodist University. Gaston died in 1996, a few months after he celebrated his one hundredth birthday.
2. Frederick G. Lieb, "Mental Disintegration Huggins' Fear," *New York Evening Telegram*, April 8, 1925.
3. J. Roy Stockton, "Second Baseman Dissatisfied in St. Louis Uniform," *St. Louis Post-Dispatch*, October 31, 1924.
4. *New York Evening Telegram*, November 13, 1924. The *New York American* reported just the opposite, that Sisler offered to trade Shocker for Hoyt during the season, but Huggins refused. October 15, 1924. Up until 1926, Huggins went back and forth on whether to trade Hoyt (and Bob Meusel, too), or whether to work out the challenges they presented to him. Ultimately, he chose the latter course.
5. Jones won only nine games in 1924, though his earned run average remained constant at 3.63, the same as in 1923. Hoyt won eighteen games in 1924, but his earned run average had risen from 3.02 to 3.79 that year.
6. Wally Pipp was still the club's regular first baseman. In his tenth Yankees season, he had another solid year, hitting .296 in 153 games.
7. Undated Lou Gehrig clip provided by Norman Macht, March 30, 2003.
8. Dan Daniel, "Daniel's Dope," *New York World-Telegram*, July 7, 1941. The *New York Evening World* of September 13, 1924, said the Yankees had offered Bush and Gehrig to the Browns for Shocker.
9. *St. Louis Post-Dispatch*, June 20, 1924. Arthur Kamp was killed on March 16, 1923. The Shockers reportedly settled for only six hundred dollars.
10. Caught on the Fly, *Sporting News*, December 18, 1924.
11. The Browns hit .295 in 1924, better than the league average of .290. Their pitching staff, however, had an earned run average of 4.57, well above the league's mark of 4.23.
12. Giard won 20 games for Toledo of the American Association that year. The Yankees sent infielder Mack Hillis, and the Browns sent pitchers Billy Bayne and George Lyons and infielder Dutch Schliebner to Toledo for Giard. *St. Paul Pioneer Press*, December 25, 1924. All four played for Toledo in 1925.
13. In the past four seasons, Bush's batting average was .316 with 432 at-bats.
14. "Shocker Goes on Trade Block," *Sporting News*, November 6, 1924.
15. Joseph Gordon, "Trade Favors Yanks," *New York Daily Mirror*, December 18, 1924.

16. Arthur Mann, "The Mouse Who Proved Himself a Man," *Sporting News*, November 2, 1939.
17. Joseph Gordon, "Shocker's Temperament," *New York Daily Mirror*, December 23, 1924.
18. Ray Gillespie, "Star Slabman Wishes Browns Best of Fortune," *St. Louis Star*, December 18, 1924.
19. Ford Frick, "Shocker in No Danger," *New York American*, January 8, 1925. The word "tumor" may have been used more broadly in the 1920s than today. It was a fatty growth of some kind and may have been a cyst.
20. "Huggins Outlines His Plans for 1925," *New York Times*, January 30, 1925.
21. Shocker was actually two years older than Bush, but listed his year of birth as 1892, the same as Bush's actual birth year. And while Bush pitched about 550 innings for the Athletics from 1913 to 1915, Shocker was pitching more than 650 innings in the Minors those years.
22. Ford Frick, Frick's Comments, *New York Evening Journal*, June 11, 1925.
23. Billy Evans, "Speaker Owns Critical Eye, Shocker Says," *Alton [IL] Evening Telegraph*, February 20, 1924.
24. W. O. McGeehan, Down the Line, *New York Herald Tribune*, December 23, 1924.
25. *New York Sun* morgue file, December 18, 1924, housed at the New York Public Library.
26. Monitor, "Shocker Best Pitcher in Baseball," *New York World*, January 22, 1925.
27. *New York Tribune*, September 28, 1921.
28. Henry L. Farrell, "'Heart' the Biggest Asset in Sport," *Lubbock Morning Avalanche*, February 22, 1925.

22. CLOUDS APPROACHING

1. *Atlanta Constitution*, December 18, 1924.
2. Frederick G. Lieb, "Yank Regulars Take First Trouncing from Yannigans," *New York Evening Telegram*, March 7, 1925.
3. Charles A. Taylor, "Spitballer Surrenders to Huggins in Hospital," *New York American*, January 24, 1925.
4. Ford Frick, "Pennock Agrees to Sign," *New York Evening Journal*, March 13, 1925.
5. *New York Herald Tribune*, February 25, 1925.
6. *New York World*, March 6, 1925.
7. E-mail from Dr. Ronald Siegel, cardiologist, January 11, 2016. Ronald Siegel has over forty years of experience in the treatment of cardiovascular disease

and has been a professor of medicine, Section of Cardiology, at the University of Wisconsin.

8. Commissioner Landis bestowed the moniker on Hyland, who received his medical degree from St. Louis University Medical School. Early in his career he was the surgeon for the city's streetcar and bus companies. See Steinberg, *Baseball in St. Louis*, 124.
9. Hyland likely continued as Shocker's personal physician when he was traded back to the Yankees. Shocker kept his home in St. Louis and probably felt his "secret" was more secure with his doctor in the Midwest. His medical records are almost certainly long gone, and I have not been successful in locating Hyland's papers.
10. E-mail from Dr. Ronald Siegel, January 11, 2016.
11. Bill Corum, "Sports: The Holdout," *New York Journal-American*, February 15, 1957. Corum passed away the following year.
12. "Yankees to Bury Mascot," *New York Times*, January 18, 1935.
13. Morris, "Eddie Bennett," 265–68.
14. The Athletics won the American League pennant four times in the five years Van Zelst (1895–1915) was their mascot. See Mack, *Connie Mack and the Early Years of Baseball*, 464–65, 481.
15. Bob Shawkey, *New York Evening Journal*, October 29, 1929.
16. Ford Frick, "Mr. Urban Shocker Sure It Is a Personal Matter," *New York Evening Journal*, April 22, 1927.
17. Will Wedge, Games, Gossip, and Guff, *New York Sun*, December 18, 1924.
18. Detroit's Hooks Dauss had served up 13 home runs to the Babe through 1924, the most of any pitcher to that point. Walter Johnson and Howard Ehmke had also given up at least as many home runs to Ruth as had Shocker. Ruth's eventual all-time "favorite" would be Rube Walberg, off whom he hit 17.
19. O'Neill had caught for spitball pitchers Stan Coveleski in Cleveland and Jack Quinn in Boston.
20. Vance did not win his first Major League game until 1922. In 1924, he posted a 28-6 record and also led the league in earned run average and strikeouts.
21. Vance's 262 strikeouts were almost double those of the second-place figure, spitballer Burleigh Grimes's 135.
22. Ford Frick, "Pennock Agrees to Sign," *New York Evening Journal*, March 13, 1925.
23. "Harris and Huggins Enter Early Claims for Pennant Honors," *Sporting News*, April 9, 1925.
24. William Hennigan, "Pitcher Unafraid," *New York World*, December 21, 1924.
25. John B. Foster, *New York Sun*, March 27, 1925.

26. Montville, *The Big Bam*, 201–5. Ruth's surgery was done at St. Vincent's Hospital in Greenwich Village.
27. Ironically, one of the men the Yankees sent to St. Louis in the Shocker deal, Joe Giard, was traded back to the New York organization in early 1927, along with outfielder Cedric Durst, for Sam Jones. In early 1926, the Yankees sent Wally Schang to St. Louis for former Yankees pitcher George Mogridge. But Mogridge exercised his rights as a ten-year veteran to turn down the deal and signed with the Boston Braves instead. Huggins had clashed with Mogridge before he traded him in December 1920. He was planning to send the pitcher to Salt Lake City as partial payment for their acquisition of Tony Lazzeri. After the players' union disbanded in early 1917, ten-year veterans retained the right to turn down a deal that would send them to the Minor Leagues.
28. Frederick G. Lieb, "Shocker's Work Justifies Deal," *New York Evening Telegram*, April 15, 1925.
29. Joe Vila, Setting the Pace, *New York Sun*, April 15, 1925.
30. Harold C. Burr, "Old Yank Star Dies in Denver," *Brooklyn Daily Eagle*, September 10, 1928.

23. THE SEASON THAT WASN'T

1. Martin J. Haley, "Shocker Hurls Ruthless Yanks," *St. Louis Globe-Democrat*, May 9, 1925.
2. Dent McSkimming, "Shocker Holds Browns to Five Hits," *St. Louis Post-Dispatch*, May 9, 1925.
3. Joe Vila, Setting the Pace, *New York Sun*, May 25, 1925.
4. Will Wedge, "Huggins Defends Yankees," *New York Sun*, March 19, 1926.
5. Scribbled by Scribes, *Sporting News*, August 6, 1925.
6. Joe Vila, "Huggins' 'Broadway Butterflies' Charged with Mutiny in Gossip," *Sporting News*, June 11, 1925.
7. Joe Vila, "Youngsters Instill New Spirit into Wavering Ranks of Yanks," *Sporting News*, June 18, 1925.
8. Smelser, *The Life That Ruth Built*, 317.
9. For Huggins's midseason moves, see Steinberg and Spatz, *The Colonel and Hug*, 230. Pipp was hit on the head during batting practice. The injury put him in the hospital, but that was not until a month after Gehrig had started in place of him.
10. Huggins struggled in his relationship with Hoyt and Meusel, though he did not trade either man. See Steinberg and Spatz, *The Colonel and Hug*, 248. Ruth was coming off a terrific 1924 season and was still a big box-office draw.

11. Mosedale, *The Greatest of All*, 143.
12. Harry Schumacher, "Huggins May Move Meusel," *New York Globe and Commercial Advertiser*, March 29, 1923.
13. Obituary, "Bob Meusel," *Sporting News*, December 17, 1977.
14. Lane, "A Masterful Pitching Craft," 395.
15. Heywood Broun, It Seems to Me, *New York World-Telegram*, December 18, 1933.
16. Lane, "A Masterful Pitching Craft," 395.
17. Pennock finished the year with a 16-17 record. In seven of his losses, he pitched complete games. Two defeats came in relief, both by one run. His earned run average of 2.96 was the best on the Yankees and the second-best in the American League in 1925.
18. James R. Harrison, "Yanks Divide Day; Take First in 15th," *New York Times*, July 5, 1925.
19. Herb Pennock, "My Greatest Diamond Thrill," *Sporting News*, May 4, 1944.
20. Ford Frick, Frick's Comments, *New York Evening Journal*, June 11, 1925.
21. "Shocker Dies; Yanks Grieve," *New York Sun*, September 10, 1928.
22. On July 10 Shocker led, 6–0, after 6 innings against Danforth and the Browns; the Yankees lost, 9–8. On July 18 he led the Tigers, 3–0, after 7; New York lost, 7–3. On July 29 he led the Browns, 4–0, after 6; the Yankees won in 12 innings, 8–7. Shocker was not around at the finishes of any of these games; he had been replaced by relief pitchers.
23. Montville, *The Big Bam*, 206.
24. John E. Wray, Wray's Column, *St. Louis Post-Dispatch*, August 31, 1925.
25. "Spanking Baseball's Baby and Petting Its Paragon," *Literary Digest*, September 19, 1925, 64.
26. Damon Runyon, Th' Mornins' Mornin', *New York American*, September 3, 1925.
27. Montville, *The Big Bam*, 209, and Ray Gillespie, "Ruth Is Suspended and Fined $5,000," *St. Louis Star*, August 29, 1925.
28. Dent McSkimming, "Yankees Pound Gaston in Eighth," *St. Louis Post-Dispatch*, August 30, 1925.
29. Technically, one starter on the 1925 Yankees had a winning record. The obscure and star-crossed Ben Shields won both of his starts, with the help of Babe Ruth's home runs. Nowlin, "Ben Shields," SABR BioProject, sabr.org/bioproject.
30. Berger, "Earle Combs," SABR BioProject, sabr.org/bioproject.
31. "Only Two Yankees Hurlers Sure of Jobs in 1926," *St. Louis Post-Dispatch*, December 5, 1925.

24. HOPE SPRINGS ETERNAL

1. Pennock (32), Shocker (35), Shawkey (35), and Jones (35) were the veterans, while Waite Hoyt was the youngster at 26.
2. Warren Brown, "Yankees Are Rated as a Doubtful Proposition," *New York American*, March 10, 1926.
3. John Kieran, *New York American*, March 15, 1926. Kieran was quoting Brown.
4. Steinberg and Spatz, *The Colonel and Hug*, 244, quoting Pegler, *Chicago Daily Tribune*, March 6 and March 14, 1926.
5. Ritter, *The Glory of Their Times*, 90.
6. Babe Ruth, "My Stomach Is Where It Belongs," *New York World*, March 12, 1926.
7. *New York Evening Telegram*, March 30, 1926.
8. Frederick G. Lieb, "Joke of the Camp Begins to Show Signs of Class," *New York Evening Telegram*, March 25, 1926.
9. Frederick G. Lieb, *New York Evening Telegram*, April 1, 1926.
10. James R. Harrison, "Three Yankee Pitchers Turn Back Braves," *New York Times*, March 18, 1926.
11. Will Wedge, "Shocker a Big Yank Asset," *New York Sun*, May 18, 1926.
12. In chapter 12 on the 1919 season, I explore Shocker's slow ball and wonder just how slow it really was.
13. Shirley Povich, This Morning with Shirley Povich, *Washington Post*, August 2, 1938. Five years later, Povich referenced Shocker in a column about Rip Sewell's "blooper" or "blimp" pitch. *Washington Post*, August 9, 1943. Povich was a reporter or editor for the *Post* from 1923 until his death in 1998.
14. Will Wedge, "Yankees Have Narrow Escape," *New York Sun*, March 8, 1926. The other Yankees on the boat were trainer Doc Woods and catcher Benny Bengough.
15. Lazzeri hit 60 home runs with Salt Lake City, many in the high desert air.
16. Ed Barrow, *My Fifty Years in Baseball*, 147.
17. Dave Newhouse, "A Golden Team's Sole Survivor: Mark Koenig, the Last of the 1927 New York Yankees," *Sports Illustrated*, September 3, 1990. Hoyt's father-in-law, under whom he apprenticed in the mortuary business, was a funeral home director.
18. John Kieran, *New York American*, March 15, 1926.
19. Frederick G. Lieb, "Robbie Pities Pitchers Who Face Yank Murderers' Row," *New York Evening Telegram*, April 5, 1926. The Brooklyn Dodgers were called the Robins during Robinson's years as their manager, 1914–31.
20. Frederick G. Lieb, "Lieb Selects Yankees and Pirates as Pennant Winners," *New York Evening Telegram*, April 12, 1926.

21. Ford Frick, *New York Evening Journal*, March 4, 1926.
22. Frederick G. Lieb, *New York Evening Telegram*, April 1, 1926.
23. "Colonel Ruppert, 'Only a Fan,' Makes Some Critical Deductions," *Sporting News*, April 1, 1926.

25. THE COMEBACK

1. Hugh Bradley, "The Barrow Story: Built an Empire but Always Considered Himself a Player," December 1953, *New York Journal-American* morgue files, Harry Ransom Humanities Research Center, University of Texas at Austin.
2. Westbrook Pegler, "Nobody's Business," *Washington Post*, October 14, 1928.
3. James R. Harrison, "Yankee Bludgeons Quell Coveleski," *New York Times*, May 1, 1926.
4. Frederick G. Lieb, *New York Evening Telegram*, May 18, 1926. Lieb noted that six of the ten hits and all three runs Shocker allowed came with two outs.
5. George Moriarty, "Shocker Is Rated with Ed Walsh," 1928 newspaper article in the Bill Loughman clippings.
6. In the 1920s, there was no distinction in box scores between sacrifice bunts and sacrifice flies, with both listed as "SH." And from 1920 to 1930, a sacrifice was credited for any fly ball on which a runner advanced, not just when he scored.
7. In 1926 and 1927 combined, Shocker had sacrifice hits in more than 20 percent of his plate appearances. For his career, his sacrifice rate of 9.3 percent ranks him first among pre-Expansion Era players, with Herb Pennock second and Ray Chapman third. E-mail from sabermetrician Cyril Morong, November 7, 2015.
8. Will Wedge, "Shocker a Big Yank Asset," *New York Sun*, May 18, 1926.
9. James R. Harrison, "Huggins Talks of Flag Outlook," *New York Times*, May 12, 1926.
10. Will Wedge, "Bob Meusel to the Reds," *New York Sun*, October 17, 1929.
11. Graham, *The New York Yankees*, 165.
12. Trachtenberg, *The Wonder Team*, 41.
13. Monitor, *New York World*, June 3, 1926.
14. The Pirates sold Bush to the New York Giants during the 1927 season. So he was not with Pittsburgh when the club met the Yankees in the World Series that fall.
15. Ruth led the league in many offensive categories, including on-base percentage, slugging percentage, OPS, runs, and walks.
16. Robinson, "Profile: The Babe," 16.

17. Creamer, *Babe*, 301.
18. "Climbs Notch," [Charleston] *Daily Mail*, May 8, 1926.
19. Gaston led the league in losses in 1926 with eighteen.
20. Both Lazzeri and Koenig played shortstop in the Minors, and Huggins decided Lazzeri would make the switch to second base more easily than the sensitive and anxious Koenig.
21. Arthur Daley, Sports of the Times, *New York Times*, August 9, 1946.
22. The Yankees were drawing big crowds on the road, and in the Chicago game (40,000 fans), thousands on the field distorted play by shrinking the size of the playing field. Three routine fly balls hit by the White Sox became "synthetic" two-base hits and ruined Shocker's "best exhibition of pitching" of the season. The Yankees hit no balls into the crowd. James R. Harrison, *New York Times*, June 21, 1926.
23. *Brooklyn Daily Eagle* morgue file, Brooklyn Public Library.
24. Dave Newhouse, "Yankee Hermit: Mark Koenig and His Memories," *Sporting News*, July 5, 1980.
25. The Yankees first extended their lead to ten games on June 13, when their record was 40-15. On July 1, their 49-23 record matched that lead.
26. Billy Evans, Billy Evans Says, syndicated column, June 4, 1926.
27. M. W. K., Sport Thoughts, *Bradford [PA] Era*, April 23, 1927.
28. W. B. Hanna, "Box Score Is Form Chart to Urban Shocker," *New York Herald Tribune*, July 26, 1925.
29. Bender won 193 games for the Athletics, while suffering only 102 losses. His A's won five pennants, and he had a 6-4 record in World Series games.
30. "Chief Bender Says Pitching Has Declined," *Boston Daily Globe*, August 9, 1925.
31. Ford Frick, "Urb Shocker Big Factor in Yankee Comeback," *New York Evening Journal*, July 8, 1926.
32. Rucker won 134 games in a ten-year career for Brooklyn, from 1907 to 1916. One reporter called his slow curve "the slowest ball in the history of the Majors," and Dan Daniel called it "one of the most amazing phenomena of baseball history." Enders, "Nap Rucker," SABR BioProject, sabr.org/bioproject.
33. Frederick G. Lieb, *New York Evening Telegram*, July 20, 1926.
34. Frederick G. Lieb, *New York Evening Telegram*, June 3, 1926.
35. Joe Vila, "Yank Boss Makes a Few 'Mind Bets,'" *Sporting News*, July 29, 1926.
36. Ford C. Frick, "Hugmen Again Show Class in Red Sox Contest," *New York Evening Journal*, September 8, 1926.

37. James R. Harrison, "Yanks Lose Fourth to the Indians, 3–1," *New York Times*, September 19, 1926.
38. Severeid caught 180 games that Shocker started for the Browns, including 15 shutouts. E-mail from sabermetrician Walt Wilson to Lyle Spatz, December 3, 2015.
39. The Yankees got both Severeid and Ruether from the Washington Senators, in part because the Yankees had helped them the previous year by sending veterans Everett Scott, outfielder Bobby Veach, and pitcher Alex Ferguson to them. All three helped the Senators win their second straight AL pennant in 1925.
40. Cincinnati traded Ruether, a year after he posted a 19-6 record for the 1919 world champion Reds; Brooklyn traded him a couple of years after he had a 21-12 record for them in 1922. Now Washington gave him up after he fashioned a 30-13 mark with them in less than two seasons.
41. James R. Harrison, "Indians' Hopes Fade as Yankees Win, 8–3," *New York Times*, September 20, 1926.
42. Frank Graham, Graham's Corner, *New York Journal-American*, June 1952.
43. Eig, *The Luckiest Man*, 73–74.
44. Arthur Mann, "Gehrig Most Valuable to Yanks This Year," *New Work Evening World*, April 27, 1927.
45. Shocker did not have a performance drop-off in those last three starts. He gave up six earned runs in 21⅔ innings, for a 2.49 earned run average, better than his 3.38 ERA for the season. The league's ERA was 4.02 in 1926.
46. Frederick G. Lieb, "Doping the World's Series," *New York Evening Telegram*, October 1, 1926.

26. MOMENT IN THE SUN

1. Mays posted a 19-12 record with three September wins in 1926, but made no starts after September 14. Pipp played in every game for Cincinnati and hit .291.
2. "Yankees Beat Browns, 6–1," *New York American*, June 16, 1926.
3. The Pirates opened Forbes Field during the 1909 season and won the World Series that year. The Red Sox were champions in 1912, the year Fenway Park opened in Boston. The Athletics opened Shibe Park in 1909, and while they did not reach the World Series that year, they won it the next two seasons. And of course the Yankees won their first world title in 1923, the year Yankee Stadium made its debut.
4. Lane, "Alexander's Greatest Triumph," 292.

5. From 1915 to 1917, Alexander won 94 games, and 36 of them were shutouts, even though his home ballpark was Philadelphia's small Baker Bowl, a notorious hitters' park. Twenty-two of those 36 shutouts came at Baker Bowl.
6. Jack Kofoed, "Series Melodrama," *New York Evening Post*, October 11, 1926. On the other hand, Alexander's manager with the Cubs, Joe McCarthy, was unwilling to tolerate his drinking. This was McCarthy's first year as a Major League manager.
7. Damon Runyon, "Club Has Strength and Dashing Youth," *New York American*, October 5, 1926.
8. Lane, "Alexander's Greatest Triumph," 292.
9. Frederick G. Lieb, *New York Evening Telegram*, August 21, 1926.
10. Damon Runyon, "McGraw Has Sent Bill to Hornsby's Team," *Cleveland Plain Dealer*, October 5, 1926. Alexander's earned run average of 2.91 (in 148⅓ innings pitched) was the lowest of any Cardinals pitcher.
11. Dan Daniel, "The World's Series: Yankee Pitching Staff," *New York Evening Telegram*, October 4, 1926.
12. George Moriarty, With George Moriarty, *Morning Herald* [Uniontown, PA], October 6, 1926.
13. The Cardinals and the Browns met for an annual series in St. Louis just before the start of the season.
14. Bozeman Bulger, "Series a Dead Heat by Expert Consensus," *New York Evening World*, September 30, 1926. Bulger wrote that Shocker had beaten the Cards nine out of ten times in the city series.
15. Sid Keener, "Short Outfield Fence Brings Prediction That Home Runs Will Feature," *St. Louis Times*, September 30, 1926.
16. "4,000 Turned Away; Big Crowd Orderly," *New York Times*, October 4, 1926.
17. Gordon McNamee, "How the Game Went, as Told over Radio," *New York Times*, October 4, 1926.
18. McNamee, "How the Game Went, as Told over Radio."
19. Grantland Rice, "67,000 Cheer Alexander as Cardinals Win Second, 6–2," *New York Herald Tribune*, October 4, 1926. The three-foot-high wire screen in right field was on a low concrete base, and Ruth probably used the top of the screen to boost himself higher up.
20. Shocker pitched to one batter in the eighth and, after he gave up a hit to the lead-off man, was relieved by Bob Shawkey.
21. Grantland Rice, "67,000 Cheer Alexander as Cardinals Win Second, 6–2," *New York Herald Tribune*, October 4, 1926.
22. Ford C. Frick, "Southworth's Homer Ties Series for Cardinals," October 4, 1926.

23. *New York Herald Tribune*, October 4, 1926.
24. Rice, "67,000 Cheer Alexander as Cardinals Win Second, 6–2."
25. Ford C. Frick, "Vet's Dazzling Hurling Turns Back Hugmen, 6–2," *New York Evening Journal*, October 4, 1926.
26. Bozeman Bulger, "Series a Dead Heat by Expert Consensus," *New York Evening World*, September 30, 1926.
27. In the first two years of Yankee Stadium, Shocker, as a member of the visiting Browns, did not give up a home run there.
28. Martin J. Haley, *St. Louis Times*, October 4, 1926, and Dan Daniel, *New York Evening Telegram*, October 4, 1926.
29. "By Urban Shocker" and "By Bill Southworth," *New York World*, October 4, 1926.
30. James R. Harrison, "Cardinals Defeat Yankees, 6–2," *New York Times*, October 4, 1926. Before Shocker settled down in the fourth inning, he gave up six hits in the first three innings.
31. John McGraw, "Urb Shocker's Mistake in Pitching to Southworth's Strength," *St. Louis Post-Dispatch*, January 9, 1927. Shocker, who paid attention to the smallest of details, often said that the position of a batter's feet revealed a lot. McGraw said that Shocker did not notice that Southworth had moved his feet for a better position to pull the ball down the right-field line.
32. J. Roy Stockton, "'Old Pete' Retires 21 Consecutive Batters and Fans 10 Yankees," *St. Louis Post-Dispatch*, October 4, 1926. Tilden was the era's dominant tennis star.
33. Monitor, "Breaks of the Game, No. 5," *New York World*, November 21, 1926.
34. Damon Runyon, "McGraw Sent Bill to Hornsby's Team," *Cleveland Plain Dealer*, October 4, 1926.
35. Ruth hit two home runs in a 1923 series game. Patsy Dougherty of the Boston Americans did so in 1903, as did the Red Sox's Harry Hooper in 1915 and Benny Kauff of the Giants in 1917. Ruth would hit three again in a 1928 World Series game, including one off Alexander. The feat would not be repeated until Reggie Jackson did so for the Yankees in 1977.
36. Henry P. Edwards, "Bambino Rips Record by Smashing 3 Homers," *Cleveland Plain Dealer*, October 7, 1926.
37. Sidelights on World's Series, *Billings Gazette*, October 7, 1926.
38. J. G. Taylor Spink, Three and One, *Sporting News*, June 8, 1939.
39. Melville E. Webb, "Returns to the Red Sox after Eleven Years," *Boston Daily Globe*, January 28, 1934.
40. *New York Herald Tribune*, October 4, 1926.

41. James R. Harrison, "Cardinals Smother Yankees, 10–2," *New York Times*, October 10, 1926.
42. Mosedale, *The Greatest of All*, 40.
43. Tullius, *I'd Rather Be a Yankee*, 37. Babe Ruth said that everyone knew Alexander had gone on a binge the night before. Wagenheim, *Babe Ruth*, 155.
44. Daniel, *The Real Babe Ruth*, 56.
45. Bozeman Bulger, Looking 'em Over, *New York Evening World*, September 9, 1927. Bulger's column was on the important role veteran players filled. Having faced pressure in the past, they stayed calm in critical situations and kept their clubs on an even keel. Bulger wrote that Alexander's taking a quick drink of alcohol before he entered Game Seven was no big deal.
46. Richards Vidmer, "Valiant Alexander Turns Back Threats," *New York Times*, October 11, 1926.
47. James R. Harrison, "Alexander Again the Hero," *New York Times*, October 11, 1926. Harrison mentioned the foul Lazzeri hit for strike two only in passing.
48. "'Strain on Lazzeri, Not on Me in Seventh,' Says Alexander," *New York World*, October 11, 1926.
49. Graham McNamee, "Play in Final Game as Told over Radio," *New York Times*, October 11, 1926.
50. Carmichael, *My Greatest Day in Baseball*, 142.
51. Durant, *Highlights of the World Series*, 71.
52. Harry T. Brundidge, "Believe It or Not, Tony Lazzeri Got His Greatest Thrill When He Fanned with Bases Loaded in World's Series," *Sporting News*, December 11, 1930.
53. Lieb, *The Story of the World Series*, 183.
54. Graham, *The New York Yankees*, 125.
55. Honig, *The October Heroes*, 101.
56. Ruth's 11 base on balls in a World Series remained the record until Barry Bonds of the Giants broke it, with 13 walks in 2002. Gene Tenace of the Athletics had tied Ruth's mark in the 1973 series.
57. H. I. Phillips, "Alexander Thrifty Pitcher," *New York Sun*, October 11, 1926.
58. Richards Vidmer called it a hit-and-run play that "went wrong." Richards Vidmer, *New York Times*, October 11, 1926, and Sid Keener, *St. Louis Times*, October 11, 1926.
59. Montville, *The Big Bam*, 236.
60. Fred Merkle made a base-running blunder late in the 1908 season that was blamed for the New York Giants not winning the pennant. When he died in 1956, the headline of his *New York Times* obituary (on March 3) mentioned his

"'Boner' in Failing to Touch 2nd Led to Loss of '08 Pennant." Fred Snodgrass muffed a routine fly ball in the 12th inning of Game Eight of the 1912 World Series; he was blamed for the Red Sox losing the championship. When he died in 1974, the headline of his *New York Times* obituary (on April 6) stated, "Ball Player Muffed 1912 Fly." In both cases, the blame directed at them was unfair and a gross simplification of a complicated series of events.

61. Billheimer, *Baseball and the Blame Game*, 43–45, 150–51.
62. Glueckstein, "Tony Lazzeri," SABR BioProject, sabr.org/bioproject.
63. Bob Considine, "Sports: Fans Remember Bad Points, but Not Good Ones, Says Lazzeri," *Pittsburgh Sun-Telegraph*, September 10, 1945.
64. Joe Vila, "Several Yank Vets Stranded on Limb," *Sporting News*, October 21, 1926. The gambler is most likely Sport Sullivan, who was indicted in the Black Sox scandal, though he was never arrested or put on trial.
65. W. J. Slocum, *New York American*, December 10, 1926.
66. E-mail from Gene Karst, May 21, 2002. Karst was the first publicity manager of a Major League team when Branch Rickey of the St. Louis Cardinals hired him in 1931.
67. Letter from Bob Broeg, late May 2002. Broeg did note that Waite Hoyt told him he was "pissed off" to lose that game because of unearned runs.
68. Letter from Donald Honig, June 6, 2002. Other historians who concurred in communications with me included David Pietrusza, Glenn Stout, and Leo Trachtenberg.
69. Spatz and Steinberg, *1921*, 355–56, 361.
70. Seymour and Mills, *Baseball, the Golden Age*, 439.
71. Ed Bang, "Grover Saves Game and Title for Cardinals," *Cleveland News*, October 11, 1926.
72. Heywood Broun, *New York World*, October 10, 1926.
73. Steve Kelley, "Cox Wastes Glavine's Guts and Performance," *Seattle Times*, October 27, 1999.
74. Knoblauch's two-run home run off Tom Glavine in the eighth inning tied the game, 5–5. The Yankees won in 10 innings and finished the sweep of the Braves the following day.

27. THE MASTER AT WORK

1. While Huggins may have realized Shocker was ailing, especially as the 1927 season progressed, there is no evidence Shocker shared any specifics with his manager until 1928.
2. Ford C. Frick, "Back of the Stars," 545.

3. Christy Walsh, Babe Ruth's agent, estimated he played before two hundred thousand people in his fall 1926 tour. Eig, *Luckiest Man*, 119.
4. *La Presse* [Montreal], October 16 and 18, 1926.
5. Giard, who had followed his 10-5 1925 season with a 3-10 1926, appeared in sixteen games for the 1927 Yankees, with no decisions. That was his last season in the Majors, done at age twenty-eight.
6. Infielders Mike Gazella and Ray Morehart and outfielders Cedric Durst and Ben Paschal joined the club. The 1927 Yankees were relatively injury-free and did not have to draw on this reserve strength very often.
7. Pat Robinson, "Huggins Picks Athletics as Team Yanks Must Beat," *New York Evening Telegram*, April 9, 1927.
8. Will Wedge, *New York Sun*, March 10, 1927, and *New York World*, March 12, 1927.
9. Yankees' salaries from an American League office letter to Ed Barrow, May 23, 1927, National Baseball Hall of Fame Library and Archives.
10. Ford C. Frick, "Yank Veteran Takes Rookie Pitchers under His Wing," *New York Evening Journal*, March 19, 1927.
11. Ford C. Frick, "Yankees Drop Two," *New York Evening Journal*, August 12, 1926.
12. Frederick G. Lieb, "Eleven Years in Game, Still the 'School Boy,'" *Sporting News*, March 3, 1927.
13. John B. Sheridan, Back of the Home Plate, *Sporting News*, February 4, 1926.
14. Cook, *Waite Hoyt*, 81–82.
15. Trachtenberg, *The Wonder Team*, 104. Trachtenberg noted that Hoyt's unpublished manuscript was housed at the Cincinnati Historical Society.
16. Frederick G. Lieb, *New York Evening Post*, May 17, 1928.
17. A couple of other spitball pitchers were still working effectively. Clarence Mitchell was thirty-six and would win twenty-one games for the Giants in 1930–31 and pitch into 1932. And Bill Doak, also thirty-six, would win eleven games for Brooklyn in 1927.
18. Steinberg, "The Spitball and the End of the Deadball Era," 16.
19. Steinberg, "The Spitball and the End of the Deadball Era," 8. The quotes are from the May 2 and June 13, 1914, issues of *Harper's Weekly*.
20. Bloodgood, "The Vanishing Spitball Pitcher," 318.
21. Rommel hit only three batters in 1927, and two were these of Shocker.
22. *New York American* and *New York Sun*, July 5, 1927.
23. "Yankee Trials Multiply in Journey through West," *New York Evening Telegram*, August 23, 1927.

24. In their 22nd and final meeting of the season, on September 11, Milt Gaston beat the Yankees, allowing the Browns to salvage a 1-21 record against New York in 1927.
25. James R. Harrison, "Ruth's 8th Homer Helps Yankees Win," *New York Times*, May 12, 1927.
26. Fleming, *Murderers' Row*, 143. The comment appeared in Frank Graham's column in the May 13 *New York Sun.*
27. Hack Wilson would set the new RBI mark in 1930 with 191. This remains the all-time record. Gehrig would knock in 185 the following year, still the American League record.
28. Because of rainouts earlier in the season, the Yankees had to play four doubleheaders in five days at the end of May. They won six of their nine games in that stretch.
29. Mosedale, *The Greatest of All*, 158.
30. Fleming, *Murderers' Row*, 221.
31. Ford C. Frick, "Mr. Urban Shocker Sure It Is a Personal Matter," *New York Evening Journal*, April 22, 1927.
32. Gallagher, *The Yankee Encyclopedia*, 198.
33. Bozeman Bulger, *Newspaper Alliance*, September 28, 1929.
34. Fleming, *Murderers' Row*, 156.
35. Moore appeared in fifty games, twelve as a starter. He was retroactively awarded thirteen saves for the Yankees, under the original, liberal 1969 definition of a save.
36. Smelser, *The Life That Ruth Built*, 353.
37. Frank Graham, "Yankees Release Shocker," *New York Sun*, July 7, 1928.
38. Moore saved Shocker's 3–2 win against the Red Sox on June 22, his 5–2 win over the White Sox on July 23, and his 4–3 victory, also over the White Sox, on August 7.
39. On April 20, Shocker took the loss after Moore let his runners score. Ten days later, Shocker took a 2–0 shutout against the Red Sox into the ninth inning. Moore came in with the score tied and let the winning run cross the plate; Shocker again took the loss. On June 28, Shocker took a 9–0 shutout against the Athletics into the ninth. After he gave up three runs, Moore came in and could not get anyone out. Two more New York pitchers finally put down the uprising, as the Yankees held on for a 9–8 win.
40. Rogers, "Billy Werber," SABR BioProject, sabr.org/bioproject. The Yankees signed Werber "under the table" in 1927 to preserve his college eligibility.

They paid him a large bonus and agreed to finance his college education. He joined the team after he graduated in 1930.

41. Werber and Rogers, *Memories of a Ballplayer*, 3.
42. Liepa, "George Pipgras," SABR BioProject, sabr.org/bioproject.
43. Dave Newhouse, "Yankee Hermit: Mark Koenig and His Memories," *Sporting News*, July 5, 1980.
44. Robert Edgren, "Babe Follows Through; Lou Chops at Ball," *New York Evening World*, August 13, 1927.
45. Fleming, *Murderers' Row*, 327.
46. Mosedale, *The Greatest of All*, 89.
47. Edgren, "Babe Follows Through; Lou Chops at Ball."
48. Fleming, *Murderers' Row*, 240.
49. Mosedale, *The Greatest of All*, 130.
50. Frank Graham, "Yanks Finish in West Today," *New York Sun*, August 29, 1927.
51. Mosedale, *The Greatest of All*, 178.
52. My son and I visited Hopkins at his Connecticut apartment late in his life and presented him with a print of a Charles Conlon photograph of him. Hopkins died in 2004 at the age of ninety-nine.
53. Joe Vila, "Huggins Figures Pitching Staff Good as Anything in National," *Sporting News*, September 29, 1927.
54. Arthur Mann, "Yankees vs. Pirates: The Pitchers," *New York Evening World*, October 2, 1927. Shocker was actually far more effective against weak teams in 1927. He had a 5-4 record with a 3.97 ERA against the league's three teams with winning records (Philadelphia, Washington, and Detroit). Against the weakest four teams, he had a 13-2 mark and a 2.41 ERA.
55. While early on in heart disease, a patient may gain weight because of fluid retention, in the final stage of the disease, known as cardiac cachexia, the patient is catabolic and suffers severe weight loss.
56. "Yanks in Pittsburgh Preparing for Series," *New York Evening World*, October 3, 1927.
57. Honig, *Baseball When the Grass Was Real*, 127–28. A pitcher is able to control a rough ball more than a smooth, fresh one.
58. Herb Pennock, "My Greatest Diamond Thrill," *Sporting News*, May 4, 1944.
59. Dan Daniel, "Pennock Poetry in Motion on Mound," *Sporting News*, February 11, 1948.
60. The Yankees had also won the 1923 World Series.
61. The National League's Chicago Cubs swept the Detroit Tigers in 1907. (There

was one tie game.) The Boston Braves won four straight against the Philadelphia Athletics in the 1914 World Series, and the New York Giants had swept the Yankees in the 1922 World Series, though there was one tie game (called because of darkness).

62. Joe Vila, "If Shocker Quits, Then Yanks Have Bigger Pitching Problems," *Sporting News*, February 23, 1928.
63. See http://www.mekulius.com/Library/obg/mlbsimSeries.html and http://www.thefreelibrary.com/mlb+Advanced+Media+Unveils+New+Simulation+Game%3b+Baseball+Weekly+Is . . .-a079613043.
64. Reba Shimansky in Schacht, *Mudville Diaries*.

28. PROMISES AND SECRETS

1. John B. Sheridan, Back of the Home Plate, *Sporting News*, March 10, 1927. "Stuff" is defined in the *Dickson Baseball Dictionary* as "a pitcher's assortment or repertoire of pitches collectively, together with his ability to deliver and control them in the proper sequence at the right velocity to the desired area of the strike zone" (837).
2. James, *Bill James Historical Baseball Abstract*, 420–21.
3. Pennock and Hoyt won more games (241 and 237, respectively) than Shocker and Shawkey (187 and 195, respectively). But while Shocker lost only 117 games, Pennock lost 162, and Hoyt lost 182. (Shawkey lost 150.) Pennock and Hoyt had far higher earned run averages, 3.60 and 3.59, respectively, compared with Shocker's 3.17 and Shawkey's 3.09.
4. James, *Bill James Historical Baseball Abstract*, 421.
5. Batter Up, *New York Evening Post*, August 19, 1926.
6. See http://baseballhall.org/hof/youngs-ross.
7. Cardiac cachexia, or body wasting, is the medical term. E-mail from Dr. Stephen Boren, November 2, 2002. Dr. Boren referred to the article on cardiac cachexia in the *International Journal of Cardiology* 85 (September 2002): 51–66.
8. Bill Corum, "Sports: The Holdout," *New York Journal-American*, February 15, 1957.
9. H. G. Salsinger, "Ty Cobb's Own Story," *Minneapolis Morning Tribune*, December 24, 1924.
10. Paul Neumann, "Effects of Sports on Hearts Still Thing of Conjecture," *New York Evening Post*, January 4, 1926.
11. Max Kase, "Does 'Athletic Heart' Bring Stars to Untimely End?" *New York Evening Journal*, January 11, 1928.

12. Gene Tunney, "Athletics Lengthen, Not Shorten Life," *New York Evening Journal*, March 16, 1928.
13. While I discussed the subject of Shocker's heart failure with a number of doctors, a layman's article by Dr. Thomas Lee on heart failure, including mitral valve disease, gave an overview in *Newsweek*, October 3, 2005.
14. "Yanks Don't Think Shocker Will Retire," *New York Herald Tribune*, February 18, 1928.
15. "Yanks Not Worried If Shocker Quits," *New York Times*, February 18, 1928.
16. "Urban Shocker, Yankee Pitcher, Quits Baseball," *New York Sun*, February 17, 1928.
17. John Kieran, "Urban the Stubborn," Sports of the Times, *New York Times*, February 19, 1928.
18. "Shocker to Enter Aviation School," *New York Evening Post*, February 21, 1928.
19. Faber, "Marvin Goodwin," SABR BioProject, sabr.org/bioproject. Goodwin pitched for the Cardinals during four seasons that Shocker was with the Browns, 1919 to 1922. He flew in the U.S. Army Air Corps during World War I. He was in the Army Service Reserve and was killed when his plane crashed in Texas.
20. *Okmulgee Democrat*, February 17 and 20, 1928.
21. Will Wedge, Games, Gossip, and Guff, *New York Sun*, February 23, 1928.
22. Gentile, *The 1928 New York Yankees*, 45.
23. "Huggins Still in Dark on Shocker's Return," *New York Times*, April 19, 1928.
24. James R. Harrison, "Shocker Lets Fall a Hint He May Sign," *New York Times*, March 8, 1928.
25. "Huggins Still in Dark on Shocker's Return," *New York Times*, April 19, 1928.
26. Frederick G. Lieb, "Change of Climate No Boon to Yanks," *New York Evening Post*, April 6, 1928, quoting a Nashville reporter.
27. Frederick G. Lieb, "Doping the Big League Races," *New York Evening Post*, April 9, 1928.
28. Letter from American League president E. S. Barnard to Miller Huggins, *714 Gallery* eBay auction item, December 24, 2008. The letter confirmed the contract's $15,000 salary.
29. *New York American*, April 25, 1928.
30. Bill Corum, "Sports: The Holdout," *New York Journal-American*, February 15, 1957.
31. Arthur Mann, "Gamest of the Game," *Sporting News*, August 11, 1938.
32. Bill Corum, "Sports: The Holdout," *New York Journal-American*, February 15, 1957.

33. A line drive off the bat of Yankees catcher Johnny Grabowski hit Shocker in the wrist in mid-May. *New York Herald Tribune*, May 16, 1928. The jawbone infection occurred during the western road trip of early June. *New York Sun*, July 7, 1928.
34. Arthur Mann, "Gamest of the Game," *Sporting News*, August 11, 1938.
35. Bill Corum, "Sports: The Holdout," *New York Journal-American*, February 15, 1957.
36. Frank Graham, "Yankees Release Shocker," *New York Sun*, July 6, 1928.
37. Frederick G. Lieb, Cutting the Plate, *New York Evening Post*, July 7, 1928.
38. Ford Frick, *New York Evening Journal*, July 7, 1928.
39. The other three at the bridge table were Ruth, Gehrig, and utility infielder Mike Gazella, according to Frick. Ruth's reference to Shocker's usually stocky appearance as a "tendency to a rather aldermanic bay window" surely came from his ghost writer.
40. A high-altitude location, such as Denver, is not a good place for a patient suffering from heart failure to recover because the partial pressure of oxygen is much lower that at lower altitudes. E-mail from Dr. Ron Siegel, January 11, 2016.
41. Frank Graham, "Yankees Release Shocker," *New York Sun*, July 6, 1928. Bennett had been his roommate since Shocker's return to the Yankees in 1925.
42. James R. Harrison, "Shocker Released as a Free Agent," *New York Times*, July 7, 1928.
43. Arthur Mann, "Gamest of the Game," *Sporting News*, August 11, 1938.
44. Arthur Mann, "Gamest of the Game," *Sporting News*, August 11, 1938.
45. Joe Williams, As Joe Williams Sees It, *Cleveland Press*, July 9, 1928. Right up to the end of his career, reporters mistook Shocker's slow ball for his spitball.
46. Frederick G. Lieb, Cutting the Plate, *New York Evening Post*, July 7, 1928.
47. Will Wedge, Games, Gossip, and Guff, *New York Sun*, February 23, 1928.
48. Frank Graham, "Yankees Release Shocker," *New York Sun*, July 6, 1928.

29. A STAR SURFACES AND CRASHES

1. Bill Haraway sold his chain to Safeway in the 1930s and joined the national chain as a district manager.
2. While tuberculosis is primarily a lung disease, the infection can affect any part of the body. Spinal TB usually attacks children and can cause paralysis of the legs. The term "extrapulmonary tuberculosis" refers to the infection occurring outside of the lungs; "osseous tuberculosis" refers specifically to the infection in the bone.

3. Phone conversation with Frank Haraway, May 16, 2000.
4. The Yankees' record on August 1 stood at an impressive 70-31. However, they had gone 20-15 in July, while the Athletics were a scorching 25-8.
5. Williams won the 100m race in Hamilton, Ontario, and matched the time set by British star Harold Abrahams (subject of the 1981 movie *Chariots of Fire*) in the 1928 Olympics.
6. See http://www.olympic.org/percy-williams.
7. "Entry List of Sixteen Breaks All Marks in History of Meet," *Denver Post*, July 29, 1928.
8. "Huge Treat in Store for Post Baseball Fans," *Denver Post*, August 4, 1928.
9. Walter Judge, "Indians Down Piggly Wiggly, 5–2, as Rube Schauer Stars," *Denver Post*, August 6, 1928. When Shocker left the game, Cheyenne was leading, 5–1. They won the game, 5–2. The Indians were beaten in the tournament final by the surprise winners, a team from tiny Texon, Texas. The following year, Bill Haraway brought Schauer to Piggly Wiggly and won the tournament. Sanford, *The Denver Post Tournament*, 32–34.
10. Sanford, *The Denver Post Tournament*, 32.
11. Phone conversation with Frank Haraway, May 16, 2000.

30. A DAY OF DEATH AND REBIRTH

1. New York teams had already won nine pennants in the 1920s: the Giants in 1921, 1922, 1923, and 1924; the Yankees in 1921, 1922, 1923, 1926, and 1927.
2. Dan Daniel, "Five Games with Harris Tribe Vital to Champs," *New York Evening Telegram*, September 5, 1928.
3. "Extra Police Ready for Stadium Jam," *New York Times*, September 8, 1928.
4. "Police Disperse Fans Trying to Buy Tickets," *New York World*, September 7, 1928.
5. Richards Vidmer, "Police Quell Riot at Yankee Offices," *New York Times*, September 8, 1928.
6. Phone conversations with Billy Rogell (1904–2003), May 20 and August 17, 1999. I visited Rogell a few weeks before his death in 2003.
7. *Chicago Daily Tribune*, September 9, 1928.
8. Richards Vidmer, "Two Defeats by Senators Drop Yanks into First-Place Tie," *New York Times*, September 8, 1928.
9. Ford Frick, "Athletics Favored to Take Series from Yankees," *New York Evening Journal*, September 8, 1928.
10. Robert Edgren, *New York Evening World*, "Time Takes Heavy Toll among Top-Notchers," September 8, 1928.

11. "Crowd of 85,265, Baseball Record, Sees Yanks Win Two," *New York Times*, September 10, 1928.
12. Curley Grieve, "Urban Shocker, Great Pitcher of New York Yankees, Dies in Denver of Athletic Heart," *Rocky Mountain News*, September 10, 1928. The quote in this article came from Shocker's wife.
13. Frank O'Neill, "Drama, Thrills Galore on Stadium Green," *New York Evening Journal*, September 10, 1928.
14. Dan Daniel, "Mackmen Again Victims of Champs' Indian Signs," *New York Evening Telegram*, September 10, 1928.
15. The head-to-head matchups between the Yankees and the Athletics determined the race. New York's record against the six teams other than the A's was 85-47. Philadelphia's record against the six teams other than the Yankees was 92-39, an edge of 7½ games.
16. Durocher, *Nice Guys Finish Last*, 53.
17. "Shocker Dies; Yanks Grieve," *New York Sun*, September 10, 1928.
18. Foxx had hit the first of his 534 home runs off Urban Shocker in 1927.
19. Liepa, "George Pipgras," SABR BioProject, sabr.org/bioproject.
20. Joe Williams, *New York Evening Telegram*, September 10, 1928.
21. Lou Gehrig, "Oh, What a Day! Sighs Lou," *New York American*, September 10, 1928.
22. "'The Same Old A's,' Chant the Yankees," *New York Times*, September 10, 1928.
23. Graham, *The New York Yankees*, 146. Graham wrote that club secretary Mark Roth broke the news to the players.
24. Pennock was suffering from neuritis, and his last 1928 appearance was on August 12. Combs ran into the outfield wall in Detroit near the end of the season and had only one plate appearance in the World Series. Lazzeri's shoulder was so sore that he could throw only underhand during the Series.
25. Alexander, now forty-one, had an earned run average of 19.80 in the Series. He did post a 16-9 record during the regular season.
26. Honig, *Baseball When the Grass Was Real*, 128.
27. Curley Grieve, "Urban Shocker, Great Pitcher of New York Yankees, Dies in Denver of Athletic Heart," *Rocky Mountain News*, September 10, 1928. Doctors had told her that, had he not pitched that game in the Denver tournament, he would have lived another six months.

EPILOGUE

1. Dent McSkimming, "Shocker Holds Browns to Five Hits," *St. Louis Post-Dispatch*, May 9, 1925.

2. Frederick G. Lieb, "Yank Regulars Take First Trouncing from Yannigans," *New York Evening Telegram*, March 7, 1925.
3. Monitor, "Ruth Victim of Boils, Carbuncles and Blisters," *New York World*, March 6, 1925.
4. Joe Williams, "The Value of Color in Baseball," *New York Evening Telegram*, July 9, 1928.
5. Cooke, *Wake Up the Echoes*, 71.
6. Daher, "The Spitter Hits the Trail," 442.
7. Sid C. Keener, On the Side Line, *St. Louis Times*, July 30, 1929.
8. John B. Sheridan, Back of the Home Plate, *Sporting News*, August 11, 1927. Sheridan had seen a lot of pitchers; he covered baseball for more than forty years, including more than a dozen as a regular columnist for the sports weekly.
9. Will Wedge, Games, Gossip, and Guff, *New York Sun*, February 23, 1928.
10. E-mail from Mark Wernick, September 23, 2012. Shocker's ERA+ of 124 ranks ahead of 40 Hall of Fame pitchers (39, per Wernick, plus Tom Glavine, inducted in 2014). Shocker's WAR (Wins above Replacement) of 54.9 is better than that of 18 Hall of Fame pitchers. His APR (Adjusted Pitching Runs) of 234 exceeds that of 28 Hall of Famers, and his APW (Adjusted Pitching Wins) of 23.54 is better than that of 27 pitchers in the Hall.
11. Bill James, "Measuring Consistency."
12. Frank Graham, "What Price Smart Pitching?" *New York Sun*, July 11, 1928.
13. Damon Runyon, Runyon Says, *New York American*, October 12, 1927. Runyon was wondering if the 1927 Yankees would "survive the test of time" as one of the greatest teams ever.
14. Hutton, *History as an Art of Memory*, 2, 25, 168. Hutton wrote that the historian's task is "one of re-creating the imagination of the past for a world that acknowledged there could be no repetition of its events" (156).
15. George B. Underwood, "Those Were the Days," chapter 21, *New York Evening Telegram*, March 16, 1924.

Bibliography

Grantland Rice was a prominent sportswriter of the first half of the twentieth century. Known as the "Dean of American Sportswriters," his work played a key role in making the 1920s the "Golden Age of Sports." His syndicated sports columns included poems, thousands of which he penned over the years. The Grantland Rice Papers are housed at Vanderbilt University, Special Collections and University Archives, Nashville, Tennessee.

Allardice, Bruce. "Sport Sullivan." SABR BioProject, sabr.org/bioproject.

Allen, Mel. "Pitching Style." *Sport*, October 1950, 9.

Anderson, David W. "Billy Evans." SABR BioProject, sabr.org/bioproject.

Appel, Marty. *Pinstripe Empire: From before the Babe to after the Boss*. New York: Bloomsbury, 2012.

Bak, Richard. *A Place for Summer: A Narrative History of Tiger Stadium*. Detroit: Wayne State University Press, 1998.

Barrow, Ed, with James M. Kahn. *My Fifty Years in Baseball*. New York: Coward-McCann, 1951.

Barry, John. *The Great Influenza: The Epic Story of the Deadliest Plague in History*. London: Penguin, 2004.

Baseball Reference at www.baseball-reference.com.

Berger, Ralph. "Earle Combs." SABR BioProject, sabr.org/bioproject.

Bevis, Charlie. "Frank 'Shag' Shaughnessy." SABR BioProject, sabr.org/bioproject.

———. "Tim Murnane." SABR BioProject, sabr.org/bioproject.

Billheimer, John. *Baseball and the Blame Game: Scapegoating in the Major Leagues*. Jefferson NC: McFarland, 2007.

Bingay, Malcolm W. *Detroit Is My Own Home Town*. Indianapolis: Bobbs-Merrill, 1946.

Blau, Cliff. "Draft." http://cliffblau.ucoz.com/ml_draft.htm.

———. "Options." http://cliffblau.ucoz.com/options.htm.

———. "Waivers." http://cliffblau.ucoz.com/waivers.htm.

Bloodgood, Clifford. "He Never Pitched under the .500 Mark!" *Baseball Magazine*, June 1928, 318 (2).

———. "The Vanishing Spitball Pitcher." *Baseball Magazine*, June 1927, 387 (3).

Bohn, Terry. "Rube Schauer." SABR BioProject, sabr.org/bioproject.

Borst, Bill. *Still Last in the American League*. West Bloomfield MI: A & M, 1992.

Borst, Bill, Jim Scott, and George Walden, eds. *From Ables to Zoldak*. 3 vols. St. Louis: St. Louis Browns Fan Club, 1988–89.

Bradley, Hugh. "Baseball's Biggest Gamble." *Baseball Magazine*, May 1933, 535 (3).

Carmichael, John P., ed. *My Greatest Day in Baseball*. Lincoln: University of Nebraska Press, 1996. Originally published by G. P. Putnam's Sons, 1955.

Cataneo, David. *Baseball Legends and Lore*. New York: Galahad Books, 1995.

Cauz, Louis. *Baseball's Back in Town: From the Don to the Blue Jays, A History of Baseball in Toronto*. Toronto: Controlled Media Corp, 1977.

Cook, William A. *Waite Hoyt: A Biography of the Yankees' Schoolboy Wonder*. Jefferson, NC: McFarland, 2004.

Cooke, Bob, ed. *Wake Up the Echoes: From the Sports Pages of the New York Herald Tribune*. Garden City NY: Hanover House.

Cooper, Brian. *Red Faber: A Biography of the Hall of Fame Spitball Pitcher*. Jefferson, NC: McFarland, 2007.

Costello, Rory. "Bob Quinn." SABR BioProject, sabr.org/bioproject.

Creamer, Robert. *Babe: The Legend Comes to Life*. New York: Penguin, 1974.

Curran, William. *Big Sticks: The Batting Revolution of the Twenties*. New York: William Morrow, 1990.

Daher, Naiph. "The Spitter Hits the Trail." *Baseball Magazine*, July 1931, 441 (3).

Daniel, Dan. *The Real Babe Ruth*. St. Louis: Sporting News, 1948.

Davenport, Frederick M. "Christy Mathewson, Special Correspondence." *Outlook*, August 30, 1922, 704–5.

Dickson, Paul. *The Dickson Baseball Dictionary*. 3rd ed. New York: W. W. Norton, 2009.

Durant, John. *Highlights of the World Series*. New York: Hastings House, 1971.

Durocher, Leo. *Nice Guys Finish Last*. New York: Simon & Schuster, 1975.

Edwards, Henry P. "A Bluff Old Fighter Passes On." *Baseball Magazine*, December 1933, 313 (2).

Eig, Jonathan. *Luckiest Man: The Life and Death of Lou Gehrig*. New York: Simon & Schuster, 2007.

Eller, Hod. "Why the New Pitching Rules Are Unjust." *Baseball Magazine,* August 1920, 433 (3).

Enders, Eric. "Nap Rucker." SABR BioProject, sabr.org/bioproject.

Faber, Charles. "Marvin Goodwin." SABR BioProject, sabr.org/bioproject.

Faber, Charles F., and Richard B. Faber. *Spitballers: The Last Legal Hurlers of the Wet One*. Jefferson NC: McFarland, 2006.

"Famous Magnates of the Federal League." *Baseball Magazine*, October 1915, 66 (9).

Field, Russell. "Before the Lynx Went on the Prowl: Ninety-Five Years of Professional Baseball in the Nation's Capital." *Dugout*, October 1993, 25–30.

———. "On the Waterfront: Toronto's Professional Baseball Heritage." *Dugout*, April 1993, 5–11.

Fleming, G. H. *Murderers' Row: The 1927 New York Yankees*. New York: William Morrow, 1985.

Fohl, Lee. "Baseball Brains: The Rare Mental Talent Which So Few Ball Players Possess." *Baseball Magazine*, June 1918, 280 (3).

Fountain, Charles. *Sportswriter: The Life and Times of Grantland Rice*. Bridgewater NJ: Replica Books, 1993.

Frick, Ford. "Back of the Stars That Shine." *Baseball Magazine*, November 1928, 545 (4).

Frommer, Harvey. *Five O'clock Lightning: Babe Ruth, Lou Gehrig, and the Greatest Baseball Team in History, the 1927 New York Yankees*. New York: John Wiley and Sons, 2008.

Gagnon, Cappy. "Red Murray." SABR BioProject, sabr.org/bioproject.

Gallagher, Mark. *The Yankee Encyclopedia*. Champaign IL: Sagamore, 1996.

Gentile, Charlie. *The 1928 New York Yankees: The Return of Murderers' Row*. New York: Rowman & Littlefield, 2014.

Gibson, Sally. *More Than an Island: A History of the Toronto Island*. Toronto: Irwin, 1984.

Glueckstein, Fred. "Tony Lazzeri." SABR BioProject, sabr.org/bioproject.

———. "Wilcy Moore." SABR BioProject, sabr.org/bioproject.

Godin, Roger. *The 1922 St. Louis Browns: The Best of the American League's Worst*. Jefferson NC: McFarland, 1991.

Graham, Frank. *The New York Yankees: An Informal History*. New York: G. P. Putnam's Sons, 1943.

Greene, Lee. "George Sisler, Picture Player." *Sport,* March 1963, 50 (4).

Harper, William A. *How You Played the Game: The Life of Grantland Rice*. Columbia: University of Missouri Press, 1999.

Heller, Dave. "Carl Weilman: The Life and Death of Carl Weilman." http://seamheads.com/2010/01/10/the-life-and-death-of-carl-weilman/.

Hoefer, W. R. "Durable Dave Davenport: Star Twirler of the St. Louis Browns." *Baseball Magazine*, February 1917, 34 (3).

———. "The Reign of the Wallop." *Baseball Magazine*, July 1923, 365 (3).

———. "The Return of the Player-Manager." *Baseball Magazine*, January 1924, 345 (2).

Honig, Donald. *Baseball When the Grass Was Real*. Lincoln: University of Nebraska Press, 1993.

———. *The Greatest First Basemen of All Time*. New York: Crown, 1988.

———. *The Man in the Dugout: Fifteen Big League Managers Speak Their Minds*. Lincoln: University of Nebraska Press, 1977.

———. *The October Heroes: Great World Series Games Remembered by the Men Who Played Them*. Lincoln: University of Nebraska Press, 1979.

Huhn, Rick. *The Sizzler: George Sisler, Baseball's Forgotten Star*. Columbia: University of Missouri Press, 2004.

Husman, John. "Toledo's Flash." *Toledo Magazine*, June 18–24, 1989.

Hutton, Patrick H. *History as an Art of Memory*. Hanover: University Press of New England, 1993.

Inabinett, Mark. *Grantland Rice and His Heroes: The Sportswriter as Mythmaker in the 1920s*. Knoxville: University of Tennessee Press, 1994.

Infantry Journal, 85th Division. Washington DC: U.S. Infantry Association, July 1926.

Istorico, Ray. *Greatness in Waiting: An Illustrated History of the Early New York Yankees, 1903–1919*. Jefferson NC: McFarland, 2008.

James, Bill. *Bill James Historical Baseball Abstract, 1st Edition*. New York: Villard, 1985.

———. "Measuring Consistency." *Bill James Online*, September 19, 2007.

Jenkinson, Bill. *The Year Babe Ruth Hit 104 Home Runs*. New York: Carroll & Graf, 2007.

Jennings, Hugh. "Will George Sisler Equal Ty Cobb?" *Baseball Magazine*, March 1921, 468 (3).

Kofoed, J. C. "Control among Pitchers." *Baseball Magazine*, February 1923, 413 (2).

Lamberty, Bill. "George Sisler." SABR BioProject, sabr.org/bioproject.

Lammers, Craig. "Bob Quinn and the Farm System." http://sabr.org/bioproj/topic/bob-quinn-and-farm-system.

Lane, F. C. "Alexander's Greatest Triumph." *Baseball Magazine*, December 1926, 291 (3).

———. "The All-America Baseball Club of 1920." *Baseball Magazine*, December 1920, 339 (6).

———. "The All-America Baseball Club of 1921." *Baseball Magazine*, December 1921, 584 (7).

———. "The All-America Baseball Club of 1922." *Baseball Magazine*, December 1922, 307 (6).

———. "The All-America Baseball Club of 1923." *Baseball Magazine*, December 1923, 307 (6).

———. "Baby Doll Jacobson: A True Clean-Up Slugger." *Baseball Magazine*, October 1920, 533 (2).

———. *Batting*. SABR, 2001.

———. "Brooklyn's New Business Manager." *Baseball Magazine*, December 1933, 301 (3).

———. "A Catching Hercules." *Baseball Magazine,* October 1924, 501 (2).

———. "A Great Natural Ballplayer Is Tony Lazzeri." *Baseball Magazine*, December 1927, 305.

———. "Has the 'Lively' Ball Revolutionized the Game?" *Baseball Magazine*, September 1921, 435 (7).

———. "The Home-Run Epidemic." *Baseball Magazine*, July 1921, 339 (4).

———. "How a Wrecked Career Produced a Good Scout." *Baseball Magazine*, March 1924, 442 (2).

———. "A Master of Pitching Craft." *Baseball Magazine*, February 1929, 395 (3).

———. "The Much Discussed Menace of the Lively Ball." *Baseball Magazine*, October 1929, 593 (5).

———. "The Prosaic Career of Elam Van Gilder." *Baseball Magazine*, February 1928, 411–12.

———. "The Sensational Rube Benton Affair." *Baseball Magazine*, May 1923, 538 (3).

———. "Should the Spitball Be Abolished?" *Baseball Magazine*, June 1919, 67 (4).

———. "Those Mid-Summer Trades." *Baseball Magazine,* October 1922, (504) 5.

———. "Urban Shocker, One of the Great Pitchers of 1920." *Baseball Magazine*, January 1921, 381–82.

———. "Why Dave Danforth Has Been a Storm Center." *Baseball Magazine*, July 1924, 353 (2).

Larson, David. "Fielder Jones." SABR BioProject, sabr.org/bioproject.

Lee, Thomas H. "Health for Life: When Should You Start to Worry?" *Newsweek*, October 3, 2005.

Levitt, Daniel R. *Ed Barrow: The Bulldog Who Built the Yankees' First Dynasty*. Lincoln: University of Nebraska Press, 2008.

——. "Paul Krichell." SABR BioProject, sabr.org/bioproject.

Lewis, Franklin. *The Cleveland Indians*. New York: G. P. Putnam's, 1949.

Lieb, Frederick G. *The Baltimore Orioles*. Carbondale: Southern Illinois University Press, 2001. Originally published by G. P. Putnam's, 1955.

——. *Baseball as I Have Known It*. Lincoln: Bison Books, 1996. Originally published by Coward, McCann, and Geoghegan, 1977.

——. *The Story of the World Series*. New York: G. P. Putnam's Sons, 1965.

——. "What 'Color' Means to a Ball Player." *Baseball Magazine*, January 1924, 349 (3).

Liepa, John. "George Pipgras." SABR BioProject, sabr.org/bioproject.

Livacari, Gary. "Jimmy Burke." SABR BioProject, sabr.org/bioproject.

Loughman, Bill. Newspaper Clippings Private Collection. This collection, owned by Bill Loughman, has been dispersed and is no longer available. It was made available to me in the early 2000s.

Lowenfish, Lee. *Branch Rickey: Baseball's Ferocious Gentleman*. Lincoln: University of Nebraska Press, 2007.

Macht, Norman. *Connie Mack and the Early Years of Baseball*. Lincoln: University of Nebraska Press, 2012.

Mahl, Tom E. *The Spitball Knuckleball Book*. Elyria OH: Trick Pitch Press, 2009.

Mallory, Patrick. "The Game They All Played: Chicago Baseball, 1876–1906." PhD diss., Loyola University, 2013.

Mason, Ward. "An Innovation in Big League Management." *Baseball Magazine*, June 1916, 45 (4).

McKenna, Brian. "Logan Squares." SABR BioProject, sabr.org/bioproject.

Meany, Tom. *Babe Ruth: The Big Moments with the Big Fellow*. A. S. Barnes, 1947.

——. *Baseball's Greatest Hitters*. New York: A. S. Barnes, 1950.

——. *Baseball's Greatest Teams*. New York: A. S. Barnes, 1949.

Mercer, Sid. "The Supreme Value of 'Color' in Baseball." *Baseball Magazine*, August 1920, 423 (5).

Montville, Leigh. *The Big Bam: The Life and Times of Babe Ruth*. New York: Doubleday, 2006.

Morgan, T. Kent, and David Jones. "Russ Ford." SABR BioProject, sabr.org/bioproject.

Morris, Peter. "Eddie Bennett." In *Scandal on the South Side: The 1919 Chicago White Sox*, ed. Jacob Pomrenke, 265–68. Phoenix: Society for American Baseball Research, 2015.

Mosedale, John. *The Greatest of All: The 1927 New York Yankees*. New York: Dial Press, 1974.

Murdock, Eugene C. *Ban Johnson: Czar of Baseball*. Westport CT: Greenwood, 1982.

———. *Baseball between the Wars: Memories of the Game by the Men Who Played It*. Westport CT: Meckler, 1992.

———. *Baseball Players and Their Times: Oral Histories of the Game, 1920–1940*. Westport CT: Meckler, 1991.

Newhouse, Dave. "A Golden Team's Sole Survivor: Mark Koenig Is the Last of the 1927 New York Yankees." *Sports Illustrated*, September 3, 1990, 129 (6).

Neyer, Rob, and Bill James. *The Neyer/James Guide to Pitchers*. New York: Fireside, 2004.

Norman L. Macht Baseball Research Collection. DeGolyer Library, Southern Methodist University.

Nowlin, Bill. "Baby Doll Jacobson." SABR BioProject, sabr.org/bioproject.

———. "Ben Shields." SABR BioProject, sabr.org/bioproject.

———. "Jack Tobin." SABR BioProject, sabr.org/bioproject.

———. "Frank Gilhooley." SABR BioProject, sabr.org/bioproject.

———. "Milt Gaston." SABR BioProject, sabr.org/bioproject.

Okkonen, Marc. *The Ty Cobb Scrapbook: An Illustrated Chronology of Significant Dates in the 24-Year Career of the Fabled Georgia Peach*. New York: Sterling, 2001.

Phelon, W. A. "When the Big League Clubs Strike Their Stride." *Baseball Magazine*, August 1919, 67 (5).

"Philip DeCatesby Ball." *Reedy's Mirror*, December 18, 1914, 74–75.

Pietrusza, David. *Judge and Jury: The Life and Times of Judge Kenesaw Mountain Landis*. South Bend IN: Diamond Communications, 1998.

———. *Minor Miracles: The Legend and Lure of Minor League Baseball*. Chicago: Taylor Trade, 1995.

Pietrusza, David, Matthew Silverman, and Michael Gershman, eds. *Baseball: The Biographical Encyclopedia*. Kingston NY: Total Sports Illustrated, 2000.

"Pitching to Babe Ruth." *Baseball Magazine,* November 1923, 540.

Porter, Roy. *The Greatest Benefit to Mankind: A Medical History of Humanity*. New York: W. W. Norton, 1999.

Reisler, Jim. *Babe Ruth: Launching the Legend*. New York: McGraw-Hill, 2004.

———. *Before They Were Bombers: The New York Yankees' Early Years, 1903–1915*. Jefferson NC: McFarland, 2002.

Rice, Grantland. *The Tumult and the Shouting: My Life in Sport*. New York: A. S. Barnes, 1954.

Rice, Stephen V. "Bob Shawkey." SABR BioProject, sabr.org/bioproject.

Ritter, Lawrence S. *The Glory of Their Times: The Story of the Early Days of Baseball by the Men Who Played It*. New York: Quill, 1984. Originally published by Macmillan in 1966.

Robinson, Arthur. "Profile: The Babe." *New Yorker*, July 31, 1926, 15–17.

Robinson, Ray. *Iron Horse: Lou Gehrig in His Time*. New York: W. W. Norton 1990.

Rogers, C. Paul, III. "Billy Werber." SABR BioProject, sabr.org/bioproject.

Ruppert, Jacob. "Building a Winning Club in New York." *Baseball Magazine*, June 1918, 203 (4).

Ruth, Babe, and Bob Considine. *The Babe Ruth Story*. New York: E. P. Dutton, 1948.

Sanborn, Irving. "Consider the Pitchers: They Shine Not; Neither Shall They Spit." *Baseball Magazine*, September 1920, 475 (4).

Sanford, Jay. *The Denver Post Tournament*. Cleveland: Society for American Baseball Research, 2003.

Sarnoff, Gary A. *The First Yankees Dynasty: Babe Ruth, Miller Huggins, and the Bronx Bombers of the 1920s*. Jefferson NC: McFarland, 2014.

Schacht, Mike. *The Mudville Diaries: A Book of Baseball Memories*. New York: Avon, 1996.

Seymour, Harold, and Dorothy Seymour Mills. *Baseball: The Golden Age*. New York: Oxford University Press, 1971.

Shalin, Mike, and Neil Shalin. *Out by a Step: The 100 Best Players Not in the Hall of Fame*. Lanham: Diamond Communications, 2002.

Shatzkin, Mike, ed. *The Ballplayers*. New York: Arbor House William Morrow, 1990.

Shawkey, Bob. "The Veteran of the Yankees' Hurling Staff." *Baseball Magazine*, July 1926, 349–50.

———. "What I Have Learned from Seven World Series." *Baseball Magazine*, November 1930, 541 (3).

Shirley, Daniel. "Mark Koenig." SABR BioProject, sabr.org/bioproject.

Shocker, Urban. "Pitching to Babe Ruth." *Baseball Magazine*, November 1923, 540.

Sisler, George. "The Inside Story of Sisler's Great Comeback." *Baseball Magazine*, August 1924, 396 (2).

Smelser, Marshall. *The Life That Ruth Built: A Biography*. New York: Quadrangle, 1975.

Smith, David. "Home Team Scoring Advantage in the First Inning Largely Due to Time." http://www.retrosheet.org/Research/SmithD/HomeTeamScoringAdvantageRelatedToTime.pdf.

Smith, Robert. *Babe Ruth's America: A Warm and Rollicking Portrait of the Babe and His Times*. New York: Robert Crowell, 1974.

Sobol, Ken. *Babe Ruth and the American Dream*. New York: Ballantine Books, 1974.

Sowell, Mike. *The Pitch That Killed*. New York: Macmillan, 1989.

"Spanking Baseball's Baby and Petting Its Paragon." *Literary Digest*, September 19, 1925, 58–67.

Sparks, Barry. *Frank "Home Run" Baker: Hall of Famer and World Series Hero*. Jefferson, NC: McFarland, 2006.

Spatz, Lyle. *New York Yankee Openers: An Opening Day History of Baseball's Most Famous Team, 1903–1996*. Jefferson NC: McFarland, 1997.

———. "Dan Parker." In *Dictionary of Literary Biography—American Sportswriters and Writers on Sport*, ed. Richard Orodenker, 241:196–204. Farmington Hills MI: Gale Group, 2001.

———. "Wally Pipp." SABR BioProject, sabr.org/bioproject.

———. *Yankees Coming, Yankees Going: New York Yankee Player Transactions, 1903 through 1999*. Jefferson NC: McFarland, 2000.

Spatz, Lyle, and Steve Steinberg. *1921: The Yankees, the Giants, and the Battle for Baseball Supremacy in New York*. Lincoln: University of Nebraska Press, 2010.

Steinberg, Steve. "Back Where I Belong." *NINE: A Journal of Baseball History and Culture* 11, no. 2 (2003): 162–67.

———. *Baseball in St. Louis, 1900–1925*. Charleston: Arcadia, 2004.

———. "Dave Danforth." SABR BioProject, sabr.org/bioproject.

———. "Dave Danforth: Baseball's Forrest Gump." *National Pastime* 22 (2002): 50–54.

———. "Del Pratt." SABR BioProject, sabr.org/bioproject.

———. "For the Good of the Game, 1923." *NINE: A Journal of Baseball History and Culture*, 19, no. 1 (2010): 108–18.

———. "The Little World Series of 1922: The Most Heartbreaking Loss in St. Louis Baseball History." *National Pastime* 28 (2008): 7–14.

———. "Pitchers in Pinstripes: Unheralded Stars of the 1920s." *New York Yankees Official 2006 Yearbook*, 474–94.

———. "Ray Caldwell." SABR BioProject, sabr.org/bioproject.

———. "Roaring Race: Yanks Took 1922 Pennant after Epic Battle with the St. Louis Browns." *New York Yankees Official Playoff Program*, 2005, 70–86.

———. "A Shocker on the Island." In *Dominionball: Baseball above the 49th*, ed. Jane Finnan Dorward, 118–19. Lincoln: University of Nebraska Press.

———. "The Spitball and the End of the Deadball Era." *National Pastime* 23 (2003): 7–17.

———. "Urban Shocker: Free Agency in 1923." *National Pastime* 20 (2000): 121–23.

Steinberg, Steve, and Lyle Spatz. *The Colonel and Hug: The Partnership That Transformed the New York Yankees*. Lincoln: University of Nebraska Press, 2015.

Stewart, Wayne. "The Man Who Owned Babe Ruth." *Sports Heritage,* May–June 1987, 54–57.

Stockton, J. Roy. "The Men Who Lead St. Louis' Pennant Battle." *Baseball Magazine*, October 1922, 492 (5).

———. "The Star of the Late World's Series." *Baseball Magazine*, December 1927, 293 (3).

Stout, Glenn, and Richard Johnson. *Yankees Century*. Boston: Houghton Mifflin Harcourt, 2002.

Trachtenberg, Leo. "Bob Meusel." *Yankees Magazine*, June 25, 1987, 23–24, 26.

———. "Earle Combs." *Yankees Magazine*, January 26, 1984, 22–24.

———. "The Last Link to Murderers' Row." *Yankees Magazine*, June 8, 1993, 68–69.

———. "Mark Koenig, a 1927 Yankee." *Yankees Magazine*, June 4, 1987, 56–58.

———. "Tony Lazzeri." *Yankees Magazine*, August 4, 1983, 32–33.

———. "Urban Shocker." *Yankees Magazine*, May 5, 1988, 70–72.

———. *The Wonder Team: The True Story of the Incomparable 1927 New York Yankees*. Bowling Green: Bowling Green State University Press, 1995.

Tullius, John. *I'd Rather Be a Yankee*. New York: Macmillan, 1986.

Vaccaro, Frank. "Herb Pennock." SABR BioProject, sabr.org/bioproject.

Wagenheim, Kal. *Babe Ruth: His Life and Legend*. New York: Henry Holt, 1974.

Walsh, Christy. *Baseball's Greatest Lineup*. New York: A. S. Barnes, 1952.

Wancho, Joe. "Ken Williams." SABR BioProject, sabr.org/bioproject.

———. "Urban Shocker." SABR BioProject, sabr.org/bioproject.

Ward, John J. "Lee Fohl's Unique Career." *Baseball Magazine*, August 1924, 396 (2).

———. "A Rival for Babe Ruth." *Baseball Magazine*, July 1922, 350 (2).

———. "Tobin the Transcendent." *Baseball Magazine*, September 1921, 447 (2).

Werber, Bill, and C. Paul Rogers III. *Memories of a Ballplayer: Bill Werber and Baseball in the 1930s*. Cleveland: Society for American Baseball Research, 2001.

Wolf, Gregory H. "Waite Hoyt." SABR BioProject, sabr.org/bioproject.

Wolinsky, Russell. "Can of Corn: Urban Shocker, Forgotten Spitballer." National Baseball Hall of Fame Library and Archives.

Wright, Craig. "The Murnane Benefit Game." *Pages from Baseball's Past*, http://baseballspast.com.

Zerby, Jack. "September 27, 1917: All-Stars Turn Out for Tim Murnane Benefit." SABR Games Project, sabr.org/gamesproject.

Index

Page numbers in italics indicate illustrations